John Mason Neale, Guillaume Durand, Benjamin Webb

The Symbolism of Churches and Church Ornaments

John Mason Neale, Guillaume Durand, Benjamin Webb

The Symbolism of Churches and Church Ornaments

ISBN/EAN: 9783337811587

Printed in Europe, USA, Canada, Australia, Japan

Cover: Foto ©Lupo / pixelio.de

More available books at **www.hansebooks.com**

THE SYMBOLISM OF CHURCHES

Uniform with this volume, Crown 8vo, cloth

I

SYMBOLISM

OR EXPOSITION OF THE

DOCTRINAL DIFFERENCES

BETWEEN

CATHOLICS AND PROTESTANTS

As evidenced by their Symbolical Writings

By JOHN ADAM MOEHLER, D.D.

II

Hours with the Mystics

By the late ROBERT ALFRED VAUGHAN, B.A.

'There is not a page nor a paragraph in these "Hours" in which there is not something worth recollecting, and often reflections very wise and very weighty indeed. No one can rise from the perusal of the book without finding himself, if not a better, at least a more thoughtful man, and perhaps a humbler one also, as he learns how many more struggles and doubts, discoveries, sorrows, and joys the human race has passed through than are contained in his own private experience.'—CHARLES KINGSLEY.

OF

Churches and Church Ornaments

A TRANSLATION OF THE FIRST BOOK OF THE

Rationale Divinorum Officiorum

WRITTEN BY

WILLIAM DURANDUS
SOMETIME BISHOP OF MENDE

WITH AN INTRODUCTORY ESSAY AND NOTES

BY

THE REV. JOHN MASON NEALE, B.A.

AND

THE REV. BENJAMIN WEBB, B.A.

OF TRINITY COLLEGE, CAMBRIDGE

New York
CHARLES SCRIBNER'S SONS
743 AND 745 BROADWAY
1893

DEDICATED

TO

THE CAMBRIDGE CAMDEN SOCIETY

BY

TWO OF ITS FOUNDERS

PREFACE

THE interest which has lately been displayed, as on all subjects connected with Ecclesiology, so more especially on the symbolical bearing of Church Architecture, has led us to imagine that a translation of the most valuable work on Symbolism which the middle ages can furnish, might not, at the present time, be unacceptable to churchmen.

Written, however, at a period when Christian Architecture had not attained its full glory, it necessarily leaves untouched many arrangements of similar tendency, subsequently adopted; addressed to those who had not yet learnt to doubt everything not formally proved, it assumes many points which may now seem to require confirmation : and composed for the use of a clergy habituated to a most figurative ritual, it passes over much as well known, which is now forgotten or neglected. On these accounts we have considered it necessary to prefix an Essay on the subject; in which we have endeavoured to prove that Catholic Architecture must necessarily be symbolical; to answer the more common objections to the system; and to elucidate it by reference to actual examples, and notices of the figurative arrangements of our own churches. We have also added notes, where any obscurity seemed to require explanation; and we have, both in them and in the Appendix, thrown together such passages from Martene, Beleth, S. Isidore of Seville, Hugo de S. Victore, and other writers, as tended to explain and to enforce the remarks of Durandus.

With reference to the author himself, but little is known; and that little has been told before.

William Durandus was born at Puy-moisson, in Provence, about the year 1220. A legend of his native country is told in the present work.* He became the pupil of Henry de Luza, afterwards Cardinal of Ostia; and taught canon law at Modena. On this subject he composed a most learned work, the *Speculum Juris;* from which he obtained the title of *Speculator:* as also another treatise called *Repertorium Juris:* and a *Breviarium Glossarum in Textum Juris Canonici.* His high attainments marked him † out for the office of Chaplain to Pope Clement IV. He was afterwards Auditor of the Sacred Palace; and Legate to Pope Gregory X at the Council of Lyons. He was then made Captain of the Papal forces; in which post he assisted at the reduction of several rebellious cities, and behaved with great courage. He finally became Bishop of Mende in 1286. While in this post, and resident at Rome (for he did not personally visit his diocese till 1291, the administration of the diocese being perhaps left to a nephew of the same name, who succeeded him), he finished the work, of the first book of which a translation is presented to the reader. But it probably

---

* See p. 126

† *Mutata fortuna,* says Doard: to what this refers, we know not.

was commenced before; for we find from a passage in its latter half, that so far had been written during the course of this same year 1286. And there is no difficulty in the title, *Episcopus Mimatensis*, which he gives himself in the Proeme, as this could easily have been added afterwards. But it was certainly published, as Martene observes, before 1295; because Durandus speaks of the Feasts of the Holy Apostles as *semi-doubles*, whereas in that year, by a constitution of Pope Urban, they were commanded to be observed as *doubles*. The time at which the treatise was written more especially demands our attention; because, did we imagine it only a few years later than it really was, we might well be astonished at finding no reference to the Symbolism of the Decorated Style. The interruptions amidst which the *Rationale* was written are feelingly alluded to by its author, in the Epilogue (p. 161). He also wrote a treatise *De Modo Concilii Generalis habendi*, probably either suggested by, or preparatory to, that of Lyons. He afterwards went on an embassy from the Pope to the Sultan; and is by some said to have ended this life at Nicosia in Cyprus. But the fact is not so: for having governed his diocese ten years, and having refused the proffered Archbishopric of Ravenna, he departed at Rome on the Feast of All Saints, 1296, being buried in the Church of Sancta Maria super Minervam, where his monument is yet to be seen, with the following inscription :—

> Hic jacet egregius doctor prœsul Mimatensis,
> Nomine Duranti Guillelmus regula morum :
> Splendor honestatis et casti candor amoris

Altum consiliis spatiosum mente serenum
Hunc insignibat immotum turbine mentis.
Mente pius, sermone gravis, gressuque modestus,
Extitit infestus super hostes more leonis :
Indomitos domuit populos, ferroque rebelles,
Impulit, Ecclesiæ victor servire coëgit.
Comprobat officiis, paruit Romania sceptro
Belligeri comitis Martini tempore quarti :
Edidit in Jure librum, quo jus reperitur :
Et Speculum Juris, et patrum Pontificale :
Et Rationale Divinorum patefecit :
Instruxit clerum scriptis, monuitque statutis :
Gregorii deni, Nicolai scita perenni
Glossa diffudit populis, sensusque profundos :
Jure dedit mentes et corpus luce studentum :
Quem memori laude genuit Provincia dignum :
Et dedit a Podio Missone diæcesis illum :
Inde Biterrensis, præsignis curia Papæ :
Dum foret ecclesiæ Mimatensis sede quietus,
Hunc vocat octavus Bonifacius ; altius illum
Promovet ; hic renuit Ravennæ præsul haberi.
Fit comes invictus simul hinc et marchio tandem,
Et Romam rediit : Domini sub mille trecentis
(Quatuor amotis) annis : tumulante Minerva.
Surripit hunc festiva dies, & prima Novembris.
Guadia cum Sanctis tenet Omnibus inde sacerdos :
Pro quo perpetuo datur haec celebrare capella.

The *Rationale* was the first work, from the pen of an uninspired writer, ever printed. The *editio princeps* appeared at the press of Fust in 1459; being preceded only by the Psalters of 1457 and 1459. It is, of course, of the most extreme rarity: the beauty of the typography has seldom been exceeded. Chalmers mentions, besides this, thirteen editions in the fifteenth, and thirteen in the sixteenth century : all of them are very rare.

The editions with which we are acquainted, are those of Rome 1473 ; Lyons 1503, 1512, 1534, 1584 ; Antwerp

1570; Venice 1599, 1609. The translation has been made from the editions of 1473 and 1599. The former is a magnificent specimen of typography : the words are excessively contracted ; and there are double columns to each page. Our copy is partially illuminated ; and the binding is ornamented with a border of the Evangelistic Symbols. The latter contains also the first edition of the work of Beleth, and is a reprint of Doard's Lyons edition of 1565. Doard dedicated it to his brother, Bishop of Marseilles ; and prefixed a Preface, in which he bestows a well-merited eulogium on Durandus, and mentions the care taken in correcting and revising the work. He also added some notes, of little worth. The Venice reprint is so vicious a specimen of typography, that from it alone the sense could in many places hardly be explained. Our copy belonged to Bishop White Kennett, who appears to have studied it diligently.

We must now say a few words as on our own share in the work. With respect to the Introduction, fully convinced as we are of the truth and importance of the general principle maintained in it, we do not wish to press, as matter of certainty, all or any of the minor details into which that theory is carried. We believe, indeed, that the more the subject has been studied, the more truthful our views will appear to be : but we wish the reader to bear in mind, that the weakness of any portion of them is no argument against their reception, as a whole. At the same time, none can be more aware than ourselves how much more ably such views might have been advocated : we have not, however, spared time or pains in the study of the subject; 'and if we have done meanly, it is that we could attain unto.'

In the Translation, we have endeavoured, too often unsuccessfully, to retain the beautiful simplicity of the original. In the obscure passages, of which there are not a few, we have mentioned the difficulty in the notes, lest the reader, by our mistake, should be led into error himself.

The quotations from Holy Scripture are given in the authorised version, except where, to bring out the author's full meaning, it was necessary to have recourse to the Vulgate; and we have then translated literally from that.

We have felt no small pleasure in thus enabling this excellent prelate, though at so far distant a land from his own, and after a silence of nearly six hundred years, being dead, yet to speak: and if the following pages are at all useful in pointing out the sacramental character of Catholic art, we shall be abundantly rewarded, as being fellow-workers with him in the setting forth of one, now too much forgotten, Church principle.

J. M. N.
B. W.

Michaelmas, 1842.

INTRODUCTORY ESSAY

SACRAMENTALITY: A PRINCIPLE OF ECCLESIASTICAL DESIGN

ANALYSIS OF THE INTRODUCTORY ESSAY

INTRODUCTION.
1. Spread of the study of Church Architecture.
2. Obvious, but indefinable, difference between old and new churches.
   Wherein this consists.
   Not in association,
   Nor in correctness of details,
   Nor in the Picturesque,
   Nor in the Mechanical advantages,
   But in Reality
      considered, in an enlarged view, as Sacramentality.
3. This probable,
      from examples, and
         promises in Holy Scripture.
         Catholic consent,
         examples to the contrary,
         philosophical reasons.
4. Enunciation of the subject.
5. Writers on the subject,
      Pugin, Poole, Lewis, Coddington, the writers of the Cambridge Camden Society.

A. ARGUMENTS FOR SYMBOLISM.
   I. A PRIORI.
      Symbolising spirit of Catholic Antiquity,
         in (a) Interpretation of Holy Scriptures.
            (b) Analogy of the Jewish Ceremonies.
            (c) Private manners.
            (d) Emblems in Catacombs, etc.
            (e) Symbolical interpretation of Heathen writers.
   II. ANALOGICAL.
      i. Examples of other nations.
         (a) Jews.
            (1) Temple rites.
            (2) Legal observances.
            (3) Sacred books.
         (b) Turks.
         (c) Infidels.
            (1) Hindu and Egyptian Mythology.
            (2) Persian Poetry.
         (d) Heretics.

    ii. From Nature.
        (a) Trinity.
        (b) Resurrection.
        (c) Self-sacrifice.
   iii. From Art.
        (a) Sculpture.
        (b) Painting.
        (c) Music.
        (d) Language of Flowers.
   iv. Parabolical teaching.

III. PHILOSOPHICAL.

   Objective answering to Subjective.
   All effect sacramental of the efficient.
   Sacramentality of all Religion.
   Ritualism peculiarly and necessarily sacramental.
   Church Architecture, a condition of Ritualism.
   Necessities induce accidents: and these material expressions.
   Example:
   Necessities of Ritualism, and their expressions in earlier and later ages.
   Hence Symbolism.
        Essential.
        Intended.
        Conventional, which again becomes intended.

IV. ANALYTICAL.
   1. Cruciformity.
   2. Ascent to Altar.
   3. Orientation.
   4. Verticality.

V. INDUCTIVE.
   Express and continuous testimony.
      (a) Apostolical Constitutions.
      (b) Eusebius.
      (c) Symbolical writers.
   Actual examples.

VI. RECAPITULATION.

B. EXAMPLES OF SYMBOLISM.
   I. DOCTRINES.
      (a) The Holy Trinity, set forth in
         i. Nave and Two Aisles.
         ii. Chancel, Nave and Apse.
         iii. Clerestory, Triforium, and Pier Arches.
         iv. Triple windows.
         v. Altar steps.
         vi. Triplicity of mouldings.
         vii. Minor details.
      (b) Regeneration.
         i. The octagonal form of Fonts.
         ii.   „   „   „   Piers.
         iii. Fishes.

(c) Atonement.
> i. Cruciformity.
> ii. Deviation of Orientation.
> iii. Double Cross.
> iv. The great Rood.
> v. Details.

(d) Communion of Saints.

II. DETAILS.

(a) Windows : a series of examples.
(b) Doors.
> i. Norman tympana.
> ii. Double doors in Early English.

(*a*) These explained in two ways,
> (1) Christ's entrance into the world.
> (2) Our entrance into the kingdom of heaven.

(*b*) Difference between mouldings of Chancel arches and doors.
(c) Porches.
(d) Chancel Arch and Rood Screen.
(e) Monuments.
> (*a*) Difference of ancient and modern symbolism in these.
>> (1) Sceptical character of the present age.
>> (2) Paganism of modern design.
>> (3) Reality of ancient design.
>
> (*b*) Historical details of Monuments.

(f) Gurgoyles and Poppyheads.
(g) Flowers used in architecture.

C. OBJECTIONS ANSWERED.
1. Inequality of type and antitype.
2. Difference of Symbolism in the same arrangement.
3. Mechanical origin.

D. HISTORY OF SYMBOLISM.
1. Norman ; as symbolising facts.
2. Early English ; as symbolising doctrines.
3. Decorated ; as symbolising the connection of doctrines.
4. Perpendicular ; as symbolising the progress of Erastianism.
5. Flamboyant, etc.
6. Post Reformation Symbolism.

E. CONCLUSION.
> Contrast between a modern and ancient Church.

Laus Deo

INTRODUCTORY ESSAY

CHAPTER I

INTRODUCTORY

THE study of Church Architecture has within the last few years become so general, and a love for it so widely diffused, that whereas, in a former generation it was a task to excite either, in the present it is rather an object to direct both. An age of church-building, such as this, ought to produce good architects, not only from the great encouragement given to their professional efforts, but from the increasing appreciation of the principles and powers of their art. And yet it cannot be denied, however we may account for the fact, that (at least among those for whom we write, the members of our own communion), no architect has as yet arisen, who appears destined to be the reviver of Christian art. It is not that the rules of the science have not been studied, that the examples bequeathed to us have not been imitated, that the details are not understood. We have (though they are but few) modern buildings of the most perfect proportions, of the most faultless details, and reared with lavish expense. It is that there is an undefined—perhaps almost undefinable—difference between a true 'old church,' and the most perfect of modern temples. In the former, at least till late in the Perpendicular era, we feel that, however strange the proportions, or extraordinary the details, the effect is church-like. In the latter, we may not be able to blame; but from a certain feeling of unsatisfactoriness, we cannot praise.

The solution of the problem,—What is it that causes this difference? has been often attempted, sometimes with partial, but never with complete, success. That most commonly given is the following:—The effect of association in old buildings,—the mellowing power of time,—the evident antiquity of surrounding objects,—the natural beauties of foliage, moss, and ivy, that require centuries to reach perfection;—as on the other hand, the bareness, the newness, nay even the sharpness and vigour of new work; these, it is said, are sufficient to stamp a different character on each. There is doubtless something in this; but that it is not the whole cause is evident from the fact, that give a modern church all the above mentioned advantages on paper, and an experienced eye will soon detect it to be modern.

Those writers who, as Grose, Milner, and Carter, lived before the details of Christian art were understood, seem to have placed its perfection in a thorough knowledge of these: experience has proved them wrong. Others, as Mr Petit,* have made a kind of ideal picturesque; and, having exalted the phantasm into an idol, have fallen down and worshipped it. Others, again, have sought for an explanation of the difficulty in mathematical contrivance and mechanical ingenuity; and the result has been little more than the discovery of curious eave-drains, and wonderful cast-iron roof-work. Lastly, Mr Pugin (*cum talis sis, utinam noster esses!*) has placed the thing required in *Reality*. That is, to quote his own words, in making these the two great rules of design:—

---

* See the review of his work in the *Ecclesiologist*, vol. i, pp. 91-105.

'1. That there should be no features about a building which are not necessary for convenience, construction, or propriety: 2. That all ornament should consist of enrichment of the essential construction of a building.'* And we may add, as a corollary, still quoting the same writer:—'The smallest detail should have a meaning or serve a purpose: the construction itself should vary with the material employed: and the designs should be adapted to the material in which they are to be executed.' Still, most true and most important as are these remarks, we must insist on one more axiom, otherwise Christian art will but mock us, and not show us wherein its great strength lieth.

A Catholic architect must be a Catholic in heart. Simple knowledge will no more enable a man to build up God's material, than His spiritual temples. In ancient times, the finest buildings were designed by the holiest bishops. Wykeham and Poore will occur to every churchman. And we have every reason to believe, from God's Word, from Catholic consent, and even from philosophical principles, that such must always be the case.

Holy Scripture, in mentioning the selection of Bezaleel and Aholiab, as architects of the Tabernacle, expressly asserts them to have been filled 'with the Spirit of God in wisdom, and in understanding, and in knowledge, and in all manner of workmanship, to devise cunning works, to work in gold, and in silver and in brass, and in cutting of stones to set them, and in carving of timber, to work in all manner of workmanship.' And this indeed is only a part of the blessing of the pure in heart: they see God, the Fountain of Beauty, even in this life; as they shall see Him, the Fountain of Holiness, in the

---

* Pugin's 'True Principles,' p. 1.

next. From Catholic consent we may learn the same truth. Why else was Ecclesiastical Architecture made a part of the profession of Clerks, than because it was considered that the purity and holiness of that profession fitted them best for so great a work?*

Nay, we have remarkable proofs that feeling without knowledge will do more than knowledge without feeling. There are instances of buildings—Lisbon cathedral and S. Peter's College chapel, Cambridge, are cases in point—which, with Debased or Italian details, have nevertheless Christian effect. And we have several similar cases, more particularly in the way of towers.

Now, allowing the respectability, which attaches itself to the profession of a modern architect, and the high character of many in that profession, none would assert that they, as a body, make it a matter of devotion and prayer; that they work for the Church alone regardless of themselves; that they build in faith, and to the glory of God.

In truth, architecture has become too much a profession: it is made the means of gaining a livelihood, and is viewed as a path to honourable distinction, instead of being the study of the devout ecclesiastic, who matures his noble conceptions with the advantage of that profound meditation only attainable in the contemplative life, who, without thought of recompense or fame, has no end in view but the raising a temple, worthy of its high end, and emblematical of the faith which is to be maintained within its walls. It is clear that modern architects are in a very different position from their predecessors, with respect to these advantages. We are not prepared to say that none but monks ought to design churches, or that it is impossible for a professional

---

* Compare the general drift of the Address to Paulinus. *Eusebius.* II. E. X. 4.

architect to build with the devotion and faith of an earlier time. But we do protest against the merely business-like spirit of the modern profession, and demand from them a more elevated and directly religious habit of mind. We surely ought to look at least for church-membership from one who ventures to design a church. There cannot be a more painful idea than that a separatist should be allowed to build a House of God, when he himself knows nothing of the ritual and worship of the Church from which he has strayed; to prepare both font and altar, when perchance he knows nothing of either Sacrament but that he has always despised them. Or, again, to think that any churchman should allow himself to build a conventicle, and even sometimes to prostitute the speaking architecture of the Church to the service of Her bitterest enemies! What idea can such a person have formed of the reality of church architecture? Conceive a churchman designing a triple window, admitted emblem of the Most Holy Trinity, for a congregation of Socinians! We wish to vindicate the dignity of this noble science against the treason of its own professors. If architecture is anything more than a mere trade; if it is indeed a liberal, intellectual art, a true branch of poesy, let us prize its reality and meaning and truthfulness, and at least not expose ourselves by giving to two contraries one and the same material expression.

It is objected that architects have a right to the same professional conscience that is claimed, for instance, by a barrister. To which we can only reply, that it must be a strange morality which will justify a pleader in violating truth; and how much worse for an architect to violate truth in things immediately connected with the House and worship of God? It may be asked, Do we mean to imply then that a church architect ought never to undertake any secular building? Perhaps, as things are, we cannot expect so much as this now: but we can never believe that the man who engages to design union-houses, or prisons, or assembly-rooms, and gives the dregs of his time to church-building, is likely to produce a good church, or, in short, can expect to be filled from above with the Spirit of Wisdom. The church architect must, we are persuaded, make very great sacrifices: he must forego all lucrative undertakings, if they may not be carried through upon those principles which he believes necessary for every good building; and particularly if the end to be answered, or the wants to be provided for, are in themselves unjustifiable or mischievous. Even in church-building itself, he must see many an unworthy rival preferred to him, who will condescend to pander to the whims and comfort of a church-committee, will suit his design to any standard of ritualism which may be suggested by his own ignorance, or others' private judgment, who will consent to defile a building meant for God's worship with pews and galleries and prayer-pulpits and commodious vestries. But hard as the trial may be, a church architect must submit to it, rather than recede from the principles which he knows to be the very foundation of his art. We would go further even, and deny the possibility of any architect's success in all the different styles of Pointed architecture, not to mention the orders of Greece and Rome, Vitruvian, Palladian, Cinque Cento, Wrennian, nay even Chinese, Swiss, Hindoo, and Egyptian at once. We have not even now exhausted the list of styles in which a modern architect is supposed to be able to design. It is even more absurd than if every modern painter were expected, and should profess, to paint equally well in the styles of Perugino, Francia, Raphael, Holbein, Claude, the Poussins, Salvator Rosa, Correggio, Van Eyck,

Teniers, Rubens, Murillo, Reynolds, West, Gainsborough, Overbeck, and Copley Fielding all at once! An architect ought indeed to be acquainted, and the more the better, with all styles of building : but if architecture, as we said before, *is* a branch of poesy, if the poet's mind is to have any individuality, he must design in one style, and one style only. For the Anglican architect, it will be necessary to know enough of the earlier styles to be able to restore the deeply interesting churches, which they have left us as precious heirlooms ; enough of the Debased styles, to take warning from their decline : but for his own style, he should choose the glorious architecture of the fourteenth century ; and, just as no man has more than one hand-writing, so in this one language alone will he express his architectural ideas.

We cannot leave this topic without referring to what the Cambridge Camden Society has said with respect to architectural competition.* *It is a fact* that at this time many competing designs are manufactured in an architect's office, by some of his clerks, as if by machinery : if a given plan is chosen, the architect is summoned, and sees *his* (!) design for the first time, when he is introduced to the smiling committee-men. It is another fact that there is at this time in London a small body of persons, with no other qualification than that of having been draughtsmen in an architect's office, who *get up* a set of competing designs for any aspirant who chooses to give them a few instructions, and to pay them for their trouble. How much it is to be wished that there were some examination of an architect's qualifications, before he should be allowed to assume the name! It seems strange that the more able members of the profession do not themselves feel some *esprit de corps*, and do not at

* See *Ecclesiologist*, vol. i, pp. 69, 85.

least endeavour to claim for their art its full dignity and importance. We fear however that very few, as yet, take that *religious* view of their profession, which we have shown to be seemly, even if not essential. If, however, we succeed in proving that religion enters very largely into the principles of church architecture, a religious *ethos*, we repeat, is *essential* to a church architect. At all events, in an investigation into the differences between ancient and modern church architecture, the contrast between the ancient and modern builders could not be overlooked: and it is not too much to hope that some, at least, may be struck by the fact, that the deeply religious habits of the builders of old, the hours, the cloister, the discipline, the obedience, resulted in their matchless works; while the worldliness, vanity, dissipation, and patronage of our own architects issue in unvarying and hopeless failure.

We said that there were philosophical reasons for the belief that we must have architects—before we can have buildings—like those of old. If it be true that an esoteric signification, or, as we shall call it, *Sacramentality*,* ran through all the arrangements and details of Christian architecture, emblematical of Christian discipline, and suggested by Christian devotion; then must the discipline have been practised, and the devotion felt, before a Christian temple can be reared. That this

---

* It may be proper to distinguish between five terms, too generally vaguely employed in common, and which we shall often have occasion to use: we mean, *allegorical, symbolical, typical, figurative,* and *sacramental*.

'Allegory employs fictitious things and personages to shadow out the truth: Symbolism uses real personages and real actions (and real things) as symbols of the truth:' *British Critic,* No. lxv. p. 121. Sacramentality is symbolism applied to the truth κατ' ἐξοχήν, the teaching of the Church, by the hands of the teacher: a Type is a symbol intended from the first: a Figure is a symbol not discovered till after the thing figurative has had a being.

esoteric meaning, or symbolism, does exist, we are now to endeavour to prove.

We assert, then, that *Sacramentality* is that characteristic which so strikingly distinguishes ancient ecclesiastical architecture from our own. By this word we mean to convey the idea that, by the outward and visible form, is signified something inward and spiritual: that the material fabric symbolises, embodies, figures, represents, expresses, answers to, some abstract meaning. Consequently, unless this ideal be itself true, or be rightly understood, he who seeks to build a Christian church may embody a false or incomplete or mistaken ideal, but will not develope the true one. Hence, while the Parthenon, or a conventicle, or a modern church, may be conceived to have, on the one hand, so much *truthfulness*, as to symbolise respectively the graceful, but pagan, worship of Athene—the private judgment of the dissenter—and the warped or ill-understood or puritanised religious ethos of the modern churchman; and, on the other hand, to have so much *reality* as to carry out most satisfactorily Mr Pugin's canons; yet, inasmuch as in neither case was the builder's ideal the true one, so in neither case is his architecture in any way adapted to, or an embodiment of, the ideal of the Church. Reality, then, is not of itself sufficient. What can be more *real* than a pyramid, yet what less Christian? It must be Christian reality, the true expression of a true ideal, which makes Catholic architecture what it is. This Christian reality, we would call *Sacramentality*; investing that symbolical truthfulness, which it has in common with *every* true expression, with a greater force and holiness, both from the greater purity of the perfect truth which it embodies, and from the association which this name will give it with those adorable and consummate examples of the same principle, infinitely more developed, and infinitely more holy in the spiritual grace which they signify and convey,—the Blessed Sacraments of the Church.

The modern writers who have treated on Symbolism seem to have taken respectively very partial views of the subject. Mr Pugin does not seem in his books to recognise the particular principle which we have enunciated. We have shown that his law about Reality is true so far as it goes, but that it does not go far enough. He himself, for example, is now contemplating a work on the reality of domestic, as before of ecclesiastical, architecture. Now, nothing can be more true, nothing more useful, than this. Yet even he does not seem to have discerned that as contact with the Church endues with a new sanctity, and elevates every form and every principle of art: so in a peculiar sense the sacred end to which church architecture is subservient, elevates and sanctifies that reality which must be a condition of its goodness in common with *all* good architecture; in short, raises this principle of Reality into one of Sacramentality. We should be sorry to assert that Mr Pugin does not feel this, though we are not aware that he has expressed it in his writings: but in his most lasting writings, his churches namely, it is clear that the principle, if not intentionally even, and if only incompletely, has not been without a great influence on that master mind. Yet even in these we could point to details, and in some of his earlier works to something more than details, which shew that there is something wanting; that in the bold expedients and fearless licence which his genius has led him to employ, he has occasionally gone wrong; not from the fact of his departure from strict precedent, and his vindication of a certain architectural freedom, but because in these escapements from authority, he has not invariably kept in view the principle now advocated. However the author of the 'True Principles' might point to his churches, to prove that a reverent and religious mind, employed in administering to the material wants of the Church, (even though that reverence be misapplied, and that Church in a schismatical position), cannot fail to succeed, at least in some degree, in stamping upon his work the impress of his own faith and zeal, and in making it, at least to some extent, a living development and expression of the true ideal.

Mr Poole, the author of the 'Appropriate Character of Church Architecture,' would appear to believe the symbolism of details rather than any general principle. He was the first, we think, to reassert that the octagonal form of fonts was figurative of Regeneration. In the latter edition of his Book he has adopted several of the symbolical interpretations advanced by the writers of the Cambridge Camden Society.

Mr Lewis, in his illustrations of Kilpeck church (in an appendix to which he has printed a translation of some part of the 'Rationale' of our author), has given a treatise on symbolism generally, and has applied his principles to the explanation of the plan and details of that particular church. His book excited some attention at the time of publication, and was met by considerable ridicule in many quarters. To this we think it was fairly open, since the author did not seem to have grasped the true view of the subject. He appears to believe that, from the very first, *all* church architecture was *intentionally* symbolical. Now this is an unlikely supposition, inasmuch as till church architecture was fully developed, we do not think that its real significancy was understood to its full extent by those who used it. That it was, in its imperfect state, symbolical, we should be the last to deny; but it seems more in accordance with probability, and more in analogy with the progress of other arts, to believe that at first certain given wants induced and compelled certain adaptations to those wants: which then *did* symbolise the wants themselves; and which afterwards became intentionally symbolical. Now such a view as this will explain satisfactorily how a Christian church might be progressively developed from a Basilican model. Mr Hope, in his essay on Architecture, carries us back to the very earliest expedient likely to be adopted by a savage to protect him from weather, and from this derives every subsequent expansion of the art. Which may be true, and probably is true, so far at least as this: that, however first acquired, the elementary knowledge of any method of building would be, like all other knowledge, continually receiving additions and improvements, till from the first bower of branches sprang the Parthenon, and from that again Cologne or Westminster. But then it is clearly necessary to show some moral reason for so strange a development, so complete a change of form and style. Now the theory that the ethos of Catholic architects working upon the materials made to hand, namely, the ancient orders of pagan architecture and (say) the Basilican plan, gradually impressed itself upon these unpromising elements, and progressively developed from them a transcript of that ethos in Christian architecture, is intelligible at least, and presents no such difficulty as Mr Lewis's supposition that ancient architects (he does not say when, or how long—but take Kilpeck church and say *Norman* architects) designed intentionally on symbolical principles. We want in this case to be informed when the change took place, from what period architects began to symbolise intentionally, at what time they forgot the traditions of church-building, which they must have had, and commenced to carry new principles into practice. Nor, on this supposition, do we see why there should have been any progressive development, why the Basilican and Debased-Pagan trammels were not cast away at once; nor why, if the *ideal* of the Norman architect was true and perfect (that is if he were a true Catholic), its expression should not have been so too: nor why any Norman symbolism, thus originated, should ever have been discarded (as it has been in later styles), instead of remaining an integral and essential part of the material expression of the Church's mind. Now our view appears to be open to no such objection. On the one hand there are given materials to work upon, and on the other a given spirit which is to mould and inform the mass. The contest goes on: mind gradually subdues matter, until in the complete development of Christian architecture we see the projection of the mind of the Church. It is quite in analogy with the history and nature of the Church, and with the workings of God's providence with respect to it, that there should be this gradual expansion and development of truth. We foresee the objection that will be raised against fixing on any period as that of the full ripeness of Christian art, and are prepared for many sneers at our advocacy of the perfection of the Edwardian architecture. But we are assured that, if there is any truth (not to say in what is advanced in this essay, but) in what has ever been proposed by any who have appreciated the genius of Pointed Architecture—to confine ourselves to our own subject—no other period can be chosen at which all conditions of beauty, of detail, of general effect, of truthfulness, of reality are so fully answered as in this. And from this spring two important considerations. Firstly, the decline of Christian art—which may be traced from this very period, if architecture be tried by any of the conditions which have been laid down—was confessedly coincident with, and (if what we have said is true) was really symbolical of, those corruptions, which ended in the great rending of the Latin Church; the effects of, and penalties for, which remain to this day in full operation in the whole of Western Christendom. Secondly, the Decorated style may be indeed the finest development of Christian architecture which the world has yet seen; but it does not follow that it is the greatest perfection which shall ever be arrived at. No: we too look forward, if it may be, to the time when even a new style of church architecture shall be given us, so glorious and beautiful and true, that Cologne will sink into a fine example of a transitional period, when the zeal and faith and love of the reunited Church shall find their just expression in the sacramental forms of Catholic art.

But besides the above objection to Mr Lewis's theory we may mention the arbitrary way in which he determines on things which are to be symbolised, and then violently endeavours to find their expected types. This is quite at variance with the practice of any sober symbolist; and more especially (as we shall hereafter have occasion to point out) with that of Durandus. This forced sort of symbolism naturally leads to a disregard of precedent and authority: and accordingly we remember to have heard of a design by this gentleman for the arrangement of a chancel which professed to symbolise certain facts and doctrines; but which, whatever might be the ingenuity of the symbolism, was no less opposed to the constant rule of arrangement in ancient churches, than it was practically absurd and inconvenient for the purpose which it was meant to answer. Indeed, while Mr Lewis insists strongly on the symbolising of facts, he does not succeed in grasping any general principle, any more than he sees the difficulty there is in the way of our receiving his supposition of an intention to symbolise from the first. No architect ever sat down with an analysed scheme of doctrines which he resolved to embody in his future building: in this, as in any other department of poesy, the result is harmonious, significant, and complete, and may be resolved into its elements, though these elements might never have been laid by the poet as the foundation upon which to raise his superstructure. That were like De La Harpe's theory that an epic poet should first determine on his moral, and then draw out such a plan for his poem as may enable him to illustrate that moral.*

The writers of the Cambridge Camden Society have carried out the system more fully and consistently than any others. It has evidently grown upon them, during the process of their inquiries: yet in their earliest publications, we trace, though more obscurely, the same thing. Their 'Few Words to Church-Builders' acknowledged the principle to a far greater length; and the *Ecclesiologist* has always acted upon it, even when not expressly referring to it. As a necessary consequence, they were the first who dwelt on the absolute necessity of a distinct and spacious chancel; the first who recommended, and

---

* It is with pain that we have spoken of Mr Lewis at all, because every Ecclesiologist owes him a debt for his great boldness in turning the public attention to the subject of symbolism. Yet we believe that a prejudice has been excited by him against that subject which it will be hard to get over; for we are constrained to say, that greater absurdities were never printed than some which have appeared in his book. His explanations of the west end of Kilpeck church—his cool assumption when any bracket appears more puzzling than usual that it is of later work, and therefore not explainable — his random perversions of Scripture — his puerile conceits about the door — deserve this criticism. This same south door he extols as a perfect mine of ecclesiastical information, while he confesses himself unable to explain the symbols wrought on the two orders of the arch—that is about two-thirds of the whole! It is strange, too, that in his restoration of the church, he should have forgotten all about the bells—and have violated a fundamental canon of symbolism, by terminating his western gable in a plain Cross.

where they could, insisted on, the re-introduction of the rood-screen; and the first to condemn the use of western triplets. The position and shape of the font, the necessity of orientation, and some few details, they have, but only in common with others, urged.

The Oxford Architectural Society have never recognised any given principles: and in consequence Littlemore is proposed by them as a model—a church either without, or else all, chancel; and either way a solecism.

As might have been expected from a separatist, Rickman, in his treatise, gives not a single line to the principle for which we contend. Mr Bloxam, in his excellent little work, though often referring to it—more especially in the later editions which have appeared since the labours of the Cambridge Camden Society—yet hardly gives it that prominence which we might have expected from one who possesses so just an idea of mediæval arrangements and art.

Among the chief opposers of the system we may mention Mr Coddington of Ware, who sees perfection in the clumsiness of Basilican arrangements, and schism in the developed art of the middle ages. This writer, as it has been observed in the *Ecclesiologist*, contends for two things:—1. That one great object of Romanism was to abolish the distinction between the clergy and laity: 2 That another great object of the same Church, acting by its monks, (or, as he calls them, schismatical communities) was to exalt the clergy unduly above the laity. The former assertion he does not attempt to prove: the latter he supports by pointing to the arrangement of the rood-screen, which, therefore, like the French Ambonoclasts, he wishes to pull down both in cathedrals and churches.

This brief review of the principal writers who have treated on the Symbolism of Churches and Church

Ornaments, concludes our first chapter. In it we have endeavoured to point out an acknowledged desideratum; to shew what suppositions have been advanced on the subject; to set forth wherein, and for what reason, they fail of being satisfactory; to enunciate the principle of *Sacramentality* as essential for the full appreciation and successful imitation of ancient church architecture; and finally, in referring to the works of some later symbolists, to shew why their hypotheses are incomplete or untenable. We have also brought under review the glaring contrasts between the methods of life of an ancient and modern architect; and, if we may so say, between the machinery of designing and the habit of mind in the two cases. We shall now proceed to examine those arguments which may lead us to suspect that some such principle as Sacramentality really exists.

CHAPTER II

THE ARGUMENT A PRIORI

IT will first be proper to consider whether, regarding the subject *à priori*, that is, looking at the habits and manners of those among whom the symbolical system originated, if it originated anywhere, we have reason to think them at all likely to induce that system. Now, as matter of fact, we know that the train of thought, the every-day observances, above all, the religious rites of the early Christians, were in the highest degree figurative. The rite of Baptism gave the most forcible of all sanctions to such a system; and while it sanctioned, it also suggested, some of the earliest specimens of Christian symbolism. Hence, when that rite was found to be, so to speak, connected with the word formed by the initial letters of our Blessed Saviour's name and titles, arose the Mystic Fish: hence, as we shall see, the octagonal baptistery and font. Indeed, almost every great doctrine had been symbolised at a very early period of Christianity. The Resurrection was set forth in the Phœnix, rising immortal from its ashes: the meritorious Passion of our Saviour, by the Pelican, feeding its young with its own blood: the Sacrament of the Holy Eucharist, by grapes and wheatears, or again by the blood flowing from the heart and feet of the Wounded Lamb into a chalice beneath: the Christian's renewal of strength thereby in the Eagle, which descending grey and aged into the ocean, rises thence with renewed strength and vigour: the Church, by the Ark, and the vessel* in which our Lord slept: the Christian's purity and innocence by the Dove: † again, by the same symbol the souls ‡ of those who suffered for the Truth: again, though perhaps not so early, the Holy Spirit: the Apostles were also set forth as twelve Doves: ‖ the Ascension of our Saviour by the Flying Bird; concerning which S. Gregory § teaches, 'rightly is our Redeemer called a Bird, Whose Body ascended freely into heaven': Martyrs also by birds let loose; for so Tertullian,¶ 'There is one kind of flesh of fishes, that is of those who be regenerate by Holy Baptism; but another of birds, that is of martyrs.' The caged bird is symbolical of the contrary; this has been found upon the phial containing the blood of a martyr. Of this, Boldetti says, 'It is represented on the mosaic of the ancient Tribune of S. Mary beyond Tiber;

---

* Naviculum quippe ecclesiam cogitate,—turbulentum mare hoc seculum.—*S. Aug. de Verb Dom.*

† Quæque super signum resident cœleste Columbæ,
Simplicibus produnt regna patere Dei.
S. Paulin. ep. 12, *ad Sever.*

‡ Cum nollet idolis sacrificare (sc. S. Reparata) ecce, gladio percutitur: cujus anima in Columbæ specie de corpore egredi, cœlumque conscendere visa est.—*Martyrol. Rom.* viii. *Id. Oct.*

Emicat inde Columba repens,
Martyris os nive candidior
Visa relinquere, et astra sequi:
Spiritus hic erat Eulaliæ
Lacteolus, celer, innocuus.
Pruden. Perist. Hymn. 9.

Compare also the Passion of S. Potitus,—Act. SS. Bollandi, 13 Jan. So, in the cemetery of S. Calistus, a piece of glass was found by Boldetti, on which S. Agnes was represented between two doves, the symbols of her Virginity and Martyrdom.

‖ Crucem corona lucido cingit globo
Cui coronæ sunt corona Apostoli,
Quorum figura est in columbarum choro.
(S. Paulin. Epp.)

§ In Evang. 29.   ¶ De Resurrect. 52.

one being seen at the side of Isaiah the Prophet, the other at that of the Prophet Jeremiah.' In the same way, partridges and peacocks, each with its own meaning are represented. So, again, lions, tigers, horses, oxen, strange fishes, and marine monsters, represent the fearful martyrdoms to which God's servants were exposed: a point which the reader will do well to bear in mind, because in treating of Norman mouldings we shall have occasion again to refer to this matter. So, again, the extended hand symbolised Providence. We have also the seven stars, the moon, and many other symbols of a similar kind. Nor must we forget the *Agnus Dei*, by which our Blessed Lord Himself was represented ; nor the *Pastor Bonus*, in which His own parable was still further parabolised. The Christian gems found in the Catacombs are all charged with some symbolical device. Upon these is the ship for the Church, the palm for the martyr, and the instrument of torture : as well as the sacred monogram expressing our Saviour's name. The same symbol blazed on the *labarum* of the first Christian Emperor ; and the very coins symbolically showed that the Church had subdued the kingdoms of this world. That fearful heresy, Gnosticism, which arose from an over-symbolising, shows, nevertheless how deeply the principle, within due limits, belonged to the Church. The Gnostic gems exhibit the most monstrous perversions of symbolical representations : the medals of Dioclesian bear a lying symbol of a crushed and expiring Christianity. Later still, new symbols were adopted: mosaics, illuminations, ornaments, all bore some holy emblems. The monogram i h s is found in every church in Western Christendom : the corresponding symbol stamps the Eucharistic wafers of the East.*

* See on this subject the Cambridge Camden Society's 'Argument for the Greek Origin of the Monogram IHS.'

The symbols of the Evangelists were also of very early date, though not, in all cases, appropriated as now: for the angel and the lion fluctuated between S. Matthew and S. Mark. Numbers, too, were fruitful of allegorical meaning; and the most ingenious combinations were used to elicit an esoteric meaning from them. By *one*, the Unity of the Deity was understood: by *two*, the divine and human Natures of the Saviour: by *three*, of course, the doctrine of the Most Holy Trinity: by *four*, the doctrine of the Four Evangelists: by *six*, the Attributes of the Deity: *seven* represented the sevenfold graces of the Holy Spirit: *eight* (for a reason hereafter to be noticed), Regeneration: *twelve*, the glorious company, the Apostles, and, tropologically, the whole Church. And when a straightforward reference to any of these failed, they were added or combined, till the required meaning was obtained. A single instance may suffice:—S. Augustine, writing on that passage of S. Paul's, 'What? know ye not that the saints shall judge the world?' after explaining (*Expos. super Psalm.* lxxxvi) the twelve thrones, which our Saviour mentions, of the whole Church, as founded by and represented in the Apostles, finds a further meaning. 'The parts of the world be four; the east, the west, the north, and the south:' and (adds the Father) 'they are constantly named in Holy Writ. From these four winds, saith the Lord in the Gospel, shall the elect be gathered together: whence the Church is called from these four parts. Called, and how? By the Trinity. It is not called, except by Baptism, in the name of the Father, and of the Son, and of the Holy Ghost. So four, multiplied by three, make twelve.' In accidental numbers, too, a meaning was often found. No wonder that some beheld, in the three hundred and eighteen trained servants wherewith Abraham, the Father of the Faithful, routed the combined kings, a type of the three hundred and eighteen Fathers of Nicæa, by whom the Faithful rose triumphant over the Arian heresy.

Again, types and emblems without number were seen in the language of the Psalmist, occurring so continuously in the services of the Church. 'His faithfulness shall be thy buckler,' gives rise to a fine allegory of S. Bernard's, drawn from the triangular shape of the buckler used at the time when that Father wrote; even as we still see it, in the effigies of early knights. It protects the upper part of the body completely: the feet are less completely shielded. And so, remarks the saint, does God's providence guard His people from spiritual dangers, imaged by those weapons which attack the upper, or more vital parts of the body: but from temporal adversities He hath neither promised, nor will give so complete protection.

To mention the symbolism which attached itself to the worship of the early Church, would be to go through all its rites. Confirmation and Matrimony, and, above all, Baptism, were attended by ceremonies in the highest degree symbolical. But it is needless to dwell on them; enough has been said to prove the attachment which the Catholic Church has ever evinced to symbolism.

But the Sign of the Cross is that which gave the greatest scope to symbolism.—Our readers will probably remember the passage of Tertullian in which he says, 'we cross ourselves when we go out, and when we come in; when we lie down, and when we rise up,' etc. Indeed, as in everything they used, so in everything they saw, the Sign of the Cross. The following lines from Donne are much to the purpose:

> Since Christ embraced the Cross itself, dare I
> His Image, th' Image of His Cross, deny?
> Would I have profit by the Sacrifice,

And dare the chosen Altar to despise?
It bore all other sins, but is it fit
That it should bear the sin of scorning it?
Who from the picture would avert his eye,
How should he fly His pains, Who there did die?
From me no pulpit, nor misgrounded law,
Nor scandal taken, shall this Cross withdraw:
It shall not—nor it cannot—for the loss
Of this Cross were to me another Cross:
Better were worse: for no affliction,
No cross were so extreme, as to have none.
Who can blot out the Cross, which th' instrument
Of God dewed on him in the Sacrament?
Who can deny me power and liberty
'To stretch mine arms, and mine own Cross to be?
Swim—and at every stroke thou art thy Cross:
The mast and yard are theirs whom seas do toss.
Look down, thou seest our crosses in small things,
Look up, thou seest birds fly on crossed wings.

We will mention but one symbolical feature more in the trains of thought which were common among the early Christians. We refer to the esoteric meaning which was supposed to exist in the writings of heathen authors: as for example, when the Pollio of Virgil was imagined to point to the Saviour, and the Fortunate Isles of Pindar to Paradise. It were easy but needless to dwell on this subject. The few instances we have given are already amply sufficient to prove to some, to remind others, how symbolical was the religion of the early Church, and (we think) to establish our case *à priori*.

CHAPTER III

THE ARGUMENT FROM ANALOGY

HAVING dealt with the argument *à priori*, we now proceed to show that, from analogy, it is highly probable that the teaching of the Church, as in other things, so in her material buildings, would be symbolical.

Firstly, let us look at other nations, and other religions. It need not be said that the symbolism of the Jews was one of the most striking features of their religion. It would be unnecessary to go through their tabernacle and temple rites, their sacrificial observances, and their legal ceremonies. The Passover, the cleansing of the leper, the scape goat, the feast of tabernacles, the morning and evening sacrifice, the Sabbatical year, the Jubilee, were all in the highest degree figurative. The very stones in the breastplate have each, according to the Rabbis, their mystical signification. And, as if still further to teach them the sacramentality, not only of things, but of events, it pleased God to make all their most famous ancestors, chiefs, and leaders, *e.g.* Abraham, Isaac, Jacob, Joseph, Moses, Joshua, David, most remarkable types of the Messiah: nay, from the beginning the principal doctrines of Christianity were, in some form or other, set forth. Regeneration and the Church, in the Flood and the Ark: the Bread and Wine in the Manna and the Stricken Rock: the two dispensations in Sarah and

Hagar. Indeed the immense extent of symbolism in the Old Testament was the mine of the Fathers. Every day they brought to light some new wealth ; and, if we press the symbolism of the Church further than it was actually intended, we are only treading in the steps of her bishops and doctors. For while, of course, in commenting on and explaining the sacrifice of Isaac, the covenant of circumcision, the captivity and exaltation of Joseph, they were only developing the real meaning which God seems to have intended should be set forth by those events, there are,—as we have already hinted,— many instances where their piety found an interpretation which was perhaps never intended. Thus, because Job, while all else that belonged to him was restored double, had only the same number of children which he had lost—they have argued, that thus the separate existence of souls was represented, as the Patriarch could not be said to have lost those who were in another state of existence.

And if in the Old Testament we find authority for the principle of symbolism, much more do we in the New. We shall presently have occasion to allude to the rise and progress of the sacramentality of Baptism : we may now refer more particularly to the frequency with which S. Paul symbolises the enactments of the law ; as in the case of the ox forbidden, while treading out the corn, to be muzzled. So again, the Revelation is nothing but one continued symbolical poem. The parabolic teaching of our Lord we shall presently notice.

To this we may add, the exoteric and esoteric signification of certain books, *e.g.*, the Song of Solomon : the double interpretation of many of the prophecies, primarily of the earthly, principally of the heavenly Jerusalem: we may refer to the symbolical meaning attached, under the Christian dispensation, to certain previously established rites, as, for instance, Holy Matrimony. With symbolical writings, enactments, events, personages, observances, buildings, vestments, for her guides and models, how could the Church Catholic fail of following symbolism, as a principle and a passion?

But not only is Christianity symbolical: every development of religion is, and must necessarily be so. On the Grecian mythology, we shall have occasion to say something more presently. The symbolism of Plato, and still further development by Proclus and the later philosophers of his school, will occur to every one. If it be asserted that the more it was touched and acted on by Christianity, the more symbolical did it become, —we only reply, So much the more to the purpose of our argument. But not only in Roman and Grecian Paganism is this the case. The Hindoo religion has much of symbolism; and some of its most striking fables, derived from whatever source—whether from unwritten tradition, or from contact with the Jews—possess this character wonderfully. Take, for instance, the example of Krishna suffering, and Krishna triumphant; represented, in the one case, by the figure of a man enveloped in the coils of a serpent, which fastens its teeth in his heel; in the other, by the same man setting his foot on, and crushing the head of the monster. Now here, it is true, the doctrine symbolised has long been forgotten among those with whom the legend is sacred: we, on the contrary, have a very plain reference to the promise concerning the Seed of the Woman and the serpent's head. This is an instance of the fact, that Truth will live in a symbolical, long after it has perished in every other form: and doubtless, when the time for the conversion of India shall have arrived, thousands will receive the truth the more willingly, in that they have had a representation of it, distorted it is true, but not destroyed, set, for so many centuries, before their eyes. Some truths, accidentally impressed on a symbolical observance, may still live, that otherwise must have perished: just as the only memory of some of the beings that existed before the flood, is to be found in the petrified clay on which they accidentally happened to set their feet.

The Mahometan religion has also, though in an inferior degree, its symbolism; and the reason of its inferiority in this respect is plain—because, namely, it is a religion of sense. Now Catholicity, which teaches men constantly to live above their senses, to mortify their passions, and to deny themselves;—nay even Hindooism, which, so far as it approximates to the truth, preaches the same doctrine, must constantly lead men by the seen to look on to the unseen. If everything material were not made sacramental of that which is immaterial, so, as it were, bearing its own corrective with its own temptation, man could hardly fail of walking by sight, rather than by faith. But now, the Church, not content with warning us that we are in an enemy's country, boldly seizes on the enemy's goods, converting them to her own use. Symbolism is thus the true Sign of the Cross, hallowing the unholy, and making safe the dangerous: the true salt which, being cast in, purified the unhealthy spring: the true meal which removed death from the Prophet's provision. Others may amuse themselves by asserting that the Church in all that she does and enacts, is not symbolical:—we bless God for the knowledge that she is.

We need not dwell on the symbolism of heretics, insomuch as we shall have occasion to refer to it in other parts of this essay. We will rather notice, that those to whom we have been but now referring, heathens and Mahomedans, have a way of discovering a subtle symbolism in things which in themselves were not intended to have any deeper meaning. We may mention the odes of Hafiz—the Anacreon, or rather perhaps, the Stesichorus, of Persia. These poems, speaking to the casual reader of nothing but love, and wine, and garlands, and rosebuds, are seriously affirmed, by Persian critics, to contain a deep esoteric reference to the communion of the soul with God; just as it has been wildly supposed, that under the name of Laura, Petrarch in fact only expressed that Immortal Beauty after which the soul of the Christian is constantly striving, and to which it is constantly advancing. So in Dante, Beatrice is not only the poet's earthly love, but, as it has been well shown by M. Ozanam, the representative of Catholic theology.

To dwell on the symbolism of Nature would lead us too far from our point. But we must constantly bear in mind that Nature and the Church answer to each other as implicit and explicit revelations of God. Therefore, whatever system is seen to run through the one, in all probability runs through the other. Now, that the teaching of Nature is symbolical, none, we think, can deny. Shall we then wonder that the Catholic Church is in all her art and splendour sacramental of the Blessed Trinity, when Nature herself is so? Shall God have denied this symbolism to the latter, while He has bestowed it on the former? Shall there be a trinity of effect in every picture, a trinity of tone in every note, a trinity of power in every mind, a trinity of essence in every substance,—and shall not there be a trinity in the arrangements and details of church art? It were strange if the servant could teach what the mistress must be silent upon: that Natural Religion should be endued with capabilities not granted to Revealed Truth.

Is not, again, the doctrine of the Resurrection wonderfully set forth by Nature? This symbolism is the more remarkable, in that to the ancients the rising of the sun and the bursting forth of the leaf must have appeared false symbolism, although they knew too well that of which autumn and evening were typical. So, to quote only one other example, the law of self-sacrifice is beautifully shadowed out by the grain that 'unless it die, abideth alone; but if it die, bringeth forth much fruit.'

We may argue next from the analogy of all art. Sculpture, perhaps, has least to offer in our support. But in painting we may refer to the conventional colours appropriated to various personages; and the mechanical symbolism of poetry is known to all. Nor must we forget the conventional use of language. Archaisms, studied inversions, quaint phrases, and the like, have always been affected by those who were treating of high and holy subjects. None has employed these with happier effect than Spenser, whose language, it need not be said, never was and never could have been really used. The solemnising effect of a judicious employment of this artifice is nowhere more strongly felt than in works of Divinity. Compare for example the English language, where the conventional Thou is always addressed to the Deity, and where a stern simplicity runs through the whole of our Divine Offices, with the French which can only employ *Vous* in prayer, and with the Portuguese, where, in the authorised translation of the Holy Scriptures, Apostles, and Prophets—nay, our Blessed Lord Himself, speak in the polite phrases of conversational elegance.*

* It is on grounds similar to these, that, in our translation of Durandus, we have adopted that conventional style which has been objected to by some recent critics:—not that anyone ever naturally conversed or wrote in it, but for the sake of producing the effect which the subject seems to require. The brilliancy of a summer's day is beautiful in its place: admitted into a cathedral, it would be totally out of character.

Music, however, has the strongest claims to our notice. We know, for example, that each instrument symbolises some particular colour. So, according to Haydn, the trombone is deep red—the trumpet, scarlet—the clarionet, orange—the oboe, yellow—the bassoon, deep yellow—the flute, sky blue—the diapason, deep blue—the double diapason, purple—the horn, violet:—while the violin is pink—the viola, rose—the violoncello, red—and the double-bass, crimson. This by many would be called fanciful:—therefore let us turn to a passage of Haydn's works, and see if it will hold. Let us examine the sun-rise in the 'Creation.' At the commencement, as it has been well observed, our attention is attracted by a soft-streaming sound from the violins, scarcely audible, till the pink rays of the second violin diverge into the chord of the second, to which is gradually imparted a greater fulness of colour, as the rose violas and red violoncellos steal in with expanding beauty, while the azure of the flute tempers the mounting rays of the violin: as the notes continue ascending to the highest point of brightness, the orange of the clarionet, the scarlet of the trumpet, the purple of the double diapason, unite in increasing splendour—till the sun appears at length in all the refulgence of harmony.

This may serve as a specimen of the manner in which the expressions of one art may be translated into that of another, because they each and all symbolise the same abstraction.

Again, the language of flowers is a case much in point. This is a species of symbolism which has prevailed among all nations, and which our devout ancestors were not slow in stamping with the impress of religion. Witness, for example, the *Herb Trinity*, now generally called *Heartsease*, the *Passion Flower*, and the *Lacrima Christi*. And in the present day, who knows not that the rose is for beauty—the violet for modesty—the sunflower for faithfulness—the forget-me-not for remembrance—the pansy for thought—the cypress for woe—the yew for trueheartedness—the everlasting for immortality? The flowers introduced into the ornament of churches we shall consider presently.

Furthermore, whatever was the character of our Lord's teaching—such is likely to be that of His Church. If the former were plain, unadorned, setting forth naked truths in the fewest and simplest words; then we allow that there is a *primâ facie* argument against the system which we are endeavouring to support. But if it were parabolic, figurative, descriptive, allegorical—why should not the Church imitate her Master? His parables are at once the surest defence, and the most probable originators, of her symbolism.

We shall have occasion in another place to draw from a consideration of the nature of our Lord's parables an argument in behalf of symbolism against one of the most formidable objections that has been raised against the system. It would here be sufficient for our purpose to notice the figurative character of our Lord's general teaching. But we have His own authority for much more than a general adoption of such a principle. Tradition hands down that He was within sight of the Temple when he pointed towards it, and uttered those gracious words, *I am the Door.* Be this as it may, we have from it a sufficient precedent to justify us in seeking for an emblematical meaning in the external world, and more particularly in the material sanctuary. S. Paul, on the same principle, allegorises the Jewish Temple, detail by detail:—the Holy of Holies was heaven; the High Priest, Christ; the veil, even his flesh. It is inconceivable that the Temple should be so symbolical, and so holy that our Lord Himself cleansed it from its defiling money-changers : and yet that a Christian church, wherein the Great Sacrifice is commemorated and our Lord is peculiarly present, should be less symbolical—particularly when its arrangement is in exact conformity to that of the temple,*—or should be less holy. At any rate the *Door* must be significant: at any rate the Altar, which S. Paul claims for the Christian Church, in opposition to those who 'serve the tabernacle.'

Again, the holy Sacraments of the Church are examples, in the highest degree, of this principle of figurative or symbolical teaching. They, indeed, are not only signs of unseen things, but the channels and instruments of grace. The latter quality we do not claim for the speaking symbolism of a material church : but architecture is an emblem of the invisible abstract, no less than Holy Baptism and the Lord's Supper. Besides the two Sacraments κατ' ἐξόχην, our Church recognises other offices, such as Marriage, Confirmation, and the like, as Sacramentals. In short the whole Church system is figurative from first to last : not indeed therefore the less real, actual, visible, and practical ; but rather the more real and practical, because its teaching and discipline are not merely material and temporary, but anticipative of the heavenly and eternal. This quality then of symbolism cannot be denied to one, and a most important, expression of the teaching of the Church, namely its architecture. The cathedral (to repeat the general in the particular) is not the less material, the less solid, the less real, because we see in it the figurative exhibition of the peculiarities of our religion and the articles of our creed.

* See Appendix A.

CHAPTER IV

PHILOSOPHICAL REASONS FOR BELIEVING IN SYMBOLISM

WE now propose to offer a few remarks on the philosophical reasons there seem to be for concluding that Ecclesiastical Architecture has some esoteric meaning, some figurative adaptation, more than can be appreciated, or even discerned, by the casual observer, to the uses which produced it, and which have always regulated it. We venture to approach this consideration, however, rather from a feeling that our Essay would be incomplete without some reference to this kind of argument, than from any idea of our own ability to treat on subjects so abstract and infinite; and fearing that we may not be able clearly to express or dissect those thoughts which, nevertheless, appear to our own minds both true and very important.

It is little better than a truism to assert that there is an intimate correspondence and relation between cause and effect: yet this thought opens the way to a very wide field of speculation. Mind cannot act upon matter without the material result being closely related to the mental intention which originated it: the fact that anything exists adapted to a certain end or use is alone enough to presuppose the end or use, who can see a ποίημα, without distinguishing its relation to the want or necessity which brought about ποίησις? In short, the ἐργόν, whatever it may be, not only answers to that which called it forth, but, in some sort, represents materially, or symbolises, the abstract volition or operation of the mind which originated it. Show us a pitcher, a skewer, or any of the simplest utensils designed for the most obvious purposes: do not the cavity of the one, and the piercing point of the other, at once set forth and symbolise the τέγος which was answered in their production? Now, from this thought, we might proceed to trace out the truthfulness and reality of every ποίημα considered in relation to the τὸ ποιοῦν; for even a deceptive thing is true and real in its relation to the mental intention of deceiving: but we intend merely to consider the way in which the abstract movements or ὀρέξεις of mind are *symbolised* by the material operations or results which they have produced. In other words, we would allege that everything material is symbolical of some mental process, of which it is indeed only the development: that we may see in everything outward and visible some inward and spiritual meaning. It is this which makes 'books in everything': finding in everything objective the material exhibition of the subjective and unseen; not claiming for the abstract mind an independence of matter, but acknowledging its union with it; and thus learning from the speculations of reason, to perceive the fitness for our nature of that system of sacramentality in which God has placed us, and to bless Him more and more for the Church, a sacramental institution, and for *the* Sacraments κατ' ἐξόχην, which it conveys. This method of viewing the subject will be our excuse for attempting on the one hand to learn by analysis from a material church itself, considered objectively, the symbolism which may be supposed to have directed its design; and on the other hand to show from the abstract necessities of the case that a material church might have been expected to be symbolically designed. But if this theory of symbolism gives light and meaning and connection to the acknowledged facts, whether abstract or material, with which we have to do; while no other view will explain *all* the phenomena;—it certainly recommends itself by its simplicity and harmony to a general reception. Considered in this light, the whole group of separate facts become linked together and adjusted, and so resolve themselves into a great fabric of truth, which (like the Pyramid of Cheops) is consistent and real and intelligible, when seen from any point, under any circumstances, or in any light.

But if it be granted that there is this mutual connection between the abstract and its material exhibition in every case, it will be readily admitted that a principle of sacramentality must be especially a condition of all religious acts. If we were merely spirits, without bodies or any necessary connection with matter, it would be possible perhaps for us to worship the Great Spirit in an abstract way by a sort of volition of devotion; but not being so, our souls cannot engage in adoration without the company of their material home. Hence every effort of devotion is attended by some bodily act. Whether we lift our eyes or hands to heaven, or kneel in prayer, we show forth this necessity of our being: our body has sinned, has been redeemed, will be punished or glorified, no less than the soul: it must therefore worship with the soul. Now the symbolism of the bodily acts of devotion is understood by all. We have even personated Prayer by a prostrate figure with uplifted hands.* It has been felt not only right but necessary, in

---

* The necessity which the body seems to feel for this symbolism may be seen in the constantly occurring fact, that in making signs, whether of in-all ages and places, to accompany the inward feeling of devotion with some outward manifestation of it. In other words, all religious actions are from their nature symbolical and figurative. But if the most obvious corporeal accompaniments to spiritual worship show this clearly, how much more evidently must all ritual systems appear to be symbolical? A system of worship, whether heathen, Christian, or heretical, is only the development and methodising of the simplest figurative acts of devotion ; the whole affected by the peculiar relation between the object of adoration and the worshippers which in each particular system may have been pre-supposed. Why does the Mussulman take off his shoes, kneel on his carpet towards Mecca, and perform his stated ablutions ? Is not each act in itself figurative and full of meaning ? How could such a system, or any other system, have been originated, but with some intended typification of certain given facts or doctrines or feelings ? Why does the heartless Quaker go with covered head into his bare conventicle, and sit in enforced silence? He will answer, to *express* his independence of idle forms, the spirituality of his worship, his repudiation of any *media* in his intercourse with the Divine Being. We thank him for his admission of a symbolical purpose, but we read the symbolism differently. We perceive it to express clearly enough the presumptuous pride and vanity of his sect, his rejection of all Sacraments, and his practical disbelief in the Communion of Saints. Again, is the pulpit of the Brownist symbolical ; and shall not our font and altar be so at least as much ? The Catholic ritual is indeed symbolical from first to last. Without the clue to its figurative meaning, we should never have understood its pregnant truthfulness and force. No one, in

quiry or adieu, to a person at a distance, we naturally *speak* the words, though inaudible to him, which the gestures we use express.

short, ever ventured to regard the ancient ritual as anything but highly figurative: this was claimed as its highest excellence by its observers and commentators, this was ridiculed and despised by the enemies of the Church; but was confessed by all. The more anyone meditates on the ancient ritual of the Church, the more this will be found not only the most prominent characteristic, but the only satisfactory explanation of many otherwise unintelligible requirements. This is not the place to go at any length into the consideration of the whole symbolism of the ritual system: it will be enough if it is granted that some prescribed ritual, however meagre, must be a necessary part of all religion; and that every such system is in some degree figurative or symbolical. Now to apply this to church architecture. No one will deny that, in a general point of view, the form of our churches is adapted to certain wants, and was chosen for this very adaptation. Indeed this is allowed by modern writers and builders: who defend a church which has no more than an altar-recess, on this very ground, that there is no longer any want of a deep chancel. 'I object to aisles,' says a modern architect, 'because the great end of a church is to be an auditorium.' 'The cross form,' says another, 'I always adopt, because then everyone can see the preacher if I place the pulpit in the middle.' But why not take a circle or octagon at once, or the form which is always adopted for the lecture-rooms at Mechanics' Institutes? For these plans are obviously *most* convenient for hearing and seeing. But then, everyone knows that these are not *church* forms. The modern builder then, trammelled, at least in this respect, by rule and precedent, chooses the cruciform plan, not (perhaps) for its true symbolism; but, by a wrong arrangement of this plan, still further symbolises (for example) his own undue estimation of the ordinance of preaching. So true it is that those who would most object to symbolism, as a rule of design, are themselves (did they but know it) symbolising, in every church they build, their own arbitrary and presumptuous ideas on the subject. It is not our intention to prove here, (what has been pointed out, however, many times), the duty incumbent upon us of following in our modern churches the ancient principles of design : we are not writing with the immediate practical end of improving modern church architecture; but are endeavouring to illustrate the symbolical principles of ancient design. We shall, however, before finishing this chapter, choose an example, which will apply to us, as well as to any other branch of the Church, to show how essentially church architecture in that respect at least is a part of the Ritual system. And if Catholic worship is expressed and represented by Catholic ritual, and if church architecture is a part of this ritual, then is church architecture itself an expression and exponent of Catholic worship. A conclusion this which will well warrant the very strong language in which the Cambridge Camden Society have always asserted the great importance of this art, and have exacted from its professors such qualifications of personal holiness and liturgical knowledge as are no less above the attainment than the aspirations of the modern school.

It may not be clear to some how in any sense architecture can be called symbolical, or the outward sign of something invisible: or rather what the process is by which a given arrangement, suggested perhaps by some necessity, becomes in turn suggestive and figurative of the very purpose for which it was planned. But let us take the case of a theatre. Here it is clearly necessary that there shall be a stage or orchestra, accommodation for spectators, and means of easy exit. Accordingly every theatre displays all these requisites. And does not the building then in turn emblem the purpose for which it was planned? The ruins of Roman theatres are not uncommon: do we fail to be recalled by them to the idea of the Roman stage? are not the several parts of the material building highly figurative and suggestive of the rules and orders of the abstract drama?

With respect to churches: let us suppose the institution and ritual of the Church to be what we know it was; and that we have to adapt some architectural arrangement to the performance of this ritual. Is there anything which will dictate any general form rather than another? Surely there is. We will not speak now of the propriety of setting aside a place for the celebration of the Holy Eucharist, or of the propriety of retaining the plan of the typical Temple; but we are considering simply what is required by practical necessity. The worshippers who are to assemble in our church are not all on an equality. There are some who are endowed with high privileges as being those consecrated to the immediate service of the sanctuary. In early times so real a thing was the distinction between the clergy and the laity, that the Church being divided into these two classes, the material edifice displayed a like division: and the nave and chancel preach to posterity the sacredness of Holy Orders, and the mutual duties arising from the relation in which the flock stand to their shepherds. But in early ages the laity were not all classed *en masse* as with us now. Among them were the Faithful, the Catechumens, who had not yet been admitted to Holy Baptism, and the Penitents or those who had lapsed. True to itself, church architecture provided then a separate place for each of these divisions. Does not the ground plan of such a church symbolise minutely the then state of church discipline and the conditions of church worship? The reality and meaning of such an arrangement may be shown thus also. After the Reformation the great distinction between clergy and laity became lost or undervalued: accordingly the chancel-screens in many places disappeared, as symbolical in their absence as in their existence. But still there was a necessity for some material arrangement to protect the Altar from insult: and so altar rails came in, manifest symbols of that spirit which made their introduction allowable, if indeed not necessary:* still these very rails, and the penned up reading-pew, teach that the clergy, at least when performing a function, are divided from the laity.

Now it is of no consequence whatever, whether the early builders of churches intended this particular arrangement to be symbolical. The arrangement being adopted becomes necessarily, even if unintentionally, symbolical, by the process we have endeavoured to trace, and so things essentially symbolical give rise to intended symbolism: for it is a simple historical fact that the weathercock, whatever practical utility may have first suggested its use and peculiar form, has been for many centuries placed on the church spire for its *intentional symbolism*.† And the process is repeated: for suppose one only of the conventional symbolical meanings of the weathercock had been discovered: the thoughtful mind

---

* In the correspondence of the Rev. W. Humphrey, whose atrocious treatment by the Church Missionary Society has so lately excited the indignation of all true churchmen, it appears that one of the noble designs of this zealous priest was to restore for the peculiar congregation over which he was appointed, consisting of Faithful, Catechumens, and Unbelievers, the distinct arrangement of the ancient Church: the modern plan of having but one area for the lay worshippers being found inconvenient and injurious. That is to say, our modern church arrangement may suit and does symbolise the present state of the Church with us, but does not suit and does not symbolise the state of the missionary Church of India.

† See Rationale, p. 27.

goes on to find out other figurative senses in which its use is appropriate, and these conventional meanings become in their turn intentionally symbolised by future church builders. This may be illustrated also in the following way: The Jews, in the rite of Baptism, had probably no other idea than a reference to 'the mystical washing away of sins.' But when S. Paul had once given to that rite the new idea of a burial with Christ in the Baptismal water, and a rising again with Him, this typical meaning became an example of intended symbolism to all those who should hereafter use it.

As we began this part of our subject with hesitation, so we finish it with some degree of apprehension. To some what has been said may seem more than ordinarily visionary and ridiculous: yet others, we hope, will feel that, however feebly and inadequately expressed, there is some truth in what has been advanced concerning the relation between the material and immaterial: that the latter welding and moulding the former into an expression of itself, makes it in turn a type of that which it expresses. So that if on the one hand, to take our particular branch of the subject, the theoretical ritual and ordinances of religion imply and require certain peculiar adaptations of the material building in which they are to be celebrated; then in turn the circumstances of the material fabric suggest and symbolise the peculiar conditions of ritual which induced them. In short we have endeavoured to prove that from our very nature every outward thing is symbolical of something inward and spiritual: but, above all things, outward religious actions are sacramental; and particularly *any* prescribed ritual, of which the first characteristic is that it is figurative: that the Catholic ritual is eminently symbolical, and from its nature very strikingly influences all its material appliances: that church architecture is the eldest daughter of Ritual : that the process, according to which architecture was influenced by the requirements of Ritualism was at first as simple as that by which the form of a theatre sprang from the conditions which were to be fulfilled by its builder : that thus a church (built in the fully developed style of Christian architecture) even if not built with any intention of symbolising, (though it is an historical fact that the symbolism of each part was known and received *before* the erection of any church of this style,) became nevertheless essentially a 'petrifaction of our religion' : a fact which, once admitted and realised, becomes to succeeding church builders, whether they will or not, a rule and precedent for intentional symbolical design.

CHAPTER V

THE ANALYTICAL ARGUMENT

WE must arrive at the same conclusion, if we consider the subject in an analytical way. For example: suppose a person, hitherto unacquainted not only with the general peculiarities of Christian churches, but also with Christianity itself, were to enter a cathedral; or (which will be a fairer case) were to visit a Catholic country, and examine its churches as a whole, would he not, if possessed of only ordinary intelligence, observe that the cross form, for example, was of most common occurrence, and, in the case of the larger buildings, was perhaps the only plan adopted? And would he not then naturally inquire why there should be this marked preference for a form, in itself inconvenient for purposes of hearing or seeing,* and open to great mechanical objections, such as the almost resistless pressure of the four arms on the piers which stand at the angles of intersection? But if he learnt that the religion for which these temples were designed was that of the Cross, he would at once see the propriety of this ground plan, and would confidently and truly conclude that this form was chosen in order to bring the Cross, by this symbolism, vividly and constantly before the eyes of the worshippers. To deny intended symbolism, in the case of such a person, would

* That is, a Catholic *arrangement* of the church being presumed.

clearly be absurd : shall it be less obvious to us ? Our traveller would probably, being satisfied on this point, examine these buildings more closely. He would find an altar raised conspicuously above the surrounding level ; and for this he might discover a practical reason ; but why in so many cases (so many as well nigh to make a rule) are the steps either *three* or some multiple of three ? Surely the fundamental doctrine of the Holy Trinity would, if explained to him, sufficiently account for this all but universal arrangement. Why, again, in every case does a screen separate one part of the church from the other ? When our inquirer learns the principle of the separation of laity and clergy, this arrangement also will be at once intelligible and figurative. How unreasonable would the position of the font by the door appear to him, till he learnt the symbolical reason for its being placed there ! And we may here remark that the practice of the last generation in removing old fonts, or using basins for substitutes, or in placing new fonts, near the altar, shows clearly enough that convenience and utility would have pointed out a very different place for the font from what is assigned by the canon, on symbolical grounds ; grounds adduced in this case, as it would seem, to give weight to a decision so clearly opposed to all merely practical and obvious reasons. Again, the marked deviation of the orientation of the chancel from that of the nave, would be quite inexplicable till the beautiful and affecting symbolism of the arrangement were pointed out.

Again, it has not been left merely to the meditative ecclesiologist to observe that Christian architecture has as decided a characteristic of verticality, as Pagan architecture had of horizontalism. A mere artist could not fail of marking the contrast between Beauvais and the temples of Pæstum. The contrast must then be admitted: but how must we explain it? Surely no accident could have developed the grovelling Pagan into the aspiring Gothic. What mechanical reasons could produce Westminster from even the Parthenon? But is not the phenomenon explained when we see in towering pier, spire, and pinnacle, the symbolical exhibition of that religion which alone aspires to things above, nay more, the figurative commemoration of that Resurrection itself, which alone originates, and only justifies, the same heavenward tendency. But if this be true; if these acknowledged peculiarities in Christian architecture be utterly unintelligible on any other supposition than this of a symbolical meaning, surely it is not unreasonable to receive so ready a solution of the difficulty: and, the principle admitted, why may not reasons of the same figurative nature be assigned for other arrangements, in themselves on any other interpretation not only meaningless but obviously useless or absurd?

CHAPTER VI

THE INDUCTIVE ARGUMENT

WE have next to show, by a process of induction, that some principles of symbolism have always been observed in designing churches: that is to say, that without any actual acquaintance with the plan, details or arrangement of existing churches, we might gather from other sources, not only the probability, but the fact, that there was some reason (not merely mechanical or accidental) for the selection and universal observation of particular forms and ornaments, and peculiar rules of distribution.

First, we shall refer to the celebrated passage of S. Clement of Rome,* about performing the Divine Offices decently and in order, as to time, and place, and circumstance. 'Where and by whom God willeth these to be performed He hath Himself defined by His most supreme will.' 'But where,' says Mede,† (discussing the passage with the view of establishing a particular point, namely, bowing towards the altar) 'hath the Lord defined these things, unless He hath left us to the analogy of the Old Testament?' This indeed is obviously S. Clement's meaning: and not to go at any

---

* S. Clem. Rom., ad Corinth. 1, 40.

† Mede, in Epist. lviii Folio, Lib. iv.

length into the consideration of all the particular forms or ceremonies of the Old dispensation which were perpetuated in the New—as the threefold Ministry deduced by S. Jerome, from the High Priest, Priests, and Levites; the Canonical Hours; the Gospel anciently laid on the altar, answering to the Two Tables, and the like—it will be sufficient to refer once more to the remarkable parallel between a Christian church and the Jewish Temple.* There can be little doubt that Mede proved his point of the propriety of genuflexion towards the altar. We are contending for a much simpler thing: for no more indeed than the concession of a probability that in the earliest Christian churches there was at least this resemblance to the Temple; that there should be in both a Holy of Holies and an outer-court. Supposing this distinction to have been only made by a curtain, our point is nevertheless gained; and we would rest here on this one particular of resemblance only (though others might be insisted on); because, any one designed parallel being granted, the inference for others is easy. And here it will be enough to observe that the almost constant practice in ancient writers of applying to some one part of a Christian church a name or names derived directly from the *Holy of Holies* is a strong argument in our favour: though the passages are often too incidental to be adduced as evidence of an intended symbolism.†
But, we repeat, the fact that a particular part of a church—(if we were now arguing for rood screens, we

---

* See this carried out by Durandus. Appendix A.

† Compare, amongst others, S. Cyprian, Ep. 55; Euseb. x, 4. τὸ ἅγιον ἁγίων θυσιαστήριον; Id. vii, 18. τὸ ἁγίασμα (the word used in the lxx for the *Sanctuary*): S. Dionys. Areop., Ep. 8, ad Demoph.; S. Athanas.. *Edit. Commel.* Tom. ii, p. 255; Theod. H. E. iv, 17, v, 18; Concil. Tours. (A. D. 557). can. 4; S. Germ. Constant. *In Theor. rer. Eccles.*; Card. Bona. *Rer Liturg.* i, xxv, 11; Dionys. *Hierarch.* cap. 2; S. Chrysost. Lib vi, *De Sacerdotio.*

should show that any such distinction of parts made a *screen of some sort* necessary, even if we did not know what sort of screens really existed)—the fact that a particular part of a church was distinguished by names directly carrying us back to the exactly corresponding particular part in the Temple, shows that in the arrangement at least, if not in the building, of the earliest churches there was, at least in this one point, an intention to produce an antitype to the typical Tabernacle. It is observed in a note to Neander's history * that if the interpretation of Michaelis be received there is evidence of a Christian church being built at Edessa, A.D. 202, with three parts, expressly after the model of the Temple.

Whatever may be the authority allowed to the Apostolical Constitutions, the fact that they touch at some length upon the form of churches is enough for our purpose. 'The church,'† they say, 'must be oblong in form, and pointing to the East.' The oblong form was meant to symbolise a ship,‡ the ark which was to save us from the stormy world. It would be perfectly unnecessary to support this obvious piece of symbolism by citations. The orientation is an equally valuable example of intended symbolism. We gain an additional testimony to this from the well-known passage of Tertullian,§ (A.D. 200,) about 'The house of our Dove.' Whether this corrupt extract be interpreted with Mede or Bingham, there can be no doubt that its

---

* Rose's Neander, i, 246.   † Apost. Const. 2, 57, (61.)

‡ See also what is said on this point by Buscemi, in his Notizie della Basilica di San Pietro. ch. iii, p. 7. The church of SS. Vincenzo and Anastatio at Rome, near S. Paolo alle Tre Fontane, built by Honorius I, (A.D. 630) has its wall *curved* like the ribs of a ship. The constitution itself refers to the resemblance of this oblong form to a ship. See also S. Clem. Alex., *Paedag*, iii, 246.

§ Tertull. advers. Valent., cap. 2.

in lucem means that the church should face the East or dayspring. The praying towards the East was the almost invariable custom in the Early Churches, and as symbolical as their standing in prayer upon the Festivals of the Resurrection.* So common was orientation in the most ancient churches, that Socrates† mentions particularly the church at Antioch as having its 'position reversed; for the altar does not look to the east but to the west.' This rule appears to have been more scrupulously followed in the East than in the West; though even in Europe examples to the contrary are exceptions.

The Apostolical Constitution in its other directions about the position of the bishop, priests, and deacons, and the separate stations for the sexes, shows (as Father Thiers‡ has remarked) that there was even then a marked distinction between the clergy and laity though the method of division is not described. At any rate, what has been here adduced—compiled from notes taken some time since for another object, and without access (from accidental circumstances) to a library— seems enough to show that in the earliest notices of Christian churches there is distinct intimation of at least three particulars of intended symbolism.

The circular form given to the church of the Holy Sepulchre was of course appropriate enough in that particular case, where the sepulchre would naturally become the centre. The circular churches of Europe were again imitated from this. The Cross form would appear to have made its first appearance in Constantinople: that is, in the city which was the first to take a

---

* See Origen, *Hom.* 5, *in Numer.* cap. 4. Tertull. *Apol.* cap. 16, and *Ad Nation.* i, 13. S. Clem. Alex. *Strom.* vii, *ante med.* quoted by Mede.

† Hist. Eccles. Lib. v, cap. κβ'.

‡ Thiers, *Dissert. de la Clôture du Chœur des Eglises.* cap. 2.

completely Christian character. For example, the church of the Apostles built by Constantine was cruciform: and the symbolism of this is pointed out by S. Gregory Nazianzen in his poem, 'the Dream of Anastasia,' quoted by Bingham.* So Evagrius describes the church of S. Simon Stylites, as cited by Buscemi,† who also mentions a Cross church founded by King Childebert, about the year 550. The cathedral of Clermont, mentioned by S. Gregory of Tours, and the church of SS. Nazarius and Celsus at Ravenna, both founded about 450, were cruciform. More than this, we have examples of an oblong church being *intentionally* made cruciform by the addition of *apsides*, as at Blachernœ by Justin Junior, instanced by Bingham out of Cedrenus and Zonaras. This has been remarked also in the case of some Italian churches: though the early churches of the West seemed to have retained the oblong form, even when the details and general arrangement were Byzantine, as in the *Capella Regia* at Messina; the more remarkable from the peculiar influence of Constantinople in the island of Sicily. But in either case there was a symbolising intention on the part of the founders of churches.

There is mention also of octagonal churches, as at Antioch and Nazianzum: but these seem to have been mere exceptions; and perhaps from being coupled with fonts in the inscription quoted by Mr Poole from Gruter, may have been intended to symbolise Regeneration. The first two lines are as follows:—

> Octachorum sanctos templum surrexit in usus:
> Octagonus fons est munere dignus eo.

Bingham mentions that the oblong form was sometimes called δρομικὸν which he explains as intimating that they

---

* Carm. ix. tom ii, p. 79.
πλευραῖς σταυροτύποις τέτραχα τεμνόμενον.
† Notizie etc. Note al Lib. 1, capo terzo. Nota 10 p. 15.

had void spaces for deambulation.* It seems however more likely that the name was derived from the resemblance between this form of church and a stadium; the apsidal end answering to the curve round the goal.

Some objection may be raised to our theory because Bingham, from whom of course almost all the existing passages in ancient writers about the form of churches might be gathered, does not recognise any such principles, and rather seems on the other hand to believe that there was at first no rule or law on these points. But it is not detracting from his fame for almost consummate learning to question whether his practical knowledge of church architecture, ancient or modern, was very deep. It might be shown indeed to be far otherwise. But at any rate the principle now contended for never entered his mind, or he would have seen that some of the very passages he adduces to show that the form of ancient churches was accidental, because (for example) they were often made out of Basilicæ or even heathen temples, really tell against such a supposition. He quotes from Socrates † a description of the conversion of a Pagan island to Christianity, about 380, and the turning the heathen temple into a church. But the words of the original, given in our note, are very remarkable: 'The guise of the temple they transformed unto the type (or pattern) of a church.' We want to prove nothing more than that there was *some* type of a church. It was not a mere ejection of idols that was required to make a temple into a church: but some change of form and arrangement. So also in a passage from Sozomen (vii, 15), ' The temple of Dionysus which

---

* Book viii, 3, following Leo Allatius and Suicer.

† Socrates iv, 24, τὸ δὲ σχῆμα τοῦ ναοῦ εἰς ἐκκλησίας τύπον μεταποιήσαντες.

they had, was changed in fittings (μετεσκευάσθη) into a church.' Again, a very interesting passage about the conversion of Iberia by means of a female captive in the time of Constantine is cited from Theodoret,* to show that churches *did exist* at that date. But we find a particular form of building clearly alluded to in the original: and, more than this, ' He Who filled Bezaleel with a wise spirit for building, judged this captive also worthy of grace, so as to design the divine temple. And so she designed, and they built.' And this passage brings us at once to the famous panegyric on Paulinus, Bishop of Tyre, and builder of the church there preserved by Eusebius. In this speech the prelate is throughout supposed to have been inspired for his work, and is compared to Bezaleel, Solomon and Zerubbabel, the builders of the Tabernacle, and the First and Second Temples. And not only is the general spirit assumed to be a directly religious one: but the details are described as having a symbolical meaning.

In the comparison between the material temple and the 'living temple' the Spiritual Church, there are several points worthy of observation. The symbolical explanation of the corner stone as our Lord, of the foundation as the Apostles and Prophets, of the stones as the members of the Church, are of course taken directly from Holy Scripture. It is scarcely necessary to remark the great authority for considering the fabric of the church as symbolical which these passages convey. Many of our readers will remember how S. Hermas carries out into considerable detail the same idea. But the Panegyrist in Eusebius distinctly refers to 'the most

---

* Theodoret I. xxiv. Τὴν ἀξιόγαστον ἐκείνην καταλαβὼν δοριάλωτον, παρεκάλει δεῖξαι τῆς οἰκοδομίας τὸ σχῆμα· Ὁ δὲ τὸν Βεσελιὴλ τῆς ἀρχιτεκτονικῆς σοφίας ἐμπλήσας καὶ ταύτην ἠξίωσε χάριτος, ὡς τὸν θεῖον διαγράψαι νεών· καὶ ἡ μὲν διέγραψεν, οἱ δὲ ἄρυττόν τε καὶ ᾠκοδομοῦν.

inward recesses [of that spiritual temple] which are unseen of the many, and are essentially holy and holy of holies';* that is, of course, to a Sanctuary; which he goes on to describe as having 'sacred inclosures,' and as being accessible to the priest alone; with a distinct reference to S. Paul's † illustration taken from the Jewish Temple. Again he proceeds to compare the Bishop Paulinus with the 'great High Priest,' not only in being permitted to enter the holy of holies, but in doing what Christ has done, just as the Son did what He saw the Father do. 'Thus he, looking with the pure eyes of his mind unto the Great Teacher, whatsoever he seeth Him doing, as if making use of archetypal patterns, has, by building ($\delta\eta\mu\iota o\nu\rho\gamma\hat{\omega}\nu$) as much like them as possible, wrought out images of them as closely as can be; having in no respect fallen short of Bezaleel, whom God Himself, having filled him with the Spirit of wisdom and knowledge and other skilful and scientific lore, called to be the builder of the material expression of the heavenly types in the symbols of the temple. In this way then Paulinus also, carrying wholly like a graven image in his soul Christ Himself, the Word, the Wisdom the Light. . . . . has constructed this magnificial temple of the most High God, resembling in its nature the pattern of the better (temple) as a visible (emblem) of that which is invisible.'‡ This remarkable passage appears to assert (i) the inspiration of the architect, (ii) the fact of this heavenly type, which (iii) material churches ought to follow; and (iv) the general symbolism of the Spiritual Church by the visible fabric. We must pass over a great deal of this oration, with a general request that such as are interested in this discussion will read

---

* Euseb. H. E., x, 4, 21.   † Hebrews, ix, 6, 7.

‡ Euseb. X, iv, 24, 25.

the whole in the original for the sake of seeing its general spirit and bearing. The description of the details is of great interest. The arrangement of the porticoes, etc., is of course quite adapted to the wants of the Church in that age: it is fair to own that the chief entrance appears to have faced the East in this church. Mention is made also of seats in order for the bishops and presbyters, and of the altar in the midst: the whole being encompassed with wooden network, exquisitely worked, in order to be made inaccessible to the multitude.* Further on† we read that Paulinus rebuilt his church, 'such as he had been taught from the delineation of the holy oracles.' And again, 'More wonderful than wonders are the *archetypes*, and the intelligent and godlike *prototypes* and *patterns* (of earthly church building): namely, I say, the renewing of the divine and reasonable building in the soul'; ‡ assuming that material churches are but copies from some heavenly type. Again, a passage, in which the ruined fabric and the persecuted Church are mixed up, speaks of the Church as 'having been made after the image of God,'§ and more to the same effect. The symbolical prophecy of the 'fair edification' of the Gentile Church ‖ is quoted as being almost literally fulfilled in the Tyrian church, and is still further symbolised by the Panegyrist.¶ The four-square atrium is said to set forth the four Gospels of the scripture.** The whole arrangement of the church is symbolised at much length, as setting forth the different divisions of the laity and the states of the faithful with respect to advance in holiness. The great portico symbolised God the Father: the side porticoes the other Two Persons of the Most Holy Trinity. The seats represented the souls of the faithful, upon which,

* Euseb. H. E., x, 43 † Ibid 53. ‡ Ibid 54. § Ibid 57.
‖ Isaiah liv, 11. ¶ Euseb. X. iv, 60. ** Ibid 61.

as on the Day of Pentecost, the cloven tongues would descend and *sit* upon each of them. 'The revered and great and only altar, what could this be but the spotlessness of soul and holiness of holies of the common Priest of us all?'* Once more, the parallel between the spiritual and the material Churches being continued, the Word, the Great Demiurgus of all things, is said to have Himself made upon earth a copy of the heavenly pattern which is the Church of the Firstborn written in heaven, Jerusalem that is above, Sion the Mount of God, and the city of the living God.

It appears then that throughout this description a symbolical meaning is found attached to the material church: and this not far-fetched or now first fancifully imagined; but appealing, as it seems, to what the auditors would be prepared to grant, and admitted by the historian without a comment, as one specimen of a class.

We have before remarked that every notice of the particular distribution of a church for the reception of the different classes of Christians, may be taken as an argument on our side: for if it can be shown that the form of churches was not arbitrary, but was adapted to certain peculiar wants, it must be granted that there was some particular law of design, and that law connected with Ritual: and then, as before pointed out, this arrangement becomes itself symbolical, and that *intentionally*. We shall only refer here to a passage quoted by Bingham,† in which S. Gregory Thaumaturgus describes the places in church assigned respectively to the five degrees of Penitents. Mede‡ argues for the *existence* of churches in the first three centuries, from the universal custom of praying towards the East, the necessity of

---

* Euseb. H. E., x, 65. † Greg. Nyssen, iii, 567.
‡ Discourse of Churches, Folio Edn., p. 333.

providing distinct places for the Penitents, Hearers, Catechumens, and Faithful, and from the patterns of the Jewish *proseuchæ* and synagogues. But all these arguments seem to tell as much for some particular form of churches as for their existence: that is they prove that the earliest churches were designed on rules which, even if not intentionally symbolical (though we have shown that many were so), became by a natural process intentional among later church-builders.

So also with respect to the great division into nave and sanctuary by a screen of some sort: concerning which the passages that might be cited from ancient writers would be innumerable. We shall only give one quoted by Father Thiers from a Poem of S. Gregory of Nazianzum, in which the *balustrade* or rood-screen is said to be 'between two worlds, the one immovable, the other changeful; the one of gods (or heaven) the other of mortals (or earth); that is to say between the choir and the nave, between the clergy and the laity.'

We have attempted to prove then that the earliest Christian churches were designed, or described, symbolically: by showing that there was a reason for their shape, whether oblong, cruciform, or circular; for their main division into choir and nave, and their subdivision for the penitents: for their orientation; and even to some extent for their minor internal arrangements: and that some type or pattern of a church was universally recognised.* It would require more reading than we can boast of to give a catena of writers who have asserted the symbolism of churches. But if the

---

* Much stress is laid by some on the acknowledged Bascilican origin of churches as an argument against the principle here contended for. But we find a great authority on the Antiquities of Christian Rome deciding differently: 'There seems to be in the building of churches, as in the mosaics, and other works of art of the old Christian times in Rome one constant type in which the art of building could show little freedom or variety.—*Beschreibung der Stadt Rom. Basiliken.* vol. i, p. 430.

point has been in any way proved for the first four centuries, enough will have been done: since from that period we can trace from existing edifices the gradual relinquishment of the peculiar Basilican plan, and general adoption of the Latin Cross, or oblong, in the West, while the East consistently retained the Greek Cross. We observe it stated * that Mr E. Sharpe, in a paper read before the Cambridge Camden Society, described the gradual '*typical* additions' to the Basilican ground plan. Indeed symbolism, to any extent, once made known, must have become a rule and precedent to later church architects.

S. Isidore, of Seville, incidentally mentions many symbolical arrangements: they will be found in the notes to the text of the Rationale. Many pieces of symbolism are to be found incidentally in the Decretum of Gratian.

In mentioning Durandus himself, it seems proper to anticipate an objection which may occur to some readers. The authority, it may be said, of that writer must be very small who can give such absurd derivations as *cemeterium* from *cime*, *altare* from *alta res*, *allegory* from *allon* and *gore*. But it must be remembered, firstly, that in the thirteenth century, Greek was a language almost unknown in Europe: next, that our author nowhere professes an acquaintance with it: further, that the science of derivation was hardly understood till within the last few years: and lastly, that Cicero's authority led Durandus into some errors; for instance, his derivation of *templum* from *tectum amplum*.

One proof of the *reality* of Durandus's principles we must not fail to notice. It is the express allusion which he makes to, and the graphical description which he

* Ecclesiologist, vol. i, p. 120.

gives of, that which we know to have been the style of architecture employed in his time. The tie beams, the deeply splayed windows, the interior shafts, all prove that we are engaged with a writer of Early English date.

It is very remarkable, that Durandus, S. Isidore, Beleth, and the rest, seem to quote from some canons of church symbolism now unknown to us. Their words are often, even where they are not very connected nor intelligible, the same. One example may suffice. ' In that this rod,' says Hugh of S. Victor, ' is placed above the Cross, it is shown that the words of Scripture be consummated and confirmed by the Cross: whence our Lord said in His Passion, " It is Finished." *And His Title was indelibly written over Him* ' (p. 200). ' In that the iron rod,' says Durandus, ' is placed above the Cross, on the summit of the church, it signifieth that Holy Scripture is now consummated and confirmed. Whence saith our Lord in his Passion, " It is Finished," *and that Title is written indelibly over Him* (p. 28). The following, by way of another instance, is the symbolical* description of a church, written on a fly-leaf, at the beginning of a MS. ' Psalterium Glossatum,' in the public library at Boulogne, though formerly in that of S. Bertin's Abbey, at S. Omer.

The text is either of the tenth or eleventh century; but it will be seen that the words of Durandus, writing at so great a distance of time and place, are nearly the same in some passages.

> Fundamentum ipsius Cameræ est Fides.
> Altitudo ejus est Spes.
> Latitudo ejus est Caritas.
> Longitudo ejus est Perseverantia.
> Latera ejus sunt Concordia et Pax.

* *British Magazine*, 1843, p. 393.

Frontes ipsius sunt Justicia & Veritas.
Pulchritudo ejus est exemplum bonorum operum.
Fenestræ ejus sunt dicta sanctorum.
Pavimentum ejus est humilitas cordis.
Camera est conversatio cœlestis.
Pilastri ejus sunt spiritales virtues.
Columnæ ejus sunt boni pontifices & sacerdotes.
Interlegatio ejus est vinculum pacis.
Tectum ejus est fidelis dispensator.
* isces ejus sunt mediatio celestis.
Mensa Christi est in camera bona conversatio.
Ministerium Christi in camera sua est bona memoria.
Facinus Christi est bona voluntas.
Canterellus Christi est nitor conscientiæ.
Cathedra Christi est serenitas mentis.
Sponsa Christi est sancta anima.
Camerariæ Christi spiritales virtutes sunt :
Prima Sancta Caritas dicta est ; illa Christi regit cameram.
Secunda est Sancta Humilitas ; illa est thesauraria in camera Christi
Tertia est Sancta Patientia ; illa facit luminaria in camera Christi.
Quarta Sancta Puritas ; illa scopat cameram Christi.

But besides, and in our opinion stronger than this express and continuous testimony to the fact that Catholic architecture is symbolical, we have the testimony of all other branches of Catholic art, which none ever did, or could deny to be figurative and sacramental. Let us take merely the rites which accompany the close of Easter week. We enter a darkened church, illuminated only by the lighted 'Sepulchre': we hear the history of the Passion chaunted by three voices in three recitatives: we have the most mournfully pathetic strain for the 'Reproaches' which perhaps the human mind ever imagined:—we pray for Pagans—and we kneel; we pray for Turks—and we kneel; we pray for the Jews, and we kneel not ; in abhorrence of the mockery that bowed the knee to the King of the Jews. We enter that church again, now perfectly darkened, except for the one lamp that renders the lectern and the books thereon just visible: the solemn litanies seem in that obscurity, and amidst the silent crowd of worshippers, more solemn than usual. There is a short pause: then in one second, priests and people, voices and instruments, burst forth with the Easter Alleluia: light pours in from every window of the cathedral: showers of rose leaves fall from the roof: bells—silent for three long days, peal from every church tower: guns fire and banners wave: *Dominus resurrexit vere, Alleluia, et apparuit Simoni Alleluia.*

Now, without being concerned to defend, or the contrary, any or all of these ceremonies, we ask:—Is it possible to conceive that the Church which invented so deeply symbolical a system of worship — should have rested content with an unsymbolical building for its practice? This consideration, perhaps, belongs to the analogical branch of our essay: yet it may also find a place here, as one of the strongest parts of the inductive argument.

Seeing then that there are strong reasons *à priori* for believing that the ritual and architecture of the Church would partake of a decidedly symbolical character: that by the analogy of the practice amongst all religionists, of the operations of God in nature, of the conditions of Art, and especially of the whole sacramental system of the Church, it is likely that church architecture itself would be sacramental: that from the nature of things everything material is in some sort sacramental, and a material fabric essentially figurative of the purpose for which it was designed: that an actual Christian church (taken as we find it) has such accidents as can be explained on no other than a symbolical supposition, and might be analysed into just those elements from which, by induction, we first constructed an hypothetical Christian church: and lastly, that from express and continuous historical testimony without any actual acquaintance with existing fabrics we might have deduced that the material church would be itself, to some extent, a figurative expression of the religion for the celebration of which it was constructed : it does not seem too much to assert that Christian architecture owes its distinctive peculiarities to its sacramental character, and that consequently we can neither appreciate ancient examples nor hope to rival them, at least in their perfection, without taking into account this principle of their design. In other words, the cause of that indefinable difference between an ancient and modern church which we were led to discover at the beginning of this treatise, is neither association of ideas nor correctness of detail, nor picturesqueness, nor of a mechanical nature, but (in the most general point of view) is the sacramentality, the religious symbolism, which distinguished and sanctified this as every other branch of mediæval art.

CHAPTER VII

EXAMPLES OF SYMBOLISM

IN endeavouring shortly to develop the practice of symbolism, according to our view of the subject, we are fully aware that to those who have never yet bestowed a thought upon it, we shall appear mere visionaries or enthusiasts. It has been the fashion of late to smile at the whole theory, as amusing and perhaps beautiful: but quite unpractical and indeed impracticable. We cannot hope to convince by æsthetics those who are deaf to more direct arguments, and who refuse to view everything, as churchmen ought to do, through the medium of the Church. But those who agree with us in the latter duty, will perhaps suffer themselves to think twice on what will be advanced before they condemn it.

We shall consider the practice of symbolism as connected with, 1. The Holy Trinity; 2. Regeneration; 3. The Atonement; 4. The Communion of Saints; and then we shall notice several parts of a church, such as windows, doors, etc., with their specific symbolical meaning.

The doctrine of the Holy Trinity has left, as might be expected, deeper traces in the structure of our churches than any other principles of our faith. We have already noticed that possibly the Basilican arrangement might be providentially ordered with reference to this. In

Saxon times we find the idea carried out, not only by the Nave and two Aisles, but also by the triple division in length, into Nave, Chancel, and Sanctum Sanctorum. This triple division is most frequently given in Norman buildings, by a central tower; with chancel and nave: we also find in this style a triple chancel arch, an arrangement never occurring at a later epoch. Thus length and breadth were made significant of this Mystery; nor was height less so. The clerestory, the triforium, and the piers cannot fail to suggest it. Indeed, where a triforium was not needed, there is often, as at Exeter and Wells, an arrangement of arcading in niches to resemble it, made that the triplicity might be retained. It is only in late Perpendicular, such as the nave of Canterbury cathedral, that the arrangement is omitted: there the eye is at once dissatisfied. Again, the triple orders of moulding, which are so much more frequent than any other number, may be supposed to refer to the same thing. The altar steps, three, or some multiple of three, certainly do. So do the three fingers with which Episcopal Benediction is given. And this is a very early symbolism. It occurs in illuminated MS. We may mention one (Harl. 5540) of the thirteenth century, where it forms a part of the first letter of S. John's gospel. So, as we shall presently see, are Eastern triplets. And reference is constantly made to the same doctrine in bosses: we may mention as a remarkable instance one that occurs in Stamford, S. Mary's, a figure with an equilateral triangle in its mouth: thereby setting forth the duty of the preacher to proclaim the doctrine of the Trinity. In large churches, the three towers undoubtedly proclaim the same doctrine. We shall hereafter show that neither in nave and aisles, in triplets, or any thing else, is the *inequality* any thing else than what might have been expected.

II. THE DOCTRINE OF REGENERATION

We know, as a fact, that from the earliest times, baptisteries and fonts were octagonal. We know also that the reason assigned, if not by S. Ambrose himself at least by one of his contemporaries, for this form was, that the number eight was symbolical of Regeneration. For as the old Creation was complete in seven days, so the number next ensuing may well be significative of the new.

Now none can deny that very much the greater number of fonts are in this shape. To prove this we will refer to those selected by the Cambridge Camden Society in the appendix to the second edition of their 'Few Words to Church-Builders.' There we find,

	Octagonal.	Of all other shapes.
In Norman	15	43
Early English	19	30
Decorated	24	1
Perpendicular	57	2
Total	115	76

Now, it is to be remembered, that the superior convenience of a cylindrical or circular form, together with the wont of Norman architects rather to symbolise facts than doctrine, accounts for the comparatively small number of octagonal fonts in that style: in later ages their preponderance is overwhelming.

The symbolism sculptured on the sides of the font hardly falls under our consideration in this place. And besides, it has been fully detailed in the publications of the Cambridge Camden Society, and of Mr Poole. Whether the general octagonal uses of piers may not arise from a similar design, we do not pretend to decide.

One of the most apposite illustrations in *corbels*,

consists in three fishes intertwined in an equilateral triangle; and thus typifying our regeneration in the Three Persons of the Ever-Blessed Trinity. For it need not be said, that the fish is the emblem of the Christian, as being born again of water. The mystical vesica piscis of this form () wherein the Divinity, and (more rarely) the Blessed Virgin are represented has no reference, except in its name to a fish; but represents the almond, the symbol of virginity, and self-production.

III. THE ATONEMENT

We will notice in the third place, the symbolical representation of the great doctrine of the Atonement, in the ground lines and general arrangement of our churches.

As soon as ever Christianity possessed temples of her own, the cruciform shape was, we have seen, sometimes adopted. And so, as we all know, has it continued down to the present day. England, perhaps, has fewer examples of cross churches than any other country: the proportion of those which bear this shape being not so much as one in ten. In France, on the contrary, the ratio would probably be inverted. Into the reason of this remarkable difference we shall not now inquire: but will merely remark, that many churches which do not, in an exterior view, appear cruciform, are nevertheless, from their internal arrangements, really so. The transepts do not project beyond the aisles: but have distinct transept arches, and a window of much larger dimensions than those in the aisles. This principally occurs in city churches, or where the founders were confined for want of room. And this is the case as well in churches which have aisles to the chancel, as in Godalming, Surrey, as where the nave alone has them, as in Holy Rood, Southampton. They will be distinguished readily on the outside by the northern and southern gable. In some cathedral churches, there is a double cross: in York, this perhaps signifies the metropolitical dignity of that church; in other cases, it was probably merely a method of imparting greater dignity to the building. Some churches—though they are not frequent—are in the form of a Greek Cross: that is, the four arms are all of equal length. Darlington, Durham, is an example: in this case there is a central tower. In some, as at Westminster, Gloucester, and S. Albans, the choir runs westward of the transept; in Seville, almost the whole of the choir is locally in the nave; in others, as Ely, it does not extend westward so far. These peculiarities, curious in themselves, do not affect the symbolism: and probably no modification of meaning is to be attached to them.

Mr Lewis has asserted, that in early churches, a cross was marked on the pavement, the upper part running into the chancel, the arms extending into the transepts, and the body occupying the nave. And some such arrangement, or rather the traces of it, we have ourselves perhaps noticed. The reason it was given up, was probably the anathema pronounced by the second Œcumenical Council, on those who should tread on that holy symbol.

Thus, in the ground plan, the Cross of Christ was preached. It is often said, that the adjacent chapels, more especially the Lady Chapel, obscured the symbolism. But it must be remembered that a ground plan can only be judged of in two methods: either from a height above, for example, the tower of the church; or when marked out on paper. It is surprising, in either of these cases, how easily the most complex cathedral resolves itself to the spectator's eyes into a cross.

In looking at the details of churches, the Cross is marked on the Dos-d'ânes and plain coffin lids of the earliest times: it commences the later inscriptions on brass: it surmounts pinnacle, and gable, and porch; it is often imprinted on the jambs of the principal entrance, showing the exact spot touched in the consecration with chrism,* and possibly having reference to the blood sprinkled at the Passover on the Door Post: and finally, in a more august form, is erected in the churchyard. And here we may notice another curious and beautiful expression of Catholic feeling.† It is very uncommon to find a plain cross surmounting a church: the whole force of Christian art has sometimes been expended in wreathing and embellishing the instrument of redemption: flowers, and figures, and foliage are lavished upon it. And why? Because that which was once the by-word of Pagans, the instrument of scorn and of suffering, has become the symbol of Hope and of Glory, of Joy, and of Eternal Felicity; and its material expression has

---

* It is proper to distinguish between Dedication Crosses, which are generally of considerable size, examples of which may be seen in Moorlinch, Somersetshire, and those small crosses in door jambs, as in Preston, Sussex, the use of which is not very clear, but which were perhaps intended to remind the entering worshipper to cross himself. At Yatton, Somersetshire, inside the northern door, and towards the east, is a large quatrefoil-fashioned cross: this perhaps pointed out a now destroyed benatura.

† That there are some plain crosses, cannot be denied—more especially that on which the weathercock is placed. A little consideration will, perhaps, clear up this difficulty. The cross may be viewed in two distinct lights. It may either set forth that on which our Redeemer suffered—in which case it is the symbol of glory: or it may image that Cross which every true Christian is to take up—in which case it may still be called the Symbol of Shame. In the latter signification, it may well be quite plain. But, inasmuch as our ancestors looked more to the Passion of Christ than to their own unworthiness, the former symbol is that which generally occurs. Yet not always on the church spire, perhaps for this reason:—the spire urges us, by its upward tendency, to press on towards our heavenly home — a home which can only be reached by the cheerful bearing of that cross by means of which (as it were) it points. The cross therefore is here, with propriety, plain.

F

altered proportionately. In that the arms frequently end in leaves and flowers, they signify the flourishing and continual increase of that Church which was planted on Mount Calvary. The Crown of Thorns is sometimes wreathed around them : but so, that it should rather resemble a Crown of Glory. The instruments of the Passion are, as every one knows, of the most ordinary occurrence. The commonest of these are—the Cross, the Crown of Thorns, the Spear, the Scourge, the Nails, and the Sponge on the pole. But in the Suffolk and Somersetshire churches many others are added. Their position is various: sometimes, as in Stogumber, Somersetshire, they appear amidst the foliage of a perpendicular capital : sometimes, as in the Suffolk churches, they are found in the open seats: often in bosses, often in brasses, often in stained glass; and sometimes the angel that supports a bracket holds them portrayed on a shield. The Five Wounds are also often found. These are represented by a heart, between two hands and two feet, each pierced ; or by a heart pierced with five wounds, as in a brass at King's College chapel, Cambridge. The instruments of the Passion may sometimes be seen amongst the volutes of the stem of the churchyard cross : examples occur at Belleville, near Havre, in Normandy, and Santa Cruz, in Madeira.

Again, the very position of our blessed Saviour on the Cross as represented in the great rood and in stained glass, is not without a meaning. In modern paintings, the arms are high above the head, the whole weight of the body seeming to rest upon them. And this, besides its literal truth, gives occasion to that miserable display of anatomical knowledge in which such pictures so much abound. The Catholic representation pictures the arms as extended horizontally : thereby signifying how the Saviour, when extended on the Cross, embraced the whole world.* Thus, as it ever ought to be, is physical sacrificed to moral truth. Perhaps for a similar reason S. Longinus is represented as piercing the Right Side, instead of the Left: and in a representation of the Five Wounds, it is the right side of the breast that is pierced (as in a brass at Southfleet, Kent); that being the side of the greatest strength, and thereby typifying the strength of that love wherewith our Redeemer loved us. [But this may be doubted. For it appears pretty clear that the ancient Church considered the Right Side to have been that which was really pierced. According to modern ideas, the effusion of the water was not a miracle. S. John undoubtedly considered it not only a miracle, but one of the most extraordinary which he had to relate, seeming to stop the mouth of the objector by insisting on the fact, that he himself was an eye-witness.] In some old roods, a still further departure was made from literal truth: the Saviour was represented on the Cross, as a crowned king, arrayed in royal apparel.† And his figure was constantly represented as larger than that of His attendants, His Blessed Mother, and S. John, thereby signifying his immeasurable superiority over the highest of human beings.

Another reference to the Atonement will be found in the deviation which the line of the chancel often presents from that of the nave. It is sometimes to the north, but more frequently to the south. There are many

---

* However, in late stained glass, the modern position is sometimes found; as in a Crucifixion represented in the east window of the north aisle, in Wiscombe church, Somersetshire.

† To this we may add the conventional representation of Royal Saints, such as S. Edmund, wearing their kingly crowns during their passion. That such conventional symbolism is *natural* to us may be shown by alluding (without irreverence in this connection) to the way in which kings are always figured with crown and orb in popular prints: and even, as in a sign-post at Leighterton, Gloucestershire, King Charles II, hiding himself in the Royal Oak, is arrayed in all the insignia of majesty.

more churches in which it occurs than those who have not examined the subject would believe: perhaps it is not too much to say that it may be noticed in a quarter of those in England. Of our cathedrals, it is most strongly marked in York and Lichfield: among the parish churches in which we have observed it, none have it so strongly as Eastbourne and Bosham, in Sussex, and S. Michael's at Coventry: in all of which the most casual glance could not but detect the peculiarity of appearance it occasions. This arrangement represents the inclination of our Saviour's Head on the Cross. In roods the Head generally inclines to the left.

Mr Poole, after noticing the fact in York minster, seems inclined to attribute it to a desire of evading the old foundation lines of that church, which induced the builders to deviate a little from the straight line, rather than encounter the difficulty of removing this obstacle. But in the first place, however much modern church builders might bethink themselves of such an expedient, it is not at all in the character of the church architects of other days: and in the second, the explanation is applicable to York alone, one only out of many hundred churches so distinguished.

IV. THE COMMUNION OF SAINTS

Next, we will notice the effect which the Doctrine of the Communion of Saints has exercised in the designs of churches.

In the ground plan of small churches there is little which seems to bear on this subject. The principal references to departed saints occur in the stained glass, in the rood screen, in niches, in the canopies of monuments, and in brasses. Monuments, in particular, often afford some beautiful ideas, among which we may notice the angels which often are seated at the head of the effigy, supporting the helmet or pillow, and seeming to point out the care of angels for the saints. In cathedrals, however, the chapels have a very considerable effect upon the ground plan : though we cannot agree with Mr Poole that such a modification of the principal lines of the building for the reception of these shrines and oratories, is necessarily uncatholic. He principally objects to the position of the Lady Chapel at the east end, above, as he expresses it, the High Altar. Now we believe the Lady Chapel to have occupied that place merely on grounds of convenience : not from any design —which it is shocking to imagine—of exalting the Blessed Virgin to any participation in the honours of the Deity. Sometimes, as at Durham, this chapel is at the west end: in country churches, it generally occupied the east end of the north or south aisle : and sometimes is placed over the chancel, as in Compton, Surrey, Compton Martin, Somerset, and Darenth, Kent ; or over the porch, as at Fordham, Cambridgeshire. At Bristol cathedral it is on the north side of the choir. That the position of the Lady Chapel at the east end adds greatly to the beauty of the building will hardly be denied on a comparison of York, or Lincoln, or Peterborough with Lichfield, *as it now is.*

CHAPTER VIII

EXAMPLES OF SYMBOLISM CONTINUED

WE come now, according to the plan we laid down, to speak of the symbolism of some particular features of a church, which do not fall so well under any of the four heads which we have been considering. And firstly, of windows.

The primary idea shadowed forth in every one of the styles, is the saying of our Lord to His disciples, *ye are the light of the world.* More simply set forth at first, this notion acquired, in the course of time, various methods of expression, and was subjected to different modifications; but we must retain it as the ground work or we shall be in danger of mistaking the true meaning of ancient church architects.

In Norman, then, and early English, the single lights north and south, set forth the Apostles and Doctors who have shined forth in their time as the lights of the Church: and the rich pattern of flowerwork wherewith the stained glass in them was decked, represented the variety of graces in each. But to have symbolised the servants without the Master, the members without the Head, had been at variance with all the Catholic Church has ever practised. Looking therefore to the east end, we behold that well-known feature, the Triplet: setting forth the Most Holy and Undivided Trinity.* Nor is this all: to denote that all the Church has, and all She is, is from above, the string course, springing from the eastern triplet, runs round the whole church (often both within and without,) binding it, as it were, in and connecting every other light, with those at the east. Again, the Western Door, as we shall see, symbolised Christ: and two lights, typical of His two natures, are therefore generally placed over it. There are, undoubtedly, instances of western triplets: though we think that the Camden Society has well explained these.

In some cases, there is a series of couplets on each side of the church: and, taking the hint from Durandus, we may interpret this arrangement of the mission of the Apostles two and two.

A series of triplets as in Salisbury cathedral, and the Lady Chapel of Bristol, is very rare: and, of course, not objectionable on any other grounds than that of the too cheap use of a most beautiful feature.

So far all is simple: but as we approach the decorated style, the symbolism becomes excessively complicated. The principal doctrines of the Catholic Church are set forth in each window: and to unravel the whole of these is often a task of no small difficulty. We shall proceed to give a few examples, with the explanation which appears to us probable: entreating the reader to remember, that if in any instance our conjectures should appear unfounded, the failure of probability in one case throws no discredit on the others, and still less does it invalidate the system. Durandus's silence on the language of tracery is easily explained by the consideration, that assign as late a date as we will to the

* We read, in the legend of S. Barbara, that, being confined by her father in a room where were two windows only, she added a third, by way of setting forth this Mystery.

publication of his work, it came forth while the Early English style was yet in existence: and his silence on triplets only proves, what is well known to ecclesiologists, that they are far less common in foreign than in our own architecture.

In Norman windows the wheel window is conspicuous. This, whether formed with the *radii* like those of Barfreston, or of the Temple church, represent (as we shall presently observe that Norman symbolism usually *does* represent) an historical fact: namely, the martyrdom of S. Catherine. The celebrity of this Virgin Martyr may tend to explain why she should be so far honoured: a celebrity which has descended to our own day in the common sign of the Cat and Wheel: as well as the firework so denominated.

Of Norman triplets there are not many to which we can refer. The tower of Winchester, however, presenting one on each face, is a noble example. The south-eastern transept of Rochester, though later, is equally in point: it contains two triplets, far apart, and one disposed above the other. The west front of S. Etienne at Caen is a well-known instance.

The earliest symbolism of Early English triplets represented the Trinity alone; the Trinity in Unity was reserved for a somewhat later period. And this was typified by the hood moulding thrown across the three lights. At other times a quatre-foiled, or cinque-foiled, circle was placed at some little distance above the triplet: thus typifying the Crown which befits the Majesty of the King of Kings. And the same Crown is often exhibited above the western couplet. But, for as much as we are 'compelled by the Christian verity to acknowledge every person by Himself to be God and Lord,' a crown is sometimes represented over each light of the triplet, as in Wimborne minster.

Another method of representing the same doctrine was by a simple equilateral triangle for a window: whether plain, of which there are many examples, or with the toothed ornament, as in the famous example at York minster.

S. Giles's at Oxford has windows, the tracery of which will serve as an example of many: it has *three* *tre*-foiled lights, with *three* quatre-foiled circles, arranged triangle-wise in the head.

This type is a little varied in S. Mary Magdalene's church, in the same city, by the introduction of the ogee form.

Berkeley church has a wheel window containing *three* quatre-foils: the *three* spaces left between them and the line being *tre*-foiled.

The east windows of Dunchurch and Fen Stanton have been explained in the publications of the Cambridge Camden Society: the former in their 'Few Words to Church-Builders,' the latter in their illustrations of monumental brasses, Part iv.

The south transept of Chichester cathedral is a glorious specimen of decorated symbolism. In the gable is a Marygold, containing two intersecting equilateral *tri*-angles: the *six* apices of these are *sex*-foiled: the interior *hex*-agon is beautifully worked in *six* leaves. The lower window seven lights: in the head is an equilateral spherical *tri*-angle, containing a large *tre*-foil, intersected by a smaller *tre*-foil. Here we have the Holy Trinity, the Divine Attributes, the perfection of the Deity.

A window in Merton College chapel has *three* lights: with a circle in the head containing *six sex*-foils.

Broughton, Oxon, has in the head of one of its windows a circle, containing two intersecting equilateral triangles, the *six* apices, and *six* spaces around, being *tre*-foiled.

The east end of Lincoln, though far inferior to the south transept of Chichester, is nevertheless highly symbolical. The east window of each of the aisles has *three* lights, with *three* foliated circles, disposed *triangle*-wise in the head. The great east window has eight lights in two divisions, each whereof has *three* foliated circles in the head: and in the apex of the window is a circle containing seven foliations. The upper window has a circle of eight foliations in the head: and in the apex of the gable is an equilateral trefoil.

The next element introduced was the consideration of the Six Attributes of the Deity. One of the simplest examples was to be found in the west window of the north aisle of S. Nicholas, at Guildford: a plain circle, containing six *tre*-foils: these are arranged in two *tri*-angles, each containing *three tre*-foils, and the two sets are varied.

The clerestory of Lichfield cathedral (circ. 1300), is a series of spherical *tri*-angles, each containing *three tre*-foils.

A similar clerestory occurs in the north-west transept of Hereford cathedral, and the same idea is repeated in its triforium: a series of *three tre*-foiled lights, with *three* circles in the head.

The east end of Lichfield symbolises most strikingly the same glorious doctrine. The apse is *tri*-gonal: the windows of each side are the same: each is of *three* lights, with six *tre*-foils (emblematical of the six attributes) disposed above in the form of an equilateral *tri*-angle.

The east end of Chichester is rather earlier, but introduces yet another element. Here we have a triplet: and at some height above it, a wheel-window of seven circles: symbolising therefore eternity and perfection.

The triforium and clerestory of Carlisle are singular

symbols of the doctrine of the Trinity. The former has in each bay three adjacent equal lancets. The latter is a series of triplets; the central window in each being composed of three lights. We may observe, by the way, that three *adjacent* equal lancets are hardly ever found, whatever the reason may be. We know but of three examples: in the churches of Bosham, Sussex, Godalming, Surrey, and S. Mary-le-Crypt, Gloucester: and in all these cases they occupy the same position, the south east end of the chancel, or chancel aisle.

Dorchester church, Oxfordshire, has for one of its windows an equilateral spherical triangle with three heads, or knops, one at each angle.

We are now in a purely decorated age. And as one of its earliest windows we may mention that in the Bishop of Winchester's Palace at Southwark. It was a wheel, and contained two intersecting equilateral *triangles*: around them were *six sex*-foiled triangles the hexagon in the centre containing a star of *six* greater and *six* smaller rays. Here, of course, the Blessed Trinity and the divine and human natures were set forth.*

---

* We may perhaps be allowed to say a few words here on the subject of those singular windows which the Cambridge Camden Society has called *Lychnoscopes*.

It appears, that in Early English churches, the westernmost window on the south side of the chancel is both lower than, and in other ways (particularly by a transom) distinguished from the rest. It is sometimes merely a square aperture, as in some churches in the Weald of Sussex: sometimes a small ogee-headed light, as in old Shoreham: sometimes, where the south side of the chancel is lighted by a series of lancets, the westernmost, as in Chiddingfold, Sussex, is transomed, where the others end, and carried down lower; sometimes the lower part appears to have been *originally* blocked, as in Kemerton, Gloucestershire, and Kingstone next Lewes, Sussex: sometimes there are remains of clamps, as at Buckland, Kent, sometimes of shutters. Again, sometimes there are two, one north, the other south of the chancel: sometimes the same arrangement is found S.E. of the nave. On the other hand, it is never found in any but a parish church: never in late work: seldom is it ornamented. We will give a few remarkable instances. 1. *Dinder*, Somersetshire. Here there is a double lychnoscope, north and south: the date is late Early

The symbolism of the more complicated decorated windows it is next to impossible to explain. Carlisle and York have doubtless their appropriate meaning; but who will now pretend to expound it?

One exception we may make:—the east window of Bristol cathedral. It is of seven lights, but so much English, and the specimen is unique from there being a rude moulding in the window arch. 2. *Othery*, Somersetshire. The lychnoscope itself is here blocked: it is square-headed, and of two lights: date probably Early Decorated. The church is cruciform, and a central perpendicular tower was subsequently erected. One of the diagonal buttresses is thrown out at a distance of some three feet from the window, so as to hide it: and an oblique square hole has been cut through the masonry of the buttress. This is the more remarkable, because there are stalls in the chancel, of perpendicular work, which would seem to render any window in that position useless. 3. *Christon*, Somersetshire. Here, *almost close to the ground*, is a horizontal slit which appears never to have been glazed. This is an early Norman church. So at Albury, Surrey, at the S.E. end of the south aisle. 4. *S. Appolline*, Guernsey. This church is of the same date as, or may be earlier than, the last. The windows are rude and square-headed slits: the lychnoscope is transomed. 5. *Preston*, Sussex. There are three windows in the south of the chancel, which rise one above the other, like sedilia, to the east. 6. *Loxton*, Somersetshire. This is an Early English church with a south western tower serving as porch. From the eastern side of this a long slit is carried through the nave wall, a distance of some twenty feet, and exactly commanding a view of the altar. It is *grated* at the west end, not glazed: the eastern end has long been blocked up. Way is made for it by a bulge of the wall in the angle formed towards the east by the tower and nave. This seems to form a kind of connecting link between the hagioscope and the lychnoscope.

With these windows we will venture to connect those extremely rare ones, three adjacent, unconnected, equal, lancets, as occurring of the same date at the same position. There is again another kind of lychnoscope only found where the chancel has aisles. A panel of the parclose, or wooden screen, behind the longitudinal stalls, is sometimes found pierced with a small quatrefoil, at the S.W. part of the chancel. This is vulgarly called a confessional. It seems, however, clearly connected with the lychnoscope. Examples are found at Erith, Kent, and Sundridge in the same county. Perhaps also the curious slit in the south wall of the chancel of S. Michael's church, Cambridge, communicating with a south chantry chapel is another variety.

From the above facts we deduce the following remarks: 1. That the necessity for a lychnoscope must in some cases have been very urgent: as may be proved by the example, at Othery, where a buttress is much injured to form one. 2. But yet this need was not universal, because there are many churches in which the arrangement does not occur. 3. That it appears, strictly speaking, a parochial arrangement, not being found in cathedral or collegiate churches. 4. That smaller buildings rather than larger are marked with it: it seldom occurs where there are aisles to the prominence is given to the three central ones, as strongly to set forth the Most Holy Trinity: over them is a crown of six leaves and by the numerous winged foliations around them, the Heavenly Hierarchy may, very probably, be understood.

chancel. 5. That, where employed, lychnoscopes were only used occasionally; else the shutters which have evidently sometimes existed, would have been useless. 6. That they are very seldom ornamented, and never have stained glass. 7. That in the Perpendicular era they generally, though not universally, ceased to be used. 8. That, a large sill seems to have been a requisite to them. 9. That, where the upper part is glazed, the lower part often was not, as in the Decorated lychnoscope at Beckford, Gloucestershire. The principal hypotheses to explain the use of this arrangement are: 1. Dr Rock's. That it was a contrivance by which lepers might see the Elevation of the Host. But the structure of the greater part of these windows forbids this idea: many instances occur in which it is splayed away from the Altar, none (except that at Loxton, and a doubtful case at Winscombe, Somersetshire, where a perpendicular addition has been made) in which it is splayed towards it. 2. That of the Cambridge Camden Society, that it was for watching the Paschal light. But this, besides being *à priori* improbable is refuted by that at Othery. Here the eye has to look through two apertures at some distance from each other, and therefore can command only a very small field on exactly the opposite side of the chancel. 3. It has been imagined by some that it was for confession. The idea of confession near an altar sufficiently refutes itself; but furthermore, some of these openings are so very low down that the thing would be impossible. Two solitary facts more, though they throw no light on the subject, may yet be mentioned. 1. In the church of S. Amaro, near Funchal, in Madeira, is a grating at the west-end like that at Loxton. Its use is *now* said to be to cool the church, though in that case one should have expected to meet it elsewhere. 2. In Sennen church by the Land's End, there is said to have been a lychnoscope (now no longer existing) used to take in the tithe-milk. We may gather on the whole, 1. that lychnoscopes could not have been used to look into a church 2. Nor to hand anything in or out. Both these are sufficiently disproved by Othery. 3. Nor to speak through. But one can hardly imagine any other use, except it were to look *out* of the church. We are inclined to think that it was in some way connected with the ringing of the bells, or of the sancte bell. Where the tower is central, we very often find it: as at Old Shoreham and Alfriston, Sussex: at Loxton it is evidently for some purpose connected with the tower. So in Beckford, which has a central tower; and Uffington, Berks, a cross church. And the place where the sancte bell was rung is exactly between a double lychnoscope. But what the particular use might have been we will not pretend to guess. We will conclude this long note by a question as to the authority for calling the small chancel door, the *Priest's Door*. It is never (originally) furnished with a lock, but always with an interior bar, thus showing that it could only have been used from the inside. So the priest could never have *entered* the church by this way, unless the door were previously opened for him.

II. Doors

Durandus has given us a clue to the symbolical meaning which these generally present, by directing our attention to that saying of our Lord's, *I am the door*. And this, uttered as tradition reports it to have been, in reference to the Gate of the Temple, on which the Saviour's eyes were then fixed, gives additional force to the allusion.

In small churches, doors are seldom the subject of much symbolical ornament, except in the Norman style; but in cathedrals, some of the most strikingly figurative arrangements are often thrown into them. The Person, the Miracles, or the Doctrines of our Lord are here frequently set forth. He is sometimes, especially in the tympanum of Norman doors, as at Egleton in Rutland, represented as described in the Apocalyptic vision; with a sword in His mouth. More frequently, however, with His Blessed Mother; in order, perhaps, to connect His *entrance* into the world with ours into the Church, which He thereby gathered together. This in the south entrance of Lincoln minster, is enclosed in a quatre-foil: because the birth of Christ is announced by the four evangelists; and angels are represented around it in attitudes of adoration. A singular, and indeed irreverent symbol, is to be seen in a door of Lisieux church: the Holy Ghost descending on the Blessed Virgin, and the infant Saviour following Him. In the entrance to the cloisters of Norwich cathedral, the door arch is filled by nine niches, the central one being occupied by the Saviour, the others by saints. But this arrangement is much more common in French churches: where two, or even three rows of saints in the architrave are not uncommon: witness the south and west doors of S. Germain, at Amiens, and a west door of S. Etienne, at

Beauvais. This is sometimes, in late Flamboyant work, carried to an absurd extent: in a south door of Gisors, two niches actually hang down out of the soffit. Early English doors are generally double, thereby representing the Two Natures of our Saviour: but embraced by one arch, to set forth His One Person. So the celebrated door in Southwell minster: the west door in the Galilee of Ely cathedral: the entrance to the chapter House, at Salisbury; the west door of the same: so the decorated west door of York; so the door to the Chapter House there, of which the inscription truly says: *Ut Rosa Phlos phlorum, sic est domus ista Domorum:* so the west door and entrance to the Chapter House of Wells. The west door of Higham Ferrars has the Saviour's triumphal entrance into Jerusalem, over the double western doors. And this is the case in one of the doors of Seville cathedral. Both these connect the ideas of His entrance into the temporal, with that of ours into the spiritual, Jerusalem. In these symbolical doorways, we have one proof of the immeasurable superiority of English over French architecture: compare any of the above named with the celebrated west door of Amiens, with its twenty-two sovereigns in its soffit. Again, by way of contrast to the second Adam, by whom we enter into Heaven, we sometimes, especially in Norman churches, have the Forbidden Tree, with Adam and Eve in the tympanum: setting forth the one man by whom sin entered into the world.

The Crucifixion seldom occurs over doors: while over porches a crucifix is very common. The cause of the difference is explained by a consideration that the former are shut, the latter open: and 'when Thou hadst *overcome* the sharpness of Death, Thou didst *open* the kingdom of heaven to all believers.' Indeed it may almost be asserted that a crucifix is never seen over a closed door, except where it forms a part of the usual representation of the Trinity. For the Trinity is also, in Norman churches, there represented: and that not inappropriately: inasmuch as the Trinity is the beginning of all things. A Holy Lamb is sometimes found in Norman tympana: as saith the Saviour, *I am the door of the sheep.* A hasty glance at Durandus * might lead us to imagine that we should find the Apostles set forth under the similitude of doors: but he there probably refers to the well-known passage in the Apocalypse. Apoc. xxi, 14.

This however leads us to another, and that a totally different, meaning attached to doors. We have already noticed the fact, that many Norman and Early English mouldings refer to various kinds of martyrdom: those which do so occur more frequently on doors than anywhere else; for it is written, 'We must through much tribulation enter into the kingdom of God.' And here we may observe a very curious aud beautiful progression in symbolism. In the early ages of Christianity, it was a matter requiring no small courage to make an open profession of Christianity, to join one's self to the Church Militant:—and this fact has left its impress in the various representations of martyrdom surrounding the nave-doors of Norman and the first stage of Early English churches: as well as in the frightful forms which seem to deter those who would enter. But in process of time, as the world became evangelised, to be a member of the visible Church was an easy matter: the difficulty was transferred from an entrance into *that*, to the so living, as to have part in the Communion of Saints:—in other words, to an entrance into the Church Triumphant. And therefore in late Early English, and Decorated, the symbols which had occupied the nave-

* Durand. i, 26.

doors in the former period, are now transferred to the chancel arch.

The different agricultural operations, the signs of the zodiac, and occupations of various kinds, sometimes found on the *outside* of Norman doors, signify that we must turn our backs on, and leave behind us, all worldly cares and employments, if we would enter into the Kingdom of God. In later porches, true love knots are sometimes found on the bosses: because part of the service of Holy Matrimony was performed there. The serpent, in which the handle is so universally fashioned, has probably reference to that text, 'They shall lay their hands upon serpents,' to signify that God's arm will protect us, when engaging, or about to engage in, His service. For the serpent with his tail in his mouth is not a Christian, and indeed by no means a desirable, emblem of eternity, and therefore the door handle cannot be so interpreted.

The doors are of course placed near the west end: for it is only by way of the Church Militant that we can hope to enter the Church Triumphant. One door, indeed, the priest's door, conducts at once into the chancel. Durandus is probably right in interpreting this of Christ's coming into the world; though it involves a little confusion of symbolism, inasmuch as the chancel, properly speaking, denotes the blessed place which He left: not the abode to which he came. It is to be noted as an instance of the decline of symbolism in the Perpendicular age, that in churches which have aisles to the chancel of that date, we sometimes, as at Bitton, Gloucestershire, Godalming, Surrey, and Wivelsfield and Isfield, Sussex, find an entrance at the east end of the south aisle. Though used as a priest's door, this is entirely to be blamed: what shall we say then of modern churches, which have two doors at the east end, one on each side of the altar, as Christchurch, Brighton? In Seville cathedral, a late, although fine flamboyant building, there are large doors at the east end of each choir aisle.

Porches are usually on the south side. For as the east was considered in an especial manner connected with the Kingdom of Heaven, so was the north imagined to be under the Prince of the Power of the Air. It is curious how diametrically opposed in both these ideas were Christianity and Paganism. For as by the latter the west was known as 'the better country, where lay the Isles of the Blest in their abundant peace,' so in the north dwelt the deathless and ageless Hyperboreans: whose state was the model of good government and secure happiness. That the belief of our ancestors is not yet extinct, a very slight knowledge of our country churchyards will prove: the north side of the churchyard has generally not more than one or two graves. To be buried there is, in the language of our eastern counties, to be buried *out of Sanctuary:* and the spot is appropriated to suicides, unbaptised persons, and excommunicates. A particular portion is, in some churchyards of Devonshire, separated for the second class and called the *chrisomer.* Where the contrary is the case, it may be worth inquiring how far it does not arise from the accidental position of the Churchyard Cross on the north side. There the spell seems broken: and the villagers' graves cluster around it, as if the presence of that sacred symbol were a sufficient protection to the sleeping dust. A remarkable instance of this occurs at Belleville, between Dieppe and Abbeville, in Normandy.

The doors in the transepts are, in small churches, almost invariably east or west: much more frequently the latter. This, however, is probably not symbolical: but an arrangement adopted to prevent any resemblance in the porches and transepts:—and it is a rule which needs to be much impressed on modern church builders.

The rule as to the western position of the doors, seems to apply generally to the churchyard.

It is worthy of remark that in the matter of doors, Protestantism presents us, as is so frequently the case, with a very unintended piece of symbolism. When we see, as in the beautiful church of Bisley, Gloucestershire, *thirteen* different openings, with external staircases, made into the church, through windows and elsewhere, can we forbear thinking of him who cometh not by the doors into the sheepfold, but climbeth up some other way?

III. CHANCEL ARCH AND ROOD SCREEN

We come now to speak of the chancel arch and the rood screen, two of the most important features in a church. These, as separating the choir from the nave, denote literally the separation of the clergy from the laity: but symbolically the division between the Militant and Triumphant Churches: that is to say, the Death of the Faithful. The first great symbol which sets this forth, is the Triumphal Cross: the Image of Him* who by His Death had overcome Death, and has gone before His people through the valley of its shadow. The images of Saints and Martyrs appear in the lower panelling, as examples of faith and patience to us. The colours of the rood screen itself represent their passion and victory: the crimson sets forth the one, the gold the other. The curious tracery of net-work typifies the obscure manner in which heavenly things are set forth, while we look at them from the Church Militant. And for as much as the Blessed Martyrs passed from this

---

* 'Let us consider Him,' says Bishop Hall, 'now, after a weary conflict with the Devil, looking down from the Triumphal Chariot of the Cross on His Church.'

world to the next through sore torments, the mouldings of the chancel arch represent the various kinds of sufferings through which they went. Faith was their support, and must be ours : and Faith is set forth either in the abstract, by the limpet moulding on the chancel arch ; or on the screen, as in Bishop's Hull, Somersetshire, by the Creed in raised gilt letters : or is represented by some notable action of which it was the source : so in Cleeve, Somersetshire, the destruction of a dragon runs along, not only the rood screen, but the north parclose also. But in that the power of evil spirits may be exercised against us till we have left this world, but not after, horrible forms are sometimes sculptured in the west side of the chancel arch. The foregoing remarks may perhaps explain what has been felt by some ecclesiologists as a difficulty : how it happens, since the chancel is more highly ornamented than the nave, that it is the western, or nave side, not the eastern or chancel side, of the chancel arch which invariably receives the greatest share of ornament. The straitness of the entrance to the Kingdom of Heaven is set forth by the excessive narrowness of Norman chancel arches. And the final separation of the Church Triumphant from everything that defileth was almost invariably represented by the Great Doom painted in fresco over the rood screen : of which there are still several examples, as the celebrated one in Trinity church, Coventry : and many more might be found, if the whitewash in that place were scraped off. And not only is the judgment of the world, but that of individuals here set forth : on the south side of the chancel wall of Preston church, Sussex, is a fresco of S. Michael weighing the souls : the Devil stands by, eager to secure his prize, but by the intervention of the Blessed Virgin, the scale preponderates in favour of the sinner. There might probably be an altar to the Blessed Virgin under this picture. Also deeds of faith are represented in similar positions: —so in the same church on the north chancel wall, is the fresco of the Martyrdom of S. Thomas of Canterbury. We have already noticed the triplicity, in some instances, of Norman chancel arches. A very curious triple chancel arch is to be seen at Capel-le-Ferne, Kent. We may also refer to those singular double ones, Wells and Finedon, and in another manner, Darlington, in Durham, and Barton, in Cumberland. It may be well, finally, to note the entire absence in the ground plans of our churches of any reference to Purgatory. The only instance in which chancel and nave are separated by any intervening object, is the chantry of Bishop Arundell in Chichester cathedral. Of the triple division of the church by two (so to speak) chancel arches, we have already spoken.

IV. MONUMENTS

We now proceed to *Monumental Symbolism*. But it will be proper first to consider a very curious subject: namely the reason of the difference between the personages with which the effigies of the departed were of old time, and are now, surrounded. In the former case they were always real: Our Lady, S. John, S. Pancras, S. Agatha, and so on. In the latter, they are always allegorical: Faith, Virtue, Courage, Eloquence and the like. Nay, in the very ground which is common to the two— the representations of angels—we may observe a great difference: in modern monuments any angel is represented: in those of ancient date the particular one is often named: S. Gabriel, S. Raphael, etc. Now there are, we think, three good reasons to be assigned for this.

1. The *enlightened*, or in plainer terms, the *sceptical* character of the present age. Unaccustomed to view

any great examples of heroic devotion and self-sacrifice now, we naturally, though scarcely allowing it to ourselves, begin to doubt whether there ever were any such. In thinking of Patience, our forefathers would naturally have had S. Vincent presented to their mind: but we, who, some of us have scarcely heard of his name, and some, are totally ignorant of his character, have of course no such ideas suggested. So again, where our ancestors would have represented S. Lawrence, we content ourselves with a representation of Fidelity. And it is in accordance with this easy and self-indulgent age, rather to personify a thing, which as having never had real existence, cannot be brought into comparison with ourselves, than by representing a really existing person, to run the risk of a contrast between his virtues and our own.

2. This allegorising spirit is more in accordance with the general paganism of our architectural designs: though, be it observed, a feature of the very worst and most corrupt state of Paganism. It is worth noting that in heathen countries, evil qualities have always been personified before good. Paganism like every other false system, became worst at its close. In the early times of Grecian mythology the attributes of purity, and truth, and mercy, were so strongly felt to reside in the gods, that a separate personification of them was needless: whereas strife, and violence and fury, qualities which had no place in heaven, demanded, and obtained a separate existence. But in process of time, when the divinities themselves became invested with the attributes of sinful humanity, the qualities of goodness which were no longer supposed theirs, found separate embodiments and expressions.

3. We may assign as a reason for the difference we have noticed the far greater reality with which our

ancestors looked on the connections subsisting between ourselves and the other world. Thus, tempests and hurricanes, which we coldly explain on philosophical principles, they considered as directly proceeding from the violence of evil spirits :*—earthquakes and volcanoes they regarded as outbreaks, so to speak, of that place of punishment, which they believed locally situated within the earth :—diseases and pestilences they held to be the immediate work of the devil : madness and lunacy were, in their view, synonymous with possession. Whether theirs, as it certainly was the most pious, were not also the most philosophical view, has been so ably discussed in the 'Church of the Fathers' under the chapter *S. Anthony in Conflict*, that we need here only allude to it. But the same spirit led them to adopt the effigies of those saints who had been members of the same Church Militant with themselves, and who now were members of that Triumphant Church which they hoped hereafter to join : and its contrary leads us to adopt the cold, vague, dreamy unsubstantialities of allegorism.

The earliest kind of monumental symbolism is that which represents the trade or profession of the person commemorated. And these principally occur on Lombardic slabs and Dos d'Anes. The distaff represents

* A Master of Philosophy travelling with others on the way, when a fearful thunderstorm arose, checked the fear of his fellows, and discoursed to them of the natural reasons of that uproar in the clouds, and those sudden flashes wherewith they seemed (out of the ignorance of causes) to be too much affrighted; in the midst of his philosophical discourse, he was struck dead with that dreadful eruption which he slighted. What could this be but the finger of that God Who will have His works rather entertained with wonder and trembling than with curious scanning? Neither is it to be otherwise in those violent hurricanes, devouring earthquakes, and more than ordinary tempests, and fiery apparitions which we have seen and heard of; for however there be natural causes given of the usual events of this kind, yet nothing hinders but the Almighty, for the manifestations of His power and justice, may set spirits, whether good or evil, on work, to do the same things sometimes in more state and magnificence of horror.—Bishop Hall, 'The Invisible World,' sect. vi.

the mother of a family:[1] a pair of gloves a glover:[2] so we have a pair of shears: and the like. But the Cross constantly appears; and in a highly floriated form: sometimes at its foot are three steps representing the Mount: sometimes a Holy Lamb.[3] And so ecclesiastical personages have their appropriate symbols: so the chalice or the ring[4] represents a priest:—another type is the hand raised in benediction[5] over a chalice: brasses abound in symbolical imagery. The animal at the feet varies with the varying circumstances of the deceased: a married lady has the dog, the emblem of fidelity: with which we may compare the speech of Clytemnestra, of her absent Lord,[6]

$$\gamma\upsilon\nu\alpha\tilde{\iota}\kappa\alpha\ \pi\iota\sigma\tau\grave{\eta}\nu\ \delta'\ \grave{\epsilon}\nu\ \delta\acute{o}\mu o\iota\varsigma\ \epsilon\ddot{\upsilon}\rho o\iota\ \mu o\lambda\grave{\omega}\nu$$
$$o\ddot{\iota}\alpha\nu\ \pi\epsilon\rho'\ o\tilde{\upsilon}\nu\ \ddot{\epsilon}\lambda\epsilon\iota\pi\epsilon\ \Delta\Omega\mathrm{MAT}\Omega\mathrm{N}\ \mathrm{KYNA}.$$

There are, doubtless, instances (there is one in Bristol, S. Peter's) where the unmarried are so represented: but they are very rare, and quite in the decline of the art. The knight again has, generally, a terrier at his feet, as the emblem of courage: sometimes the greyhound,[7] the symbol of speed. Lord Beaumont[8] has an elephant: it is a bearing in his coat-armour.

Early priests have a lion[9] also at their feet; but this typified their trampling on the devil: as servants of Him concerning whom it is written, 'And the Devil shall go forth before[10] His feet.' They have also a dragon for the same reason. And this position doubtless also has reference to the verse, 'Thou shalt tread upon the lion[11] and adder: the young lion and the

---

[1] See on this subject an interesting article in the *Church of England Quarterly*, for September, 1841. [2] As in Fletching, Sussex. [3] As in Lolworth, Cambridgeshire. [4] As in S. Mary, Castlegate, York. [5] As in Hedon, Yorkshire. [6] Agamemnon, 606. (Ed. Dindorf.) [7] As in Sir Grey de Groby, S. Alban's. [8] Engraved in the 5th number of the Cambridge Camden Society's *Illustrations of Monumental Brasses*. [9] As in Watton, Herts, and Cottingham, Yorkshire. [10] Habaccuc III. v, *Et egredietur diabolus ante pedes ejus.* [11] Psalm xc. *Qui habitat.*

dragon shalt thou trample under feet.' In the decline of the art, effigies have the crest of the departed at their feet.

Whether those knights who are represented with crossed legs are to be considered as crusaders, or at least as having taken the vow, is a question which has been much discussed. The general belief seems now to be in the negative :—and Mr Bloxam in his work on Monumental Architecture gives it as his opinion that this posture was chosen by the artist, for the more graceful arrangement of the *surcoat*. And it is to be remarked that some illuminations, as in the Life of S. Edward the Confessor, in the Cambridge University Library, represent the knights as sitting cross legged. For our own part we must confess that we incline to the old belief :—as better supported by tradition, and more in accordance with the general principles of Catholic artists. The knight's hand is sometimes represented as resting on the hilt of his sword :—or as it is called *drawing it*. We are astonished that a writer in the *Quarterly Review* should fall into this popular error: especially when the idea was completely opposed to the whole course of his argument. There can be no doubt that this typifies the accomplishment of the vow, the taking which was set forth by the crossed legs. The contrary—an act of war in the House of Peace—is not for a moment to be thought of. As emblematical of deep humility, some effigies are represented naked: some in shrouds: some, as emaciated corpse: and sometimes, still more strikingly, the tomb will be divided into two partitions: and while the departed appears in rich vests, and with a gorgeous canopy above—below there is a skeleton, or a worm eaten figure. There is a remarkable instance at Tewkesbury, in the cenotaph of the last Lord Abbot: and we may refer to the monument of William Ashton, in S. John's College chapel, Cambridge.

The symbolism of ecclesiastics, lying principally in their vestments, does not so much fall within the scope of this essay. The same may be said of the allusion to the Holy Trinity in the benedictory attitude of the bishop: and the distinction between the mitred abbot and the bishop in the former holding his pastoral staff with the crook inwards, as signifying his dominion to be *internal*, *i.e.* within his own house;—the latter outwards, to set forth his external dominion over his diocese.

The reception of the soul of the departed into Abraham's bosom is often represented. Sometimes angels are bearing it, in the likeness of a newborn child, (a figure symbolical of its having now returned into its baptismal state of purity) and presenting it before the throne. The founders or rebuilders of churches are known by the building which they hold in their hands.

The carving of the *open seats* is one of those parts of ecclesiastical symbolism, which it is very hard to explain. The monsters which constantly occur on them may be perhaps regarded as typical of the evil thoughts and bad passions which a life of ease and rest encourages, and it will be observed, that in the choir, a gentler class of ideas often is suggested: we have here flowers and fruit, and birds making their nests, and flocks feeding. There, are however, certain other types to be found here, and also in string courses, and corbel heads, of which we shall presently speak in terms of disapprobation.

Nothing, with this exception, shows the exuberance and beauty of ideas which distinguished the architects of the ages of Faith—and the depth and variety of the scriptural knowledge we are pleased to deny them—than their wood carvings.* There is perhaps hardly a scrip-

---

* The astonishing scriptural knowledge of Durandus may be judged of from the Index at the end of the volume of texts quoted by him.

tural subject which they have not handled: and it requires no small degree of ecclesiastical knowledge to be able at all to comprehend many of their allusions: while probably many more are lost to us. The Annunciation is one of the most favourite topics. The almond tree blossoming in the flower pot—the bud terminating in a cross or crucifix—the prayer desk at which the Blessed Virgin kneels—the temple seen in the distance —the Holy Dove descending on a ray of light—these are its general accompaniments. The descent of our Saviour into hell—the delivery of souls—

'Magnaque ; de magna præda petita domo :'

the visions of the Apocalypse: the final doom: the passions and triumphs of martyrs—all here find their expression.

V. CORBELS, GURGOYLES, POPPY HEADS, ETC.

The corbels which occur in the interior of churches generally represent the Heavenly Host—often with various instruments of music, as if taking a share in the devotions of the worshippers. This idea is most fully and beautifully carried out in late perpendicular roofs: where the various orders of the heavenly hierarchy hover, with outstretched wings, over the sacred building—an idea evidently derived from the cherubim that spread their wings over the ark, and the apostle's explanation, 'which things the angels desire to look into.' Often, however, benefactors to the Church are here portrayed. The gurgoyles, on the contrary, represent evil spirits as flying from the holy walls: the hideousness of the figures, so often, by modern connoisseurs, ridiculed or blamed, is therefore not without its appropriate meaning.

We must now say a few words on the least pleasing

part of the study of symbolism: we mean the satirical representations which record the feuds between the secular and the regular clergy. Thus, in the churches of the former, we have, principally as stallwork, figures of a fox preaching to geese: in those of the latter an ass's head under a cowl: or, which is very frequent, both in woodwork and as a gurgoyle, the cowled double face. As a specimen of these designs, we may mention the stalls* in East Brent, Somersetshire. A fox hung by a goose, with two cubs yelping at the foot of the gallows, a monkey at prayers, with an owl perched over his head: another monkey holding a halbert: a fox with mitre and staff, a young fox in chains, a bag of money in his right paw, and geese and cranes on each side. To these objectionable devices we may add those which to us appear simply profane or indecent :† such as the baptism of a dog in one of the Stamford churches, and others in Northampton, S. Peter's, of Norman date. One of the grossest which we have ever seen is to be found on the north side of the chancel arch of Nailsea, Somersetshire.

On the towers of some Norman churches, the evangelistic symbols are represented. So in Stow church, Lincolnshire. Tiles ought not to have the cross on them: for though Christ is indeed the foundation of the Church, yet these holy symbols should not be exposed to be trodden under foot. Heraldic devices are here more proper, to signify the worthlessness of worldly honours in the sight of God.

* Rutter's *Delineations*, p. 89.

† It is fair to observe that our designating them so *may* be the effect of our own ignorance.

CHAPTER IX

SOME OBJECTIONS CONSIDERED

SEVERAL objections to the symbolical system have been noticed and answered in the course of this treatise. We shall, however, devote a greater space to the consideration of one difficulty which has often been raised by opponents, and has often been felt even by such as have adopted the theory. It is said, for example, that to assert the nave and two aisles, or a triplet of lancets, to be symbolical of the Most Holy Trinity, is both false and profane, when, as is almost always the case, the aisles are much less broad than the nave, and the three lancets are unequal both in height and breadth: whereas in the Trinity none is afore or after other, none is greater or less than another. But the difficulty seems only to arise from carrying the similitude too far: the point of resemblance is in these cases a single one: the mere trinity of the arrangement is the only particular which gives rise to the symbol. 'Three mystic lines approach the shrine,' sings the poet of the Christian year for Trinity Sunday. The number alone is answerable for the emblem. We do not deny that an equilateral triangle is a more perfect symbol of the Blessed Trinity: but even here a captious man might object to the emblem, because the angles gain greater or less prominence according to the position in which the triangle is placed. The Catholic monogram of the Trinity, for example, assigns to the Father and the Son the upper angles of a triangle standing on the third point. On the other hand the modern triangle, generally charged with the Hebrew word Jehovah, has the third angle uppermost. We can quite conceive these differences being thought objectionable. The case is not so strong indeed as when the three members are unequal, but still it is the same in kind and in reality.

It is a condition of emblems that the points of similitude must not be pressed too far. The material Sun indeed typifies the Sun of Righteousness: but in what particulars? in its being *created*, in its rising on the dark world *every* day, in its being matter? Surely not: but in this one point, that it brings light and heat to the earth. *I am the Door*, said our Lord. In what particulars, we may again ask? It would be profane to show by examples that it is only in this point: that a door is for entrance into a material house just as we enter into the Church through Christ. The ark, our Church teaches us, was an emblem of the Church: not in its human building, nor in its final perishing; but in that it saved souls by water. Did the Paschal Lamb typify the Immaculate Victim in any thing more than its comparative purity and its bloody death? We need not multiply such examples.

But there is another consideration to be adduced. Our Lord's own parables must not be pressed too far. The history of the five wise and five foolish virgins, must not be adduced to prove that the number of the lost will equal that of the saved. This may be dangerous ground, but the assertion is true. Every parable is figurative to a certain point, and no further. Not that there is much danger of persons not knowing where the line is to be drawn: any more than there would be in the case of one of a reverent mind, who was told that the *triplicity* of aisles and windows typified a great doctrine. The *British Critic* made a very just observation on this point, that it argued a great blindness of spiritual vision to deny such an emblem, because the similitude was not complete in all points. Indeed if all points answered so closely and exactly to each other, it is not clear how a similitude would differ from a fac-simile. The very notion of a thing being like another involves the fact that the two are not identical. Nothing more is found or expected, than a similarity, an analogy, in certain qualities. For in all symbolism it is quality and not essence in which resemblance is sought.

Which leads us to consider another objection sometimes urged to the effect that if a thing mean one thing it cannot mean another. For example, if the nave and aisles represent the Holy Trinity, they cannot also represent the Church Militant here on earth, or in another point of view the true fold. Again, if the piers and arches set forth the foundation of the apostles and prophets, they must not bear a part in the representation of the Trinity together with the cleristory and triforium. But this difficulty vanishes if we remember that the resemblance, for the most part, is derived from grouping independent things together and viewing them in a particular light. We do not deny the *real* essential symbolism of a material result: but this its particular significancy need not obtrude itself at all times: the thing itself in other combinations, and viewed under other aspects, may acquire an additional and occasional meaning. For example, it is the union of the rose, thistle, and shamrock, which is the emblem of our United Empire: they have each their own figurative sense; in combination they acquire a new meaning. The harp is not less the emblem of Ireland, because it must primarily represent music. Leaven was of old the symbol of wickedness: our Lord spake of the leaven of the Scribes and Pharisees: yet we hear from His own lips, The kingdom of heaven is like unto leaven.*

Another objection is as follows: If this theory be true, how will you account for churches with nothing but a nave, or with only one aisle; how for churches with neither cleristory nor triforio; or, on the other hand, for those with double triforia, or with four or five aisles? Now we never asserted that it was necessary that all, or indeed any, given things should be intentionally symbolised. We have pointed out that some things are essentially symbolical; others accidentally and occasionally. We might attempt to classify what *must* be symbolised in church building, and what *may* be. But we decline to do so because we do not think that the principles of symbolism are yet sufficiently investigated or apprehended. However, in a general way, *every* building must, from the nature of things, have some accidents, as of material, of parts, of plan; every particular building must have particular accidents, as of use and purpose. These accidents *must* be symbolical, from their nature, in a general way: they may derive, from purpose added to their nature, a further or modified symbolism in a particular way. With the first sort it is that Durandus chiefly concerns himself. A building must have walls, must have roof, piers, windows, corners, and floor. For each then he finds a meaning. He does not quite

---

* We have the highest authority for believing that one type can symbolise two things quite independent of each other, in that the Jewish Sabbath, commanded from Sinai to be observed in commemoration of the Rest after the Creation, is enforced in Deuteronomy as the representation of the rest of the children of Israel from Egyptian bondage. 'Remember,' says Moses, 'that thou wast a servant in the land of Egypt, and that the Lord thy God brought thee out thence through a mighty hand and by a stretched out arm: *therefore* the Lord thy God commanded thee to keep the Sabbath day.'—Deut. v, 15.

neglect the second sort. Early English windows must have a splay: the spire may have a weathercock: for these then there is an appropriate signification. So we do not mean to insist that certain things *shall* be symbolised, we say they *may* be symbolised. Perhaps when more is known, we shall be able to criticise ancient buildings, to show their faults or their shortcomings in this particular. As it is, we have framed a sort of *beau ideal* of a church, fully formed and developed, which we should propose as a perfect model. We are not qualified as yet to blame the ancient churches which do not come up to this ideal, but we cannot be wrong in praiseing such as do.

In discussing Mr Lewis's illustrations of Kilpeck church, we touched upon the Basilican origin of churches considered as an argument against the reception of the symbolical theory. Our last remarks will apply to the same question. It has been thought quite sufficient ground for turning into ridicule the whole principle, that the Roman justice halls had three or more aisles, or that a barn or banquetting room may have three longitudinal divisions. But what if mechanical convenience suggested the arrangement? (though we do not grant this). It is clear that many churches, many barns, and many refectories have never had a triple arrangement. It has never been asserted that every church shall have nave and aisles: but if a church has nave and aisles it will be symbolical of a great doctrine; and for this reason it is better for a church to have nave and aisles. Why do not such writers argue that the cross form is not symbolical, because many barns are cruciform? Now it is instructive to observe that there is a great and obvious utilitarian advantage in this shape for a barn: but not in the case of churches *as anciently arranged;* in which the transepts were utterly useless for the accommodation of worshippers; and in which there is a mechanical evil (as before mentioned) from the lateral pressure on the lantern piers. Yet it is undeniable that the cross form was chosen for its symbolical meaning: and this in spite of mechanical disadvantages. A mechanical reason fails here, as in the former case, in accounting for the fact. How will they account for the cross form? Their own argument tells against them. We may still further remark that in modern times we have had some curious practical lessons upon this cross form. Messrs Britton and Hosking, in their atrocious plan for rearranging S. Mary Redcliffe church, unwittingly testified to the inconvenience, and want of any utilitarian end, of this plan by placing the pulpit under the lantern, and ranging the congregation in the four arms so as to face it. On the other hand, some modern architects confessedly employ the cross form because it allows of people arranged as in the last case, all seeing the preacher. But why do they not look deeper into things? Why have the cross at all? Why not have an amphitheatre, an octagon, an accoustically designed Mechanic's Institute Lecture Room? Then all could hear, all could see much better, and the building would not cost half so much. They may think that they are designing on utilitarian principles. In truth they are unknowingly, unwillingly, symbolising the Cross.

CHAPTER X

DEVELOPMENT OF SYMBOLISM

IT is now our intention to attempt a brief sketch of the history of symbolism, confining ourselves to its rise, progress, and decline in England. For of its earlier development we have already had occasion to speak, both in the first and in the eighth chapter, when we referred to its use among the primitive Christians, and to such particulars of information as could be gained concerning it from the later fathers, and from mediæval authors.

Among all nations the facts of Christianity have been received before its doctrines. The inhabitants of a heathen country are first called on to believe, as matter of history, that our Blessed Lord was conceived by the Holy Ghost, born of the Virgin Mary, suffered under Pontius Pilate, was crucified, dead, and buried, before any attempt is made to set before them the doctrine of the Atonement, the mystery of the Trinity, or the compatibility of God's foreknowledge with man's free action. And it is in the infancy of individuals, as in that of nations. We may therefore, from all analogy, conclude, that the things set forth in the earlier development of church art would be facts rather than doctrines.

Now, if we look to Norman buildings, we shall find this to be the case. Excepting the doctrine of the Holy Trinity (which, after all, perhaps rather ranks, through all the stages of Christian art, under the head of essential, than under that of intended symbolism), we shall find an almost exclusive reference to history, in arrangements and details. That God was the Creator of heaven and earth, is set forth in door mouldings, and capitals, sometimes by the heavenly constellations or signs of the zodiac, sometimes by the animals brought to Adam to be named, sometimes by the references to agriculture, which, as we have before seen, often occur. The Incarnation of our Saviour is set forth, as it has been already hinted, by representations so physical and earthly, as to be to our eyes almost profane. The Fall of Man, which appears on the sides of fonts, well reminds us of that stain which must be washed away in Holy Baptism. A great many of the events of our Lord's life are sculptured in various positions: above all, of course, His Passion. Again, duties are symbolically represented, so in the chancel arch of Egleton, Rutland, we have the figure of a deacon ringing a bell; doubtless to remind the worshippers of the duty of attending God's house. And a still more practical method of representing the evil consequences attending the breach of duty, and one which speaks much of the rudeness of the age, is where some local event well-known at the time of the erection of the church, finds a commemoration in it. Thus (though at a later epoch) among the capitals of the south transept of Wells cathedral, the architect has represented a theft, which doubtless, at the time, had made a considerable noise in that place. In the first group, a man is seen stealing apples; then follows the struggle and apprehension: finally, his trial and condemnation. And such practical admonitions might not have been without their use. Sometimes they are refined and exalted into such an one as may be seen in the northern apse of S. Mary's, at Guildford, where heavenly and earthly judgment are portrayed. Victory over the devil is singularly enough symbolised in Oxford, S. Peter's, by the piers which rest on, and crush, a monster. We have before noticed that Norman architecture, true to its love of facts, delighted in the representation of instruments of martyrdom, or the deeds of faith, as the victory of S. George. The final doom was also a favourite subject; so was the descent of Christ into hell. In fact, its whole character, whether in string courses, tympana, capitals, or chancel arches, was graphicalness, and that obtained sometimes at the expense of grace, sometimes almost at that of decorum, but probably well adapted to the particular development which the minds of the people had then reached. One point we must remark, to the eternal honour of the Anglo-Norman, and indeed also of the Saxon Church, deadly as was the hatred existing between the two peoples, for at least a hundred and fifty years after the conquest, it has left no symbolical trace, either in the churches of the vanquishers, or of the vanquished. Much as the one had suffered, and much as the other despised the conquered nation, this feeling vanished in the house of God.

In advancing to Early English, we still find strong traces of the historicalism of ornaments, both in some of the mouldings, as in the toothed, and in the capitals, though the latter begin now to assume a more allegorical form. Indeed, the observation seems worth making, that this style is the only one which appears to have dealt much in allegory, we mean in that sense which we have already attached to the word. That is, it employs fictitious representations to set forth real truths; as in Wells cathedral, the fall of the barren tree forms a beautiful corbel. We do, however, find some traces of this in Norman work, as the fable of the crow and the fox may occasionally be discovered in it. The works of the creation were often set forth, rather with reference to their beauty than from any other reasons. Such as the birds making their nests in the thick foliage, flowers, and fruit. Yet, on the whole, facts such as those which principally occupied the attention of Norman architects, began rather to find expression among the details, than to usurp any important part in church arrangement. We are in possession of too little wood work of this date —and in that many references of this kind were probably to be found—to be able to speak with so much certainty as we can in the later styles: but that this was the tendency of the progress of architecture, it requires but little knowledge to discover. Impressed, but evidently, now, not only essentially but intentionally, on every building, was the doctrine of the Ever Blessed Trinity: for triplets were so common at the east end as to form the rule of Early English design. Fonts, instead of bearing a representation of the Fall of Man, and thereby implying our need of regeneration, began to be octagonal, thereby setting forth the doctrine itself, a strong confirmation of our previous observation respecting facts and doctrines. The shape of piers is also to be noticed. For there appears to have been almost a rule, either that the octagonal and circular shape should alternate; or that one aisle should present the one kind, the other the other. This we can hardly, in our present state of knowledge, profess to explain. Durandus's observations about windows, their splay and shafts, are very curious: and again, he evidently recognises in the tiebeams, the knitting together of the elect in one communion and fellowship: a strong argument, this, that we are justified in regarding arrangements, which arise from mechanical necessity, as nevertheless truly and really symbolical. In the bases of piers we now often find flowers, which indeed, sometimes, as in Rochester cathedral, occur in transition work; principally the fleur de lys, which we may interpret to signify that humility is the foundation of all Christian graces.

On the whole, however, we conclude that in this style, while churches taken as a whole became more symbolical, their details, *as* details, became less so.

In proceeding to the next development of Catholic art, we are almost afraid of expressing a belief, that Decorated, in its early dawn, gave promise of a brighter day than it ever reached. It had not shown its wonderful resources and capabilities in windows and flying buttresses, before the boldness of its capitals and bases began to decline. We can imagine that, had it so been ordered, Christian architecture might, about the year 1300, have taken a different direction, and attained to a glory, inconceivable to us—perhaps attainable only when the whole Catholic Church shall be at unity. As it is, we cannot but consider, that about that period, or a few years later, it took a wrong turn, and being hurried in a short space through the hectic of a rare flush of beauty, declined thenceforward slowly but surely. Now, if we ask, why was this? it will lead us to look at Church history as connected with the development of church architecture. Contemporary with the change from Saxon to Norman (for we are none of those who hold that the former extended till Oct. 14, 1065, and the latter began the next day), was finally the victory of the Anglican Church over Paganism in the conversion and civilisation of the Danes. Contemporary with the appearance of Early English, was the great victory of the Church over Erastianism, by the martyrdom of S. Thomas of Canterbury, and the abrogation of the constitutions of Clarendon. But, hardly had Early English finished its course of splendour, when while traces of rare glory were developing daily, the statute of Mortmain began to tell upon the

Church: and though the impulse already given yet continued for some time to act, the end was near. No magnificent cathedral was built after the full effects—not so much of that act, as of the Erastianism which contrived and allowed it—were felt. The nave of Winchester can hardly be called a solitary exception; because, in truth, it may be doubted whether the pious exertions of William of Wykeham were not, so far as concerns the actual beauty of his cathedral, misplaced. Thenceforward, the State interfered more and more with the Church; and not allowed to carry out her own designs, it is no wonder if the latter quickly began to forget her own symbolical language. After, for the first few years of the fourteenth century, using it with precision and elegance before unattainable, she thenceforward began to disuse it. We need not give examples of decorated symbolism, because all that was new in it lay in its windows: and these we have already discussed at considerable length. And having sufficiently explained why there should be a decline, we have only now to examine why that decline should have been so different in England, France, and Italy. In England, from the time that Edward IV directed the execution of Archbishop Scrope, when the State interfered, it was with a strong arm, cramping and confining, obliging the Church to confine herself to ritual observances, and forbidding her to expatiate in the grand objects for which she was ordained. Now could there be a more fitting expression of this than the Perpendicular style? Does not its stiffness, its failure in harmony, its want of power and adaptation, its continual introduction of heraldry, its monotony, its breaking up by hard continued lines, its shallowness, its meretriciousness, its display—set forth what we know to have been the character of the contemporary Church? Above all, do not the reintroduction of Horizontality, the Tudor arch, the depressed pier, speak of her want of spirituality? Everything teaches us that there was no want of power in her architects; considered merely as specimens of art, King's College, and Henry the Seventh's chapels, are matchless. And here and there we may trace some tokens of vastness and holiness of conception worthy of a better age; such as the Suffolk roofs, which, as it has been well said, never attained their full development. It must be borne in mind, that Perpendicular* was the first style, which in its full development was used first for a secular building. Far be it from us, however, to depreciate the excessive magnificence it assumes in shrines and chapels: indeed, this is one of the features which Decorated has not, and the absence of which in that style renders it possible to believe that a still more magnificent may be in store for us. Perpendicular introduced no new element of symbolism.

But if this were the state of the Anglican Church, the Gallican, though not better off, was acted on in a very different manner. The State gradually interfered with it, embraced it with its dangerous friendship, made its observances meaningless, while sustaining their splendour; secularised its abbeys, by appropriating them to political ends; made statesmen of its bishops, gave it outside show, while eating out its heart. Does not Flamboyant express this? A vast collection of elegant forms, meaninglessly strung together: richness of ornament, actually weakening construction: vagaries of tracery, as if the hand possessed of church art were suddenly deprived of church feelings: nothing plain, simple, intelligible, holy: parts neglected, parts ostentatious: the west

* We deeply regret that the Oxford Architectural Society should ever have allowed itself to put on paper the opinions expressed by one of its members, that Perpendicular windows are those best suited to the spirit of Christian architecture.

front of Abbeville to a choir that would disgrace a hamlet.

In Spain, again, where Christianity unfolded itself later, so also was church art later in its development. San Miguel, at Seville, which was actually built in 1305, would, in England, be set down to the date of about 1180.

In Italy, where there was no State to interfere with the Church, Paganism, which had always been more or less at work, sprang up at once, at the time of the Great Schism, and has ever since prevailed.

But to return to England. Perpendicular, unable to express any idea by its ornaments, soon began to imitate those of earlier styles: first Early English, in the wretched banded capitals of the western counties, and then Decorated in its windows. While, however, the Church was yet united with the rest of Christendom, Paganism interfered but in a very slight degree: the Italian example of Henry the Seventh's tomb was not followed. Even after the Dissolution, there were some good churches built: the symbolism which lingered longest was that of the chancel and nave. Nor was this destroyed summarily: the importance of the chancel had been gradually, all through the Perpendicular era, weakened by chancel aisles, and the omission of the chancel arch: it was but to omit the rood screen and parclose, and (as at Hawkshead, Lancashire, circ. 1564) the mystical division vanished.

The symbolisms which Protestantism introduced were few and easily understood.

The removal, and material, of the altar, the change of vestments, the gradual introduction of close pews, the innovation of a reading pew, were all figurative enough. Something like a return to church art was made just before the great Rebellion: chancels became elongated, altars resumed their old position, copes reappeared, and the like. Details began to improve: and (which we could hardly have expected) intentional symbolism is sometimes to be discovered in them. So, in Baltonsburgh, Somersetshire, a stone pulpit of the date of 1621, has among other devices, an equilateral triangle, containing, and surrounded by, a *tre*-foil: and evidently setting forth the Holy Trinity. After the Rebellion, but still more after the Revolution, those faint traces of symbolism died away into that *ne plus ultra* of wretchedness, the Georgian style.

CHAPTER XI

GENERAL CONCLUSION

IT is very remarkable, as has been already observed, that the buildings of those who most strongly object to the principle of symbolism, do in effect contain as striking an exemplification of it as it would be possible to find.

Let us look at a Protestant place of worship. It is choked up and concealed by surrounding shops and houses, for religion, nowadays, must give way to business and pleasure : it stands north and south, for all idea of fellow-feeling with the Church Catholic is looked on as mere trifling, or worse : the front which faces the High Street is of stone, because the uniformity of the street so required it : or (which is more likely) of stucco, which answers as well, and is cheaper : the sides, however, are of brick, because no one can see them : there is at the entrance a large vestibule, to allow people to stand while their carriages are being called up, and to enter into conversation on the news of the day, or the merits of the preacher : it also serves the purpose of making the church warmer, and contains the doors and staircases to the galleries. On entering, the pulpit occupies the central position, and towards it every seat is directed : for preaching is the great object of the Christian ministry : galleries run all round the building, because hearing is the great object of a Christian congregation: the altar stands under the organ gallery, as being of no use, except once a month: there are a few free seats in out-of-the-way places, where no one could hear, and no pews would be hired, and therefore no money is lost by making the places free: and whether the few poor people who occupy them can hear or not, what matters it? The font, a cast-iron vase on a marble pillar, stands within the altar rails; because it there takes up no room: the reading pew is under the pulpit, and faces the congregation; because the prayers are to be read to them and not addressed to God. Look at this place on Sunday or Thursday evening. Carriages crash up through the cast-iron gates, and, amidst the wrangling and oaths of rival coachmen, deposit their loads at the portico: people come, dressed out in the full fashion of the day, to occupy their luxurious pew, to lay their smelling-bottles and prayer-books on its desk, and reclining on its soft cushions, to confess themselves—if they are in time—miserable sinners: to see the poor and infirm standing in the narrow passages, and close their pew doors against them, lest themselves should be contaminated, or their cushions spoilt, at the same time beseeching God to give their fellow-creatures the comfort which they refuse to bestow: the Royal Arms occupy a conspicuous position; for it is a chapel of the Establishment: there are neat cast-iron pillars to hold up the galleries, and still neater pillars in the galleries to hold up the roof; thereby typifying that the whole existence of the building depends on the good-will of the congregation: the roof is flat, with an elegant cornice, and serves principally to support a gas-lighted chandelier: and the administration of this chapel is carried on by clerk, organist, beadle, and certain bonnetless pew-openers.

We need not point out how strongly all this symbolises the spiritual pride, the luxury, the self-sufficiency, the bigotry of the congregations of too many a pew-rented Episcopal chapel.

In contrast to this, let us close with a general view of the symbolism of a Catholic church.

Far away, and long ere we catch our first view of the city itself, the three spires of its cathedral, rising high above its din and turmoil, preach to us of the Most Holy and Undivided Trinity. As we approach, the transepts, striking out cross-wise, tell of the Atonement: the Communion of Saints is set forth by the chapels clustering round choir and nave: the mystical weather-cock bids us to watch and pray and endure hardness: the hideous forms that seem hurrying from the eaves speak the misery of those who are cast out of the Church: spire, pinnacle, and finial, the upward curl of the sculptured foliage, the upward spring of the flying buttress, the sharp rise of the window arch, the high-thrown pitch of the roof, all these, overpowering the horizontal tendency of string course and parapet, teach us, that vanquishing earthly desires, we also should ascend in heart and mind. Lessons of holy wisdom are written in the delicate tracery of the windows: the unity of many members is shadowed forth by the multiplex arcade: the duty of letting our light shine before men, by the pierced and flowered parapet that crowns the whole.

We enter. The triple breadth of nave and aisles, the triple height of pier arch, triforium, and clerestory, the triple length of choir, transepts, and nave, again set forth the Holy Trinity. And what besides is there that does not tell of our Blessed Saviour? that does not point out 'Him first' in the two-fold western door: 'Him last' in the distant altar: 'Him midst' in the great rood: 'Him without end' in the monogram carved on boss and corbal, in the Holy Lamb, in the Lion of the tribe of Judah, in the Mystic Fish? Close by us is the font;

for by regeneration we enter the Church: it is deep and capacious; for we are buried in baptism with Christ: it is of stone; for He is the Rock: and its spiry cover teaches us, if we be indeed risen from its waters with Him, to seek those things that are above. Before us, in long drawn vista, are the massy piers, which are the Apostles and Prophets: they are each of many members, for many are the graces in every saint: there is delicate foliage round the head of all; for all were plentiful in good works. Beneath our feet are the badges of worldly pomp and glory, the charges of kings and nobles and knights: all in the presence of God as dross and worthlessness. Over us swells the vast 'valley' of the high-pitched roof: from the crossing and interlacing of its curious rafters hang fadeless flowers and fruits which are not of earth: from its hammer-beams project wreaths and stars, such as adorn heavenly beings: in its centre stands the Lamb as it had been slain: from around Him the Celestial Host, cherubim and seraphim, thrones, principalities, and powers, look down peacefully on the worshippers below. Harpers there are among them harping with their harps: for one is the song of the Church in earth and in heaven. Through the walls wind the narrow cloister galleries: emblems of the path by which holy hermits and anchorites, whose conflicts were known only to their God, have reached their home. And we are compassed about with a mighty cloud of witnesses: the rich deep glass of the windows teems with saintly forms, each in its own fair niche, all invested with the same holy repose: there is the glorious company of the apostles: the goodly fellowship of the prophets: the noble army of martyrs: the shining band of the confessors: the jubilant chorus of the virgins: there are kings who have long since changed an earthly for an heavenly crown: and bishops who have given in a glad account to the Shepherd and Bishop of souls. But on none of these things do we rest; piers, arch behind arch, windows, light behind light, arcades, shaft behind shaft, the roof, bay behind bay, the saints around us, the heavenly hierarchy above with dignity of pre-eminence still increasing eastward, each and all, lead on eye and soul and thought to the image of the crucified Saviour as displayed in the great east window. Gazing steadfastly on that, we pass up the nave, that is through the Church Militant, till we reach the rood screen, the barrier between it and the Church Triumphant, and therein shadowing forth the death of the faithful. High above it hangs, on His triumphal cross, the image of Him Who by His death hath overcome death; on it are portrayed saints and martyrs, His warriors, who fighting under their Lord have entered into rest and inherit a tearless eternity. They are to be our examples, and the seven lamps above them typify those graces of the Spirit, by Whom alone we can tread in their steps. The screen itself glows with gold and crimson: with gold, for they have on their heads golden crowns: with crimson, for they passed the Red Sea of martyrdom to obtain them. And through the delicate net-work, and the unfolding holy doors, we catch faint glimpses of the chancel beyond. There are the massy stalls; for in heaven is everlasting rest: there are the sedilia, emblems of the seats of the elders round the throne: there is the piscina; for they have washed their robes and made them white: and there, heart and soul and life of all, the altar with its unquenched lights, and golden carvings, and mystic steps, and sparkling jewels: even Christ Himself, by Whose only merits we find admission to our heavenly inheritance. Verily, as we think on the oneness of its design, we may say: *Jerusalem edificatur ut civitas cujus participatio ejus in idipsum.*

POSTSCRIPTUM

ON concluding their work, which from circumstances that need not be specified has been a year in the press, the writers must apologise for the numerous typographical errors which have been allowed to remain. Their separation from each other, and distance from the printer, must plead in excuse.

They take this opportunity of expressing their thanks to the Reverend Dr Mill, Christian Advocate of the University of Cambridge, and to F. A. Paley, Esq., M.A., of S. John's College, Cambridge, Honorary Secretary of the Cambridge Camden Society, for their advice and assistance.

It remains to say that some doubt has been felt by persons who have read the Introductory Essay in proofs, whether the writers have given Mr Pugin sufficient credit for several passages in his works which seem to *involve* the principle now contended for. We had thought that no misapprehension could be feared on this head. It was enough to know that the principle in question, even though *felt* (as we indeed allowed) by this architect, had not been *expressed in terms*. In short, we took this fact for our ground : that whereas Mr Pugin's book professed to assert the *true principles* of Christian architecture, yet reality, according to his definition, was not at least so accurately a 'true principle' as sacramentality. The principles themselves, as enunciated by Mr Pugin, apply as well to any secular building as to a church : they are true for *construction*, but not adequate in themselves to form a rule for ecclesiastical design.

KEMERTON, *August* 16, 1843.

The following very curious passage ought to have come in at page lxxvii of the Introductory Essay, but was not accessible at the time. It is an extract from the 'Fardle of Facions,' printed A.D. 1555.

FROM THE 'FARDLE OF FACIONS,' PRINTED 1555

Oratories, temples, or places of praier (whiche we calle churches) might not to be built without the good will of the bishoppe of the diocese. And when the timbre was redy to be framed, and the foundacion digged, it behoved them to sende for the bishoppe, to hallowe the firste corner stone of the foundacion, and to make the signe of the Crosse thereupon, and to laie it, and directe it juste easte and west. And then might the masons sette upon the stone, but not afore. This churche did they use to builde after the facion of a crosse, and not unlike the shape of a manne. The channcelle (in the whiche is conteined the highe altare and the quiere) directe fulle in the easte, representeth the heade, and therefore ought to be somewhat rounde, and muche shorter than the body of the churche. And yet upon respect that the heade is the place for the eyes, it ought to be of more lighte, and to bee seperate with a particion, in the steade of a necke, from the bodye of the churche. This particion the Latine calleth cancelli, and out of that cometh our terme channcelle. On eche side of this channcelle peradventure (for so fitteth it beste) should stand a turret; as it were for two ears, and in these the belles to be hanged, to calle the people to service, by daie and by night. Undre one of these turretts is there commonly a vaulte, whose doore openeth into the quiere, and in this are laid up the hallowed vessells and ornamentes, and other utensils of the churche. We call it a vestrie. The other parte oughte to be fitted, that having as it were on eche side an arme, the reste maye resemble the bodye with the fete stretched in breadthe, and in lengthe. On eche side of the bodye the pillers to stande, upon whose coronettes or heades the vaulte or rophe of the churche maye reste. And to the foote beneth aulters to be joyned. Those aulters to be orderly alway covered with two aulter clothes, and garnished with the crosse of Christe, or some little cofre of reliques. At eche ende a candelsticke, and a booke towarde the middes. The walls to be painted without and within, and diversely paineted. That they also should have in every parishe a faire round stone, made hollowe and fitte to holde water, in the whiche the water consecrate for baptisme maye be kept for the christening of children. Upon the right hand of the highe aulter that ther should be an almorie, either cutte into the walle, or framed upon it, in the whiche they woulde have the sacrament of the Lorde's bodye, the holy oyle for the sicke, and chrismatorie, alwaie to be locked. Furthermore they would that ther should be a pullpite in the middes of the churche, wherein the prieste maye stonde upon Sondaies and holidays to teache the people those things that it behoveth them to knowe. The channcelle to serve only for the priests and clerks; the rest of the temporalle multitude to be in the bodye of the churche, seperate notwithstanding, the men on the righte side, and the women on the left.

Here beginneth the First Book of GULIELMUS DURANDUS *his* RATIONALE *of the* DIVINE OFFICES.

THE PROEME

Importance and Difficulty of the Study of Symbolism—Necessity of its Cultivation by Priests—Consideration of Unlearned Priests—Mystical and Moral Meaning of the Law—Four-fold Sense of Scripture: the Historical, the Allegoric, the Tropologic, the Anagogic—Different Ceremonies used by Different Churches—Name of Rationale, whence derived—Division of the Work.

1. ALL things, as many as pertain to offices and matters ecclesiastical, be full of divine significations and mysteries, and overflow with a celestial sweetness; if so be that a man be diligent in his study of them, and know how to draw 'honey from the rock, and oil from the hardest stone.'[1] But who 'knoweth the ordinances of heaven, or can fix the reasons thereof upon the earth?'[2] For he that prieth into their majesty, is overwhelmed by the glory of them. Of a truth 'the well is deep, and I have nothing to draw with':[3] unless He giveth it unto me Who 'giveth to all men liberally, and upbraideth not':[4] so that 'while I journey through the mountains'[5] I may 'draw water with joy out of the wells

---

[1] Deut. xxxii, 13. [2] Job xxxviii, 33. [3] S. John iv, 11.
[4] S. James i, 5. [5] Psalm ciii. Vulgate.

of salvation.'[6] Wherefore, albeit of the things handed down from our forefathers, capable we are not to explain all, yet if among them there be anything which is done without reason, it should forthwith be put away. 'Wherefore I, William, by the alone tender mercy of God, Bishop of the Holy Church which is in Mende,'[7] will knock diligently at the door, if so be that 'the key of David'[8] will open unto me: that the King may 'bring me in to His treasury,'[9] and show unto me the heavenly pattern which was showed unto Moses in the Mount: so that I may learn those things which pertain to rites ecclesiastical, whereof they teach and what they signify: and that I may be able plainly to reveal and make manifest the reasons of them, by His help, 'Who hath ordained strength out of the mouth of babes and sucklings':[10] 'Whose spirit bloweth where it listeth,'[11] dividing to 'each severally as it will'[12] to the praise and glory of the Trinity.

2. Sacraments we have received to be signs or figures, not in themselves virtues, but the significations of virtues, by which men are taught as by letters. Now of signs there be that are natural, and there be that are positive: concerning which, and also of the nature of a Sacrament, we shall speak hereafter.

3. Therefore the priests and the bishops to whom 'it is given to know the mysteries of the kingdom of God,'[13]

---

[6] Isaiah xii, 3.
[7] 'A city of France, and capital of the department of Lozére, situated on an eminence near the Lot: before the Revolution, the See of a Bishop. The number of inhabitants is about 5000.'—Cruttwell's *Gazetteer*, s.v.
[8] Apocalypse iii, 7. [9] Cant. ii, 4.
[10] Psalm viii, 2. See also Wisdom x, 21. [11] S. John iii, 8.
[12] 1 Cor. xii, 11. [13] S. Luke viii, 10.

as He saith in Luke, and who be the stewards and dispensers of sacred things, ought both to understand the sacred mysteries, and to shine in the virtues which they signify: so that by their light others may be illuminated: otherwise 'they be blind leaders of the blind.'[14] As saith the Prophet, 'Let their eyes be darkened, that they see not.'[15] But, woe therefore is me! in these days they apprehend but little of those things which day by day they handle and perform, what they signify, and wherefore they were instituted: so that the saying of the Prophet seemeth to be fulfilled, 'As is the people, so is the priest.'[16] For when they bear the bread of Prothesis[17] to the Lord's Table and the Mysteries, they understand not its signification more than brute beasts which carry bread for the use of others. Of which ignorance they shall give account in the day of vengeance and wrath. 'When the cedars of Paradise shall tremble, what shall the bush of the desert do?'[18] For to them is that saying of the Prophet, 'They have not known My ways: so I swear in my wrath, if they shall enter into My rest.'[19]

4. Now the professors of the arts liberal, and of all other arts, seek how they may clothe, support, and adorn with causes and hidden reasons those things which be nakedly and without ornament therein set forth; painters moreover, and mechanics and handicraftsmen of what

---

[14] S. Matthew xv, 14.   [15] Psalm lxix, 23.   [16] Isaiah xxiv, 2.
[17] Here is a distinct reference to the Prothesis: the more valuable because in writers of the Middle Ages it does not hold so prominent a place as we might have expected: and the table of Prothesis appears not to have occupied a certainly defined situation in Catholic churches. There is also a reference to Lev. xxi, 8, and the showbread.
[18] S. Luke xxii, 3.   [19] Psalm xcv, 11.

sort soever, study in every variety of their works to render and to have at hand probable reasons thereof. So, also, unseemly is it to the magistrate to be ignorant of this world's laws; and to the pleader to know nothing of the law, wherein he is exercised.

5. But although learning be necessary unto priests for the sake of doctrine: yet must not scholastics think slightingly of unlettered priests; according to that saying in Exodus, 'Thou shalt not revile the gods.'[20] Whence, saith S. Augustine, they shall not deride if they hear the priests and ministers of the Church, either invoking God with barbarisms and solecisms, or not understanding and misdividing the words which they pronounce. Not but that such things are to be corrected; but they must firstly be tolerated of the more learned. But that which priests ought to learn, shall be said below.

6. Furthermore, the symbolism which existeth in things and offices ecclesiastical, is often not seen, both because figures have departed, and now it is the time of truth; and also because we ought not to judaise. But, albeit those types of which the truth is made manifest have departed, yet even to this time manifold truth is concealed, which we see not; wherefore the Church useth figures. For so by white vestments we understand the beauty in which our souls shall be arrayed, or the glory of our immortality, which we cannot manifestly behold: and in the Mass, by the oblation on the altar,[21] the

---

[20] Exodus xxii, 28.

[21] The prayer of oblation is as follows—'Suscipe, Sancta Trinitas, hanc oblationem quam Tibi offerimus *ob memoriam Passionis*, resurrectionis et ascensionis Jesu Christi Domini nostri,' etc.

Passion of Christ is represented, that it be held in the memory more faithfully and more firmly.

7. Furthermore, of the things which be commanded in the law, some be moral, and others mystical. They be moral which inform the morals, and are to be understood in the simple tenour of the words: 'Love God: honour thy father: thou shalt do no murder,' and such like. Mystical be such as are typical: where something is set forth beyond the literal meaning. Of these, some be sacramental, and some ceremonial. Sacramental be such as may be accounted for, why thus they were ordered: such as circumcision, and the observance of the Sabbath, and the like. Ceremonial be they for which no reason can be given. Such be, 'Thou shalt not plough with an ox and an ass together:'[22] 'Thou shalt not wear a garment of linen and woollen mixed.'[23]

8. Now in things that are moral commands, the law hath received no change: but in things sacramental and ceremonial its outward form is altered: yet not one of the mystical significations is done away: for the law is not done away. Though the 'priesthood being changed, there is made of necessity a change likewise of the law.'[24]

9. Now, in Holy Scriptures there be divers senses: as historic, allegoric, tropologic, and anagogic. Whence, according to Boethius, all divine authority ariseth from a sense either historical or allegorical or from both. And according to S. Hierom, we ought to study Holy Scriptures in three ways:—firstly, according to the letter; secondly, after the allegory, that is, the spiritual

---

[22] Deut. xxii, 10.   [23] Deut. xxii, 11.   [24] Hebrews vii, 12.

meaning; thirdly, according to the blessedness of the future.

History is *things signified by words:* as when a plain relation is made how certain events took place: as when the children of Israel, after their deliverance from Egypt, made a tabernacle to the Lord. And history is derived from ἱστορεῖν, which is to gesticulate:[25] whence gesticulators (that is, players) are called *histriones*.

10. Allegory is when one thing is said and another meant: as when by one deed another is intended: which other thing, if it be visible, the whole is simply an allegory, if invisible and heavenly, an *anagoge*. Also an allegory is when one state of things is described by another: as when the patience of Christ, and the sacraments of the Church are set forth by mystical words or deeds. As in that place: 'There shall come forth a rod of the stem of Jesse, and a branch shall grow out of his roots:'[26] which is in plain language, The Virgin Mary shall be born of the family of David, who was the son of Jesse. [This is an example of mysticism in words.] Truth is also set forth by mystic deeds: as the children of Israel's freedom from Egyptian slavery, wrought by the blood of a lamb, signifieth that the Church is freed by the Passion of Christ from demoniacal servitude.* The word allegory is derived from the Greek *allon*, which means *foreign*, and *gore*, which is *sense;* that is, a *foreign sense*.

11. *Tropology* is an injunction unto morality: or a moral speech, either with a symbolical or an obvious

---

[25] Here is a notable instance of Durandus's misderivations, of which we have spoken in the Introduction. [26] Isaiah xi, 1. *See Appendix I.

bearing, devised to evince and instruct our behaviour. *Symbolical;* as where he saith, 'Let thy garments be always white: and let the oil of thy head never fail.'[27] That is, let all thy works be pure, and charity never fail from thy mind. And again, It is fit that David should slay the Goliath within us: that is, that humbleness may subdue our pride. *Obvious* as in that saying, 'Deal thy bread to the hungry.'[28] And in that text: 'Let us not love in word, neither in tongue: but in deed and truth.'[29] Now tropology hath his name from *tropos*, a turning, and *logos*, which is a discourse.

12. Anagoge is so called from *ana*, which is upwards, and *goge*, a leading: as it were an upward leading. Whence the anagogic sense is that which leadeth from the visible to the invisible: as light, made the first day, signifieth a thing invisible, namely the angelic nature which was made in the beginning. *Anagoge*, therefore, is that sense which leadeth the mind upwards to heavenly things: that is to the Trinity and the orders of angels, and speaketh concerning future rewards, and the future life which is in the heaven: and it useth both obvious and mystical expressions; obvious, as in that saying, 'Blessed are the pure in heart: for they shall see God:'[30] mystical, as that, 'Blessed are they that have made white their robes: that they may have right unto the tree of life, and enter in through the gate into the city.'[31] Which signifieth, Blessed are they who make pure their thoughts, that they may have a right to see 'God, who is the way, the truth, and the life:'[32] and after

---

[27] Ecclesiastes ix, 8.   [28] Isaiah lviii, 7.   [29] 1 S. John iii, 18.
[30] S. Matthew v, 8.   [31] Apocalypse vii, 14.   [32] S. John xiv, 6.

the example of the fathers, enter into the kingdom of heaven.

In like manner, Jerusalem is understood historically of that earthly city whither pilgrims journey; allegorically, of the Church Militant; tropologically, of every faithful soul; anagogically, of the celestial Jerusalem, which is our country.[33] Of these things, more examples may be seen in the lessons for Holy Saturday.[34] But in this work many senses are applied: and speedy changes are made from one to another, as the diligent reader will perceive.

13. For as none is prohibited from using divers grounds of exception and manners of defence, so neither are they forbidden to employ divers expositions in the praise of God, so that faith be not injured.

14. Notice must also be taken of the variety of rites used in the divine worship. For nearly every Church hath her own observances, and attacheth to them a full meaning of her own: neither is it thought blameworthy or absurd to worship with various chants, or modulations of the voice, nor yet with different observances: when the Church Triumphant herself is surrounded,[35] according to the Prophet, with the like diversity, and in the administration of the sacraments themselves a variety of customs is tolerated, and that rightly.

15. Whence, according to Austin of ecclesiastical

---

[33] How beautifully, observes a writer in the *British Critic*, do old ecclesiastical writers use *patria* and *domus* of our celestial country, and our everlasting home!

[34] Reference is here apparently made to the fifth chapter of the book of Lamentations, which appears as the 3rd lesson at Matins.

[35] The author appears to refer here to the XLV Psalm, 'Eructavit cor meum.'

institutions in the divine office, some we have received from Holy Scriptures: some from the traditions or writings of the apostles, being confirmed by their successors: some, moreover, of which, however, the institution is unknown, are confirmed by custom and approved by use: and to them equal observance is due as to the others.

16. Let not, then, the reader be angry if he perchance read in this work of observances which he never saw in his own church: or does not read of some that are there in use. For we endeavour not to go through the particular rites of particular places, but those which be more common and usual: because we labour to set forth that doctrine which is of universal, and not that which is of particular bearing, nor would it be possible for us to examine the particular rites of every church. Therefore we have determined, for the health of our soul and the benefit of the readers, to set forth and to arrange the secret mysteries of divine offices in a clear state, to the best of our power and to inculcate and thoroughly to explain that which appears necessary for ecclesiastics, towards the understanding of the daily service: even as it is well known that, when in a different condition of life, we did faithfully in our *Mirror of Magistrates* do the like for the use of those who were employed in secular courts.

17. But it must diligently be noted that in the divine offices themselves [36] many ceremonies there be of usual

---

[36] This passage is worth noting, as showing that our Author does not proceed with the determination of making a meaning where he could not find one: but that he is willing to leave much, explained only in the principles of necessity, or convenience, or reverence.

employment which have, from their institution, respect neither to a moral nor mystical signification. Of these, some are known to have arisen of necessity: some of congruity: some of the difference of the Old and New Testament; some of convenience; and some for the mere honour and reverence of the offices themselves: whence saith blessed Austin, so many things are varied by the different customs of divers place, that seldom or never can those causes be discovered which men followed in constituting them.

18. This work is described as a Rationale. For as in the 'breastplate of judgment'[37] which the Jewish high priest wore was written manifestation and truth, so here the reasons of the variations in divine offices and their truths are set forth and manifested: which the prelates and priests of churches ought faithfully to preserve in the shrine of their breasts: and as in the breastplate there was a stone by the splendour of which the children of Israel knew that God was well pleased with them: so also the pious reader who hath been taught the mysteries of the divine offices from the clearness of this work will know that God is favourably disposed towards us, unless we rashly incur His indignation by our offence and fault. The breastplate was woven of four colours and of gold: and here, as we said before, the principles on which are founded the variations in ecclesiastical offices, take the hues of four senses, the historic, the allegoric, the tropologic, and the anagogic, with faith as the[38] groundwork.

[37] Vulg. In Rationali Judicii. Exodus xxviii, 3.
[38] Such appears the meaning of this beautiful comparison. The words are rather obscure, *quatuor sensibus fide media colorantur.*

19. It is divided into eight parts: which we shall go through, by the Lord's favour, in order. The first treateth of churches, and ecclesiastical places and ornaments: and of consecrations and sacraments. The second of the members of the Church, and their duties: the third of sacerdotal and other vestments: the fourth of the Mass, and of the things therein performed: the fifth of the other divine offices: the sixth of the Sundays and holydays, and feasts specially pertaining to our Lord: the seventh of Saints' days, and the feast of the dedication of a church, and the office of the dead; the eighth of the method of computing time, and the calendar.

Tractatus Gulielmi Durandi de ecclesia et ecclesiasticis locis et sacramentis et ornamentis et de consecrationibus incipit feliciter.

CHAPTER I

OF A CHURCH AND ITS PARTS

Two-fold Meaning of the Word—Different Synonyms for the Term—Form of a Church—Of the Tabernacle—The Foundation, how to be laid—To Point East, and Why—The Spiritual Church, how Built up—Of Cement—What Arms the Spiritual Church Employeth—Of the Materials of the Tabernacle—Of Shittim Wood—Analogy of a Church with the Human Body—Of what the Spiritual Church consisteth—Of its Foundations—Of the Walls—Of the Choir—Of Apses—Of the Cloister Court—Of the Towers—Of the Cock—Of the Pinnacles—Of the Windows—Of the Lattice Work—Of the Doors—Of the Piers—Of the Beams—Of the Roof—Of the Stalls—Of the Pulpit—Of the Rood Loft—Of the Hours—Of the Sanctuary—Of the Sacristy—Of the Roof Tiles—Of the Lights—Of the Crosses—Of the Cloister—Of the Bishop's Throne—Why we go together to Church—Of the Separation of the Women from the Men—Of the Covering of Women's Heads—Of Speech in Church—Of Immunity for Malefactors—Why Churches may be rebuilt in other Places.

1. FIRST of all, let us consider a church [1] and its parts. The word church hath two meanings: the one, a material building, wherein the divine offices are celebrated: the other, a spiritual fabric, which is the collection of the faithful. The Church, *that is* the people forming it, is assembled by its ministers, and collected together into

---

[1] It has been found advisable to print the word church in the following pages with a great or a small initial letter, according as 'The Blessed Company of all Faithful People,' or the material building, were intended.

one place by 'Him who maketh men to be of one mind in an house.'[2] For as the material church is constructed from the joining together of various stones, so is the spiritual Church by that of various men.

2. The Greek *ecclesia* is in Latin translated by *convocatio*, because it calleth men to itself: the which title doth better befit the spiritual than the material church.

The material typifieth the spiritual Church: as shall be explained when we treat of its consecration.[3] Again, the Church is called Catholic, that is universal, because it hath been set up in, or spread over, all the world, because the whole multitude of the faithful ought to be in one congregation, or because in the Church is laid up the doctrine necessary for the instruction of all.

3. It is also called in Greek *synagoga*, in Latin *congregatio*, which was the name chosen by the Jews for their places of worship: for to them the term synagogue more appropriately belongeth, though it be also applied to a church. But the Apostles never call a church by this title, perhaps for the sake of distinction.

4. The Church Militant is also called *Sion:* because, amidst its wanderings, it expecteth the promise of a heavenly rest: for Sion signifieth *expectation*. But the Church Triumphant, our future home, the land of peace, is called Jerusalem: for Jerusalem signifieth *the vision of peace*.[4] Also, the church is called the *House of God:* also, sometimes, κυριακή, that is, the *Lord's House*. At others *basilica* (in Latin, a royal palace), for the abodes of earthly kings are thus termed: and how much more fittingly our houses of prayer, the dwelling-places of the King of Kings! Again, it is called *temple*, from *tectum*

---

[2] Psalm lxviii (*Exsurgat Deus*), 6. [3] See below, chapter vi.
[4] So the hymn in the Parisian Breviary, for the dedication of a church:

> Urbs beata, vera pacis
> Visio, Jerusalem.

amplum, where sacrifices are offered to God: and sometimes the *tabernacle of God*, because this present life is a journey, and a progress to a lasting country: and a tabernacle is an hostelrie:[5] as will be explained when we speak of the dedication[6] of a church. And why it is called the *Ark of the Testimony*, we shall say in the ensuing chapter, under the title Altars. Sometimes it is called *Martyrium*, when raised in honour of any martyr; sometimes *capella*[7] (chapel), (see under the head Priest in the second part); sometimes *cænobium*, at others *sacrificium;* sometimes *sacellum;* sometimes *the house of prayer:* sometimes *monastery:* sometimes *oratory*. Generally, however, any place set apart for prayers is called an oratory. Again, the church is called the *Body of* Christ: sometimes a *virgin*, as the Apostle saith, 'that I may present you as a chaste virgin to Christ':[8] sometimes a *bride*, because Christ hath betrothed her to Himself, as saith the Gospel: 'he that hath the bride is the bridegroom':[9] sometimes a *mother*, for daily in baptism she beareth sons to God: sometimes a *daughter*, according to that saying of the Prophet, ' Instead of thy fathers thou shalt have children':[10] sometimes a *widow*, because 'she sitteth solitary through her afflictions, and, like Rachel, will not be comforted.' Sometimes she is set forth under the emblem of an *harlot*, because she is

---

[5] Compare Cicero de Senect. xxiii. Et ex vita ita discedo tanquam ex hospitio, non tanquam ex domo: commorandi enim Natura diversorium nobis, non habitandi dedit.

[6] Chapter vi, sect. 5, ad fin.

[7] Durandus, II. 10, 8. 'In many places, priests be called chaplains. For of old the Kings of France, when they went forth to war, carried with them the Cope of Blessed Martin, which was kept in a certain tent (where Mass was said), and from the cope (cappa) the tent was called chapel (capella).'

We may observe that chapel was used in former times with much greater latitude than now. An additional aisle or chantry was so called. So in Haddenham, Cambridgeshire, on a brass in the north aisle, *Orate pro Animabus fundatorum hujus Capellæ:* that is, the aisle itself.

[8] 2 Cor. xi, 2.   [9] S. John iii, 29.   [10] Psalm xlv (*Eructavit cor meum*), 16.

called out of many nations, and because she closeth not her bosom against any that return to her. Sometimes she is called a city, because of the communion of her holy citizens, being defended by the munitions of the Scriptures, whereby heretics are kept off: having stones and beams of divers kinds, because the merits of the saints are of divers kinds also, as shall be said below. Whatever the Jewish Church received by the law, that doth the Christian Church receive, and with large increase by grace, from Christ whose bride she is. The setting up of an oratory, or church, is not new. For the Lord commanded Moses in Mount Sinai, that he should make a tabernacle of curiously wrought materials. This was divided by a veil into two parts: the outer, called the holy place, where the people attended the sacrifices: the inner, the holy of holies, where the priests and Levites ministered before the Lord (see the Preface to the Fourth Book and also Appendix A).

5. This tabernacle having decayed through age, the Lord commanded that a temple should be built, which Solomon accomplished with wonderful skill: this also had two parts, like the tabernacle. From both of these, namely, from the tabernacle and the temple, doth our material church take its form. In its outer portion, the laity offer their prayers, and hear the Word. In the sanctuary, the clergy pray, preach, offer praises and prayers.

6. The tabernacle, built as it was amidst the journeyings of the Israelites, is sometimes taken as a type of the world which 'passeth away, and the lust thereof.'[11] Whence it was formed with curtains of four colours, as the world is composed of four elements. 'God,' said the Prophet, 'is in His tabernacle':[12] God is in this world, as in a temple dyed scarlet by the blood of Christ. The

---

[11] S. John ii, 17.   [12] Psalm xi (*In Domino confido*), 4.

tabernacle is, however, more especially symbolical of the Church Militant, which hath 'here no continuing city, but seeketh one to come.'[13] Therefore is it called a tabernacle, for tabernacles or tents belong to soldiers: and this saying, God is in his tabernacle, meaneth, God is among the faithful collected together in His name. The outer part of the tabernacle, where the people sacrificed, is the active life, wherein men give themselves up to the love of their neighbour: the interior, wherein the Levites ministered, is the contemplative life, where a band of religious men devote themselves to the love and contemplation of God. The tabernacle gave place to the temple: because after the warfare cometh the triumph.

7. Now a church is to be built on this fashion: The foundation being prepared, according to that saying, 'It fell not, for it was founded upon a rock,'[14] the bishop, or a priest[15] as the bishop's deputy, must sprinkle it with holy water, to banish the foul forms of evil spirits, and lay the first stone, whereon a cross must be engraved.[16]

8. The foundation must be so contrived, as that the head of the church may point due east (see Appendix B); that is, to that point of the heavens, wherein the sun ariseth at the equinoxes; to signify, that the Church Militant must[17] behave herself with moderation,

---

[13] Hebrews xiii, 14.

[14] S. Matthew vii, 25. In general illustration of the foregoing sections the reader is referred to the first chapter of the eighth book of Bingham's 'Antiquities.'

[15] In the account of the dedication of S. Michael the Archangel, in the Isle of Guernsey, preserved in the 'Black Book of the Bishop of Coutances,' it appears that the ceremony was performed by a priest: though it is believed that such has seldom been the case in the Anglican Church. But see chapter vi, section 2.

[16] A cross was not only inscribed on the foundation stone, but a cross was placed where the church was to be: and this in the Eastern Church; where the *Stauropegia* was a ceremony of much importance.

[17] This passage is valuable as proving that in the country of our Bishop nothing was known of a practice undoubtedly prevalent in England; the direction of a church to that part of the sky in which the sun arose on the Feast of the Patron Saint.

both in prosperity and adversity : and not towards that point where the sun ariseth at the solstices, which is the practice of some. But if the walls of Jerusalem, ' which is built as a city that is at unity with itself,'[18] were, by the Prophet's command, raised by the Jews, with how much greater zeal should we raise the walls of our churches! For the material church, wherein the people assemble to set forth God's holy praise, symboliseth that Holy Church which is built in heaven of living stones.

9. This is that House of the Lord, built with all strength, 'upon the foundations of the apostles and prophets, Jesus Christ Himself being the chief cornerstone.[19] Her[20] foundations are in the holy mountains.' The walls built upon these are the Jews and Gentiles ; who come from the four parts of the world unto Christ, and who have believed, believe, or shall believe on Him.

The faithful predestinated to eternal life, are the stones in the structure of this wall which shall continually be built up unto the world's end. And one stone is added to another, when masters in the Church teach and confirm and strengthen those who are put under them : and whosoever in Holy Church undertaketh painful labours from brotherly love, he as it were beareth up the weight of stones which have been placed above him. Those stones which are of larger size, and polished, or squared, and placed on the outside and at the angles of the building, are men of holier life than others, who by their merits and prayers retain weaker brethren in Holy Church.

10. The cement, without which there can be no stability of the walls, is made of lime, sand, and water. The lime is fervent charity, which joineth to itself the sand, that is, undertakings for the temporal welfare of

---

[18] Psalm cxxii (*Lætatus sum*), 3.　　[19] Eph. ii, 20.
[20] Psalm lxxxvii (*Fundamenta ejus*), 1.

our brethren: because true charity taketh care of the widow and the aged, and the infant, and the infirm: and they who have it study to work with their hands, that they may possess wherewith to benefit them. Now the lime and the sand are bound together in the wall by an admixture of water. But water is an emblem of the Spirit. And as without cement the stones cannot cohere, so neither can men be built up in the heavenly Jerusalem without charity, which the Holy Ghost worketh in them. All the stones are polished and squared—that is, holy and pure, and are built by the hands of the Great Workman into an abiding place in the Church: whereof some are borne, and bear nothing, as the weaker members: some are both borne and bear, as those of moderate strength: and some bear, and are borne of none save Christ, the corner-stone, as they that are perfect. All are bound together by one spirit of charity, as though fastened with cement; and those living stones are knit together in the bond of peace. Christ was our wall in His conversation: and our outer wall in His Passion.

11. When the Jews were rebuilding the walls of Jerusalem, their enemies strove hard to let the works: so that 'they built with one hand, and held their weapons of war in the other.' And round us too do enemies gather, while we are building the walls of our Church: our own sins, or ungodly men, willing to hinder our success. Whence, while we build our walls, that is, while we add virtue to virtue, we must fight with the enemy, and grasp our weapons firmly: we must 'take the helmet of salvation, the shield of faith, the breastplate of righteousness: and for our sword the word of God,'[21] that we may defend ourselves against them: and God's

---

[21] Eph. vi, 16, 17.

priest shall be unto us in Christ's stead, to teach us by his lessons, and defend us by his prayers.

12. Furthermore, of what the tabernacle was made the Lord hath told us, saying unto Moses, 'Take the first fruits,'—that is, the most precious gifts—'of the children of Israel: but from him alone who willingly offereth gold, and silver, and brass, and precious stones, and purple and linen twice dyed'; namely cloth of the colours of blue, purple, and scarlet: and of biss, which is a kind of Egyptian linen white and soft: 'and goat's hair, and rams' skins dyed red,' which we call Parthian, because the Parthians first dyed them thus, 'and purple skins and shittim wood' (shittim is the name of a mountain, and also of a tree: its leaves are like the white thorn, and to be injured neither by fire nor by decay): 'and oil for the lights, frankincense, and ointment of a sweet savour, onyx stones, and sard-onyxes, and jewels: and let them make Me a house, that I may dwell in the midst of them: and that they may not weary themselves in returning to this mountain.'[22]

14. The arrangement of a material church resembleth that of the human body: the chancel, or place where the altar is, representeth the head: the transepts, the hands and arms, and the remainder—towards the west—the rest of the body. The sacrifice of the altar denoteth the vows of the heart. Furthermore, according to Richard de Sancto Victore, the arrangement of a church typifieth the three states in the Church: of virgins, of the continent, of the married. The sanctuary[23] is smaller

---

[22] Exodus xxv, 2.

[23] The sanctuary of course means that eastermost division in churches consisting of three parts, which still remains in many Norman buildings, and of which Kilpeck, in Herefordshire, may be taken as a type. These churches are generally apsidal: but there are instances to the contrary, as Bishopstone, in Sussex. A view of the sanctum sanctorum and chancel arches in this church is given in the Cambridge Camden Society's 'Illustrations of Monumental Brasses,' part iv.

than the chancel, and this than the nave: because the virgins are fewer in number [24] than the continent, and these than the married. And the sanctuary is more holy than the chancel: and the chancel than the nave: because the order of virgins is more worthy than that of the continent, and the continent more worthy than the married.

15. Furthermore, the church consisteth of four walls, that is, is built on the doctrine of the Four Evangelists; and hath length, breadth, and height: the height representeth courage, the length fortitude, which patiently endureth till it attaineth its heavenly home; the breadth is charity, which, with long suffering, loveth its friends in God, and its foes for God; and again, its height is the hope of future retribution, which despiseth prosperity and adversity, hoping 'to see the goodness of the Lord in the land of the living.' [25]

16. Again, in the temple of God, the foundation is faith, which is conversant with unseen things: the roof, charity, 'which covereth a multitude of sins.' [26] The door, obedience, of which the Lord saith, 'If thou wilt enter into life, keep the commandments.' [27] The pavement, humility, of which the Psalmist saith, 'My soul cleaveth to the pavement.' [28]

17. The four side-walls, the four cardinal virtues, justice, fortitude, temperance, prudence. Hence the Apocalypse saith, 'The city lieth four-square.' [29] The windows are hospitality with cheerfulness, and tenderness with charity. Concerning this house saith the Lord, 'We will come unto him, and make our abode

---

[21] This passage is somewhat obscure; but the difference between the virgins and the continent appears to be this: by the former are meant those who have taken vows of celibacy; by the latter, those who practise it, without, however, having bound themselves to it by vow.

[25] Psalm xxvii (*Dominus illuminatio*), 13.   [26] 1 S. Peter iv, 8.
[27] S. Matthew xix, 17.   [28] Psalm cxix (*Adhæsit pavimento*), 25.
[29] Rev. xxi, 16.

with him.'[30] But some churches are built in the shape of a cross, to signify, that we are crucified to the world, and should tread in the steps of the Crucified, according to that saying, 'If any man will come after Me, let him deny himself and take up his cross, and follow Me.'[31] Some also are built in the form of a circle:[32] to signify that the Church hath been extended throughout the circle of the world, as saith the Psalmist: 'And their words unto the end of the world.'[33] Or because from the circle of this world, we reach forth to that crown of eternity which shall encircle our brows.

18. The choir is so called from the harmony of the clergy in their chanting, or from the multitude collected at the divine offices. The word *chorus* is derived from *chorea*, or from *corona*. For in early times they stood like a crown round the altar, and thus sung the Psalms in one body: but Flavianus and Theodorus taught the antiphonal method of chanting, having received it from S. Ignatius, who himself learnt it by inspiration. The two choirs then typify the angels, and the spirits of just men, while they cheerfully and mutually excite each other in this holy exercise. Others derive *chorus* from *concord*, which consisteth of charity; because he who hath not charity, cannot sing with the spirit. But what this choir signifieth, and why the greatest in it sit last, shall be explained in the fourth book.[34] And observe, that when one sings, it is called in Greek a *monody*, in

---

[30] S. John xiv, 23.   [31] S. Matthew xvi, 18.
[32] This of course refers to the Church of the Holy Sepulchre, the prototype of these buildings. There are four, as it is well known, in England yet standing, and two in ruins—namely, Temple Aslackby, in Lincolnshire, and the church in Ludlow Castle.
[33] Psalm xix (*Cæli enarrant*), 4.
[34] We may observe that Prynne perverts the fact, that the westernmost seats in the choir are the most honourable, to a depreciation of the Catholic custom of the position of the altar. See his 'Pacific Examination,' s.v.

Latin *tycinium*. When two sing, it is called *bicinium;* when many, a *chorus*.

19. The exedra is an apsis, separated a little from a temple or palace ; so called because it projecteth a little from the wall (in Greek ἐξέδρα), and signifieth the lay portion of the faithful joined to Christ and the Church. The crypts, or subterranean caves, which we find in some churches, are hermits who are devoted to a solitary life.

20. The open court signifieth Christ, by Whom an entrance is administered into the heavenly Jerusalem : this is also called porch, from *porta*, a gate, or because it is *aperta*, open.

21. The towers are the preachers and prelates of the Church, which are her bulwark and defence. Whence the bridegroom in the Canticles saith to the bride, 'Thy neck is like the tower of David builded for an armoury.'[35] The pinnacles of the towers signify the life or the mind of a prelate which aspireth heavenwards.

22. The cock at the summit of the church is a type of preachers. For the cock, ever watchful even in the depth of night, giveth notice how the hours pass, wakeneth the sleepers, predicteth the approach of day, but first exciteth himself to crow by striking his sides with his wings. There is a mystery conveyed in each of these particulars. The night is this world: the sleepers are the children of this world who are asleep in their sins. The cock is the preacher, who preacheth boldly, and exciteth the sleepers to cast away the works of darkness, exclaiming, 'Woe to them that sleep ! Awake thou that sleepest !'[36] And these foretell the approach of day when they speak of the Day of Judgment, and the glory that shall be revealed : and like prudent mes-

---

[35] Canticles iv, 4.   [36] Eph. v, 14.

sengers, before they teach others, arouse themselves from the sleep of sin by mortifying their bodies. Whence the Apostle, 'I keep under my body.'[37] And as the weathercock faceth the wind, they turn themselves boldly to meet the rebellious by threats and arguments: lest they should be guilty, 'when the wolf cometh, of leaving the sheep and fleeing.'[38] The iron rod, whereon the cock sitteth, representeth the discourse of the preacher, that he speaketh not of man but of God: according to that saying, 'If any man speak, let him speak as the oracles of God.'[39] But in that the iron rod is placed above the cross, on the summit of the church, it signifieth that Holy Scripture is now consummated and confirmed. Whence saith our Lord in His Passion, 'It is finished': and that title is written indelibly over Him.

23. The cone, that is the summit of the church, of great height, and of round shape, signifieth how perfectly and inviolably the Catholic faith must be held: which faith except a man do keep whole and undefiled, without doubt he shall perish everlastingly.

24. The glass windows in a church are Holy Scriptures, which expel the wind and the rain, that is all things hurtful, but transmit the light of the true Sun, that is, God, into the hearts of the faithful. These are wider [40] within than without, because the mystical sense is the more ample, and precedeth the literal meaning. Also, by the windows the senses of the body are signified: which ought to be shut to the vanities of this world, and open to receive with all freedom spiritual gifts.

25. By the lattice work* of the windows, we understand the prophets or other obscure teachers of the Church Militant: in which windows there are often two shafts,

---

[37] 1 Cor. ix, 27.   [38] S. John x, 12.   [39] 1 S. Peter iv, 11.
[40] This passage is particularly to be observed, for the reason given in the Introduction.   * See Appendix I.

signifying the two precepts of charity, or because the apostles were sent out to preach two and two.

26. The door of the church is Christ: according to that saying in the Gospel, 'I am the door.'[41] The apostles are also called doors.

27. The piers of the church are bishops and doctors: who specially sustain the Church of God by their doctrine. These, from the majesty and clearness of their divine message, are called silver, according to that in the Song of Songs, 'He made silver columns.'[42] Whence also Moses at the entering in of the tabernacle, placed five columns, and four before the oracle, that is, the holy of holies. Although the piers are more in number than seven, yet they are called seven, according to that saying, 'Wisdom hath builded her house, she hath hewn out her seven pillars':[43] because bishops ought to be filled with the sevenfold influences of the Holy Ghost:[44] and SS. James and John, as the Apostle testifieth, 'seemed to be pillars.'[45] The bases of the columns are the apostolic bishops,[46] who support the frame of the whole church. The capitals of the piers are the opinions of the bishops and doctors. For as the members are directed and moved by the head, so are our words and works governed by their mind. The ornaments of the capitals are the words of Sacred Scripture, to the meditation and observance of which we are bound.

28. The pavement of the church is the foundation of our faith. But in the spiritual Church, the pavement is the poor of Christ: the poor in spirit, who humble themselves in all things: wherefore on account of their

---

[41] S. John x, 9.   [42] Canticles viii, 9.   [43] Prov. viii, 1.
[44] Compare the *Veni Creator*:
  Thou the anointing Spirit art,
  Who dost Thy sevenfold gifts impart.
[45] Gal ii, 9.
[46] That is, it may be supposed, bishops of those sees which were founded by the apostles themselves, *e.g.* Rome, Crete, Ephesus.

humility they are likened to the pavement. Again, the pavement, which is trodden under foot, representeth the multitude, by whose labours the Church is sustained.

29. The beams [47] which join together the church are the princes of this world or the preachers who defend the unity of the Church, the one by deed, the other by argument.

30. The stalls in the church signify the contemplative, in whom God dwelleth without hindrance, who, from their high dignity and the glory of eternal life, are compared to gold. Whence He saith in the Canticles, 'He made a golden seat.'*

31. The beams in the church are preachers, who spiritually sustain it. The vaulting also, or ceiling, representeth preachers, who adorn and strengthen it, concerning whom, seeing that they are not corruptible through vice, the bridegroom glorieth in the same Canticles, saying 'the beams of our house are cedar, and its ceiling, fir.' For God hath built His Church of living stones, and imperishable wood, according to that saying, 'Solomon made himself a litter of cedar wood;' [48] that is,

---

[47] *Beams.* That is, probably, tie-beams: here is another reference to the architectural arrangements of Early English date.

[48] It is very difficult to find the right meaning of the word *ferculum* here. The English version gives the passage from the Canticles, 'King Solomon made himself a *chariot* (marg. reading, *bed*) of the wood of Lebanon. In the extremely beautiful treatise of Hugo de S. Victore, *De Nuptiis Spiritualibus* (cap. iii), the *fercula nuptialia* appear to mean the *marriage feast*, which is to perform its part in the general *Sensuum refectio*, by its sweet savours; as the bed or chariot of Solomon is noted for the odour of its cedar wood. However, the same writer devotes five Tituli of his *Erudit. Theolog. Ex Miscellan.* namely, lix—lxii of the first book, and cxxi of the second, to the consideration of this Ferculum Solomonis: which he decides to be a *lectica seu vehiculum*, a litter or sedan (such as is now used in Sicily under the name of *lettiga*), differing from the *lectulus* or *bed* (Cant. i, 16), inasmuch as this denotes the repose of the contemplative life, while the ferculum typifies the laborious exercise of the active life; and differing again from the *currus* or chariot (the only other vehicle mentioned in Holy Scripture), since the latter is drawn on the earth with a grating noise, and represents a depraved heart clinging to earthly things, but the former is borne smoothly and quietly above the ground, an image of the righteous soul despising earthly and seeking heavenly things. Lastly, the *ferculum*, or litter, typifies the Church, from carrying, *a ferendo*, as doth the Church her children unto Heavenly Rest.

* See Appendix I.

Christ, of His saints who wear the white robe of chastity. The chancel, that is, the head of the church, being lower [49] than its body, signifieth how great humility there should be in the clergy, or in prelates, according to that saying, 'And the more thou art exalted, humble thyself in all things.' The rail, by which the altar [50] is divided from the choir, teacheth the separation of things celestial from things terrestrial.

32. The seats in the choir admonish us that the body must sometimes be refreshed: because that which hath not alternate rest wanteth durability.

33. The pulpit in the church is the life of the perfect: and is so called from being public, or placed in a public place. For we read, 'Solomon made a brazen scaffold, and set it in the midst of the temple, and stood upon it, and stretching forth his hands spake to the people of God.' Esdras also made a wooden scaffold for speaking: in which when he stood, he was higher than the rest of the people.[51]

34. The analogium (rood-loft) is so called because in it the Word of God is read and delivered. Which also is called ambo, from *ambire*,[52] to surround, because it surroundeth him that entereth in.

---

[49] The fact that in many unaltered and unmutilated churches the chancel is lower than the nave, appears to have been unnoticed by ecclesiologists. Wherever it occurs, William Dowsing, or some of his puritanical coadjutors, have been supposed agents in the matter. But there exist chancels, which, whether from the height of the piscina and sedilia, or on other accounts, cannot have been lowered, to which nevertheless there is a descent from the nave. Such an one is that of S. Giles's at Cambridge: and the arrangement is very common in the little churches of the south-west part of Sussex.

[50] This is another very remarkable passage: and one which proves that the injunction of Abp. Laud for the erection of altar rails was not a novelty. And though their abolition is much to be wished, as well from the ugliness of all existing specimens, as from the irreverence which they seem to pre-suppose, the Church in England can scarcely be charged with the adoption of an innovation in giving her sanction to them.

[51] 3 Kings vi, 13.

[52] This is, of course, a false derivation. The important subject of Roodlofts has been treated with admirable learning by Father Thiers, in his treatise 'Sur les jubés,' to which the reader is referred. See also Appendix C.

35. The horologium, by means of which the hours are read, teacheth the diligence that should be in priests to observe at the proper times the canonical hours: as he saith, 'Seven times a day do I praise thee.'[53]

36. The tiles [54] of the roof which keep off the rain are the soldiers, who preserve the Church from paynim, and from enemies.

37. The circular staircases, which are imitated from Solomon's temple, are passages which wind among the walls, and point out the hidden knowledge which they only have who ascend to celestial things. Concerning the steps, by which ascent is made to the altar, hereafter.

38. The sacristy, or place where the holy vessels are deposited, or where the priest putteth on his robes, is the womb of the Blessed Mary, where Christ put on his robes of humanity. The priest, having robed himself, cometh forth into the public view, because Christ, having come from the womb of the Virgin, proceeded forth into the world.

The bishop's throne in the church is higher than the rest.

39. Near to the altar, which signifieth Christ, is placed the piscina, or lavacrum, that is, the pity of Christ, in which the priest washeth his hands, thereby denoting that by baptism and penitence we are purged from the filth of sin: which is drawn from the Old Testament. For he saith in Exodus, 'And Moses made a laver of brass, with his basin, in the which Aaron the priest and his sons should wash, before they went up to the altar, that they might offer an offering.[55]

40. The lamp in the church is Christ: as He saith, 'I am the light of the world';[56] and again, 'That was the

---

[53] Psalm (cxix), *Beati immaculati,* 164.
[54] This passage deserves to be noticed, as proving that lead was not the only roofing employed in the Norman churches.
[55] Exodus xxxviii, 8.   [56] S. John viii, 12.

true light.'[57] · Or the light in a church may denote the apostles and other doctors, by whose doctrine the Church is enlightened, as the sun and moon : concerning whom saith the Lord, 'Ye are the light of the world':[58] that is, an example of good works. Wherefore He saith to them in His admonitions, 'Let your light shine before men.'[59] But the Church is enlightened by the precepts of the Lord; wherefore it saith in the before-quoted place, 'Speak unto the sons of Aaron that they offer oil-olive most pure, that the lamp may burn continually in the tabernacle of the testimony.'[60] Moses made also seven lights, which are the seven gifts of the Holy Ghost: for they in the darkness of this world shine forth with brightness: and they rest in candlesticks, because in Christ rested 'the spirit of wisdom and knowledge, the spirit of counsel and might, the spirit of learning and piety, the spirit of the fear of the Lord, by which He preached wisdom to the captives.'[61] The number of lights showeth the number of graces in the faithful.

41. In many places a triumphal cross is placed in the midst of the church; to teach us, that from the midst of our hearts we must love the Redeemer: who, after Solomon's pattern, 'paved the midst of his litter (*ferculum*) with love for the daughters of Jerusalem:'[62] and that all, seeing the sign of victory, might exclaim, Hail, thou Salvation of the whole world, Tree of our Redemption: and that we should never forget the love of God, who, to redeem His servants, gave His only son, that we might imitate Him crucified. But the cross is exalted on high, to signify the victory of Christ. Why a church is ornamented within and not without, shall be said hereafter.

---

[57] S. John i, 6.
[58] S. Matthew v, 14.
[59] S. Matthew v, 16.
[60] Lev. xxiv, 2.
[61] Isaiah lxi, 1.
[62] Cantic. iii, 10.

42. The cloisters, as Richard, Bishop of Cremona, testifieth, had their rise either in the watchings of the Levites around the tabernacle, or from the chambers of the priests, or from the porch of Solomon's temple. 'For the Lord commanded Moses, that he should not number the Levites with the rest of the children of Israel; but should set them over the tabernacle of the testimony to carry it and to keep it.'[63] On account of which divine commandment, while the Holy Mysteries are in celebration, the clergy should in the church stand apart from the laity. Whence the Council of Mayence ordained that the part which is separated with rails from the altar should be appropriated altogether to the priests choral. Furthermore, as the church signifieth the Church Triumphant, so the cloister signifieth the celestial Paradise, where there will be one and the same heart in fulfilling the commands of God and loving Him: where all things will be possessed in common, because that of which one hath less, he will rejoice to see more abounding in another, for 'God shall be all in all.'[64] Therefore the regular clergy who live in the cloisters, and are of one mind, rising to the service of God and leaving worldly things, lead their lives in common. The various offices in the cloister signify the different mansions, and the difference of rewards in the Kingdom: for 'In My Father's House are many mansions,'[65] saith our Lord. But in a moral sense the cloister is the contemplative state, into which the soul betaking itself, is separated from the crowd of carnal thoughts, and meditateth on celestial things only. In this cloister there are four sides: denoting, namely, contempt of self, contempt of the world, love of God, love of our neighbour. Each side hath his

[63] Numbers i, 47; xviii, 6.
[64] 1 Corinth. xv, 28.   [65] S. John xv, 2.

own row of columns. Contempt of self hath humiliation of soul, mortification of the flesh, humility of speech, and the like. The base of all the columns is patience.

43. In this cloister the diversity of office-chambers is the diversity of virtues. The chapter-house is the secret of the heart: concerning this, however, we shall speak differently hereafter. The refectory is the love of holy meditation. The cellar, Holy Scripture. The dormitory, a clean conscience. The oratory, a spotless life. The garden of trees and herbs, the collection of virtues. The well, the dew of God's heavenly gifts; which in this world mitigateth our thirst, and hereafter will quench it.

44. The Episcopal throne, which according to the injunctions of Saint Peter has been of old consecrated in each city (as shall be said below), the piety of our forefathers dedicated, not in memory of confessors, but to the honour of apostles and martyrs, and especially of the Blessed Virgin Mary.

45. But we therefore go to church, that we may there ask for the pardon of our sins, and assist in the divine praises: as shall be said in the proeme of the fifth book, and that there we may hear God's proceedings[66] with the good and the ill, and learn and receive the knowledge of God, and that we may there feed on the Lord's body.

46. In church, men and women sit apart: which, according to Bede, we have received from the custom of the ancients: and thence it was that Joseph and Mary lost the Child Jesus; since the one who did not behold Him in his own company, thought Him to be with the other. . . . But the men remain on the southern, the

---

[66] Such is probably the meaning of the passage. The original is *ut ili bona sive mala judicia audiamus*.

women on the northern side: [67] to signify that the saints who be most advanced in holiness should stand against the greater temptations of this world: and they who be less advanced, against the less; or that the bolder and the stronger sex should take their place in the position fittest for action: because the Apostle saith, 'God is faithful, Who will not suffer you to be tempted above that ye are able.' [68] To this also pertaineth the vision of S. John, who 'beheld a mighty angel placing his right foot in the sea.' [69] For the stronger members are opposed to the greater dangers. But, according to others, the men are to be in the fore part [*i.e.* eastward], the women behind: because 'the husband is the head of the wife,' [70] and therefore should go before her.

47. A woman must cover her head in the church, because she is not the image of God, and because by woman sin began. And therefore in the church, out of respect for the priest, who is the vicar of Christ, in his presence, as before a judge, she hath her head covered, and not at liberty: and on account of the same reverence she hath not the power of speaking in the church before him. Of old time, men and women wearing long hair stood in church with uncovered heads glorying in their locks: which was a disgrace unto them.

48. But what should be our conversation in church the Apostle teacheth, saying, 'Speaking to yourselves in psalms and hymns and spiritual songs.' [71] Whence we must, when we be there, abstain from superfluous words:

---

[67] This is the practice in some parts of England even to this day: more especially in Somersetshire. Bp. Montague in his 'Visitation Articles' (reprinted Camb. 1841) asks (p. 17), 'Do men and women sit together in those seats indifferently and promiscuously? or (as the fashion was of old), do men sit together upon one side of the church, and women upon the other?' And, indeed, of old there was a still further separation on each side, into the married and unmarried. The restoration of the practice recommended by Bp. Montague is much to be wished.

[68] 1 Corinth. x, 13. [69] Apocalypse x, 7.
[70] Eph. v, 23. [71] Coloss. iii, 16.

according to that saying of S. Chrysostome, When thou goest into a king's palace, set in order thy conversation and thy habit. For the angels of the Lord are there: and the House of God is full of incorporeal virtues.[72] And the Lord saith to Moses, and so doth the angel to Joshua, 'Put off thy shoes from off thy feet: for the place where thou standest is holy ground.'[73]

49. In the last place, a consecrated church defendeth murderers who take sanctuary in it from losing life or limb, provided that they have not offended in it, or against it. Whence it is written that 'Joab fled to the tabernacle, and laid hold on the horns of the altar.'[74] The same privilege is possessed also by an unconsecrated church, if the divine offices be therein celebrated.

50. But the body of Christ received by such persons, doth not defend them nor those who fly to it: partly because the privilege is granted to a church as a church: and therefore not to be misbestowed on other things: partly because that food is the support of the soul, and not of the body: whence it freeth the soul and not the body.

51. Churches are moved from one place to another on three accounts. First, on account of the necessity arising from persecutors: secondly, on account of the difficulty of access or habitation, such as the unwholesomeness of air: thirdly, when they are oppressed with the society of evil men: and then with the consent of the Pope or the bishop. Wherefore he that entereth into a church fortifieth himself with the sign of the cross, shall be said in the proeme of the fifth book.[75]

---

[72] The passage referred to is as follows :—' Regiam quidem ingrediens, et habitu et aspectu et incessu et omnibus aliis te ornas et componis : Hic autem vere est Regia et plane hic talia qualia cœlestia :—et rides ? Atque scio quidem quod tu non vides. Audi autem quod ubique adsunt angeli, et maxime in Domo Dei adsistunt Regis, et omnia sunt impleta incorporeis illus Potestatibus.

[73] Exod. iii, 5. Josh. v, 15.   [74] 2 Kings i, 28.   [75] See Appendix.

CHAPTER II

OF THE ALTAR

The First Builders of Altars—The Difference between Altare and Ara—Various Significations of Various Kinds of Altars—The Ark of the Testimony—It is preserved in the Lateran Church—What a Man needeth that he may be the Temple of God—What the Table Signifieth—Of the Candlestick—Of the Ark—Of the Altar—Of the Altar Cloths—Of Steps to the Altar.

1. THE altar hath a place in the church on three accounts, as shall be said in speaking of its dedication. We are to know that Noe[1] first, then Isaac[2] and Abraham[3] and Jacob made, as we read, altars: which is only to be understood of stones set upright, on which they offered and slew the victims and burnt them with fire laid beneath them. Also Moses made an altar[4] of shittim wood: and the same was made as an altar of incense, and covered with pure gold: as we read in the xxvth chapter of Exodus, where also the form of the altar is described. From these of the ancient fathers, the altars of the moderns have their origin, being erected with four horns at the corners. Of which some are of one stone, and some are put together of many.

2. And sometimes the words altare and ara are used in the same sense. Yet is there a difference. For *altare*, derived from *alta res*, or *alta ara*, is that on which

---

[1] Gen. viii, 20.   [2] Gen. xxvi, 25; xxxiii, 20.   [3] Gen. xiii, 18.
[4] Exodus xxvii, 1.

the priests burnt incense. But *ara*, which is derived from *area*, or from *ardeo*, is that on which sacrifices were burnt.*

3. And note, that many kinds of altars are found in Scripture: as a higher, a lower, an inner, an outer; of which each hath both a plain and a symbolical signification. The higher altar is God the Trinity: of which it is written, 'Thou shalt not go up by steps to my altar.'[5] And it also signifieth the Church Triumphant: of which it is said, 'Then shall they offer bullocks upon mine altar.'[6] But the lower altar is the Church Militant, of which it is said, 'If thou wilt make an altar of stone, thou shalt not make it of hewn stone.'[7] Also it is the table of the temple. Of which he saith, 'Appoint a solemn day for your assembly even unto the horns of the altar.'[8] And in the Third of Kings, it is said that Solomon made a golden altar.[9] But the interior altar is a clean heart, as shall be said below. It is also a type of faith in the incarnation, of which in Exodus, 'An altar of earth ye shall make Me.'[10] And an interior altar is the altar of the cross. This is the altar on which they offered the evening sacrifice. Whence in the Canon of the Mass it is said, *Jube hoc in sublime Altare Tuum perferri.*[11] Moreover the external altar representeth the sacraments of the Church: of which it is said, 'Even thine altars, O Lord of hosts, my King, and my God.'[12] Again, the altar is our

---

* The true ecclesiastical distinction between *altare* and *ara* is that the former means the altar of the true God, and is therefore alone used in the Vulgate, answering to the Greek θυσιαστήριον, as opposed to *ara* (βῶμος), an altar with an image above it. See *Mede*. Folio 386.

[5] Exodus xx, 26.   [6] Psalm li (*Miserere mei*), 19.
[7] Exodus xx, 25.   [8] Psalm cxviii (*Confitemini*, 27.
[9] III Kings vi. 22.   [10] Exodus xx 26.

[11] This prayer, which immediately precedes the Commemoration of the Dead, runs thus: Supplices Te rogamus, omnipotens Deus, jube hoc perferri per manus Sancti Angeli Tui, in conspectu Divinæ Majestatis Tuæ: ut quotquot ex hac Altaris participatione sacrosanctum Filii Tui Corpus et Sanguinem sumpserimus, omni benedictione cœlesti et gratia repleamur. Per.   [12] Psalm lxxxiv (*Quam dilecta*), 4.

mortification in our heart, in which carnal motions are consumed by the fervour of the Holy Spirit.

4. Secondly, it also signifieth the Spiritual Church: and its four horns teach how she hath been extended into the four quarters of the world. Thirdly, it signifieth Christ, without whom no gift is offered acceptable to the Father. Whence also the Church addresseth her prayers to the Father through Christ alone. Fourthly, it signifieth the body of Christ, as shall be explained in the fifth book. Fifthly, it signifieth the table at which Christ did feast with His disciples.

5. It is written in Exodus, that in the Ark of the Testament or of the Testimony the witness was laid up:[13] that is, the tables on which the law was written: and it is said that the *Testimony* was there laid up, because it was a bearing witness that the law imprinted on our hearts by nature God had reimprinted by writing. Also, there was laid up the golden pot full of manna, for a testimony that He had given the children of Israel bread from heaven. And the rod of Aaron, for a testimony that all power is from God. And the second tables of the law, in testimony of the covenant in which they had said, 'All that the Lord hath spoken we will do.'[14] And on these accounts it is called the Ark of the Testimony or Testament; and also the tabernacle of the testimony thence deriveth its title. But over the ark was made a mercy seat: of which we shall speak in the proeme of the fourth book. In imitation whereof some churches have over the altar an ark or tabernacle, in which the body of the Lord and relics are preserved. The Lord also commanded that a candlestick should be made of beaten pure gold. It is written in the third book of Kings, that in the Ark of the Covenant was nothing else than the two tables of stone which Moses put therein

[13] Exodus xxv, 16.   [14] Exodus xix, 8.

in Horeb: when the Lord made a covenant with the children of Israel in the day that they came out of the land of Egypt.

6. And note that in the time of S. Silvester, Pope,[15] Constantine the Emperor built the Lateran church, in which he placed the Ark of the Testament, which the Emperor Titus had brought from Jerusalem, and the golden candlestick with his seven branches. In which ark are these things: the rings and the staves of gold: the tables of the testimony: the rod of Aaron: manna: barley loaves: the golden pot: the seamless garment: the reed: a garment of S. John Baptist, and the scissors with which the hair of S. John the Evangelist was shorn.

7. Man, if he hath an altar, a table, a candlestick, and an ark, he is the temple of God. He must have an altar, whereon rightly to offer and rightly to distribute. The altar is our heart, on which we ought to offer.

---

[15] It is very remarkable that no notice whatever is taken of these relics by Ciampini in his very minute description of the Lateran Basilica: although in his account both of this, and of all the other Basilican churches built by Constantine, he copies *verbatim* the list of the donations of the Emperor which is given in the life of Pope S. Sylvester, compiled by an unknown librarian of the Vatican. It is clear that either Durandus was misinformed, or that the present passage is corrupt. Again, it is not likely that the vest of S. John Baptist, or the scissors of S. John Evangelist would have been kept in the ark besides its proper contents. Yet Durandus had obviously some facts to go upon, since the Lateran Church, having been originally dedicated to the Saviour, was now under the Invocation of the two SS. John; and the sufferings of both these saints were depicted in a very ancient mosaic, those of the Evangelist having over them the following inscription, which we give as describing a Confession of this *Martyr in will*, now little known.

    Martyrii calicem bibit hic Athleta Johannes
    Principium Verbi cernere qui meruit.
    Verberat hunc fuste Proconsul, *forfice tondet*,
      Quem fervens oleum lædere non valuit.
    Conditus hic oleum, dolium, cruor, atque capilli,
      Quæ consecrantur libera Roma tibi.

To return, we may be satisfied that these Jewish memorials did not exist, since Ciampini, while composing his account, consulted the former writers upon the Lateran Basilica; viz. the poet Prudentius, an unedited MS. of Panvinius, Severanus De Septem Urbis Ecclesiis, and the work of Cæsar Cardinal Rasponus.

Whence the Lord commandeth in Exodus: 'Thou shalt offer burnt offerings on mine altar.'[16] Since from the heart words, set on fire of charity, ought to proceed. *Holocaust* is derived from *holos*, *whole*, and *cauma*, *a burning:* therein signifying a thing wholly burnt. On this altar we must rightly offer, and we must rightly divide. We offer rightly when we bring any good thought to perfection. But we do not rightly divide if we do it not discreetly. For a man often thinketh to do good, and doeth ill: and sometimes with one hand he doeth good and with the other ill; and thus himself buildeth, and himself knocketh down. But we then rightly divide when the good which we do we attribute, not to ourselves, but to God alone.

8. It behoveth also man to have a table, whence he may take the bread of the Word of God. By the table we understand Holy Scripture, concerning which the Psalm, 'Thou preparest a table before me in the presence of mine enemies.'[17] That is, Thou hast given me Scripture against the temptations of the devil. This table then we must have, that is, must lay up in our minds, that thence we may take the Word of God. Of the deficiency of this bread saith Jeremiah: 'The little ones sought bread, and there was none to break it unto them.'[18] It behoveth man likewise to have a candlestick, that he may shine with good works.

9. A candlestick that giveth light without is a good work, which by its good example inflameth others. Of which it is said, 'No man lighteth a candle and putteth it under a bushel, but in a candlestick.'[19] This candle, according to the Word of the Lord, is a good intention: of which He saith Himself: 'Thine eye is a light.'[20] But the eye is the intention. Therefore we ought not

---

[16] Exodus ix, 2.   [17] Psalm xxiii (*Dominus regit me*), 5.
[18] Jeremiah xvi, 7.   [19] S. Matthew v, 15.   [20] S. Matthew vi, 22.

to put the candle under a bushel, but in a candlestick. Because, if we have a good intention, we ought not to hide it: but to manifest our good deeds to others, for a light and an example.

10. Man must also have an ark. Now *arca* is derived from *arcendo:* discipline, therefore, and regular life may be called the ark; by which crimes are driven away (*arcentur*) from us. Now in the ark were the rod, the tables, and the manna: because in the regular life there must be the rod of correction, that the flesh may be chastised; and the table of love, that God may be loved. For in the tables of the law were written the commands which pertain to the love of God. Therein must also be the manna of divine sweetness: that we may 'taste and see how gracious the Lord is: for it is good to have to do with Him.'[21] According to that proverb of the prudent woman, 'She tasted and saw that it was good.'[22] Therefore, that we may be the temple of God, let us have in ourselves an altar of oblation, lest we appear empty in His presence, according to that saying, 'Thou shalt not appear empty before the presence of thy God':[23] let us have a table for refection lest we faint, through hunger, in the way: as saith the Evangelist, 'If I send them away empty, they will faint in the way,'[24] a candlestick by good works that we be not idle, as he saith in Ecclesiasticus, 'Idleness hath taught much mischief,'[25] let us have an ark, that we be not as sons of Belial, that is, undisciplined, and without the yoke: for discipline is necessary, as the Psalmist teacheth, saying, 'Be instructed, lest He be angry.'[26] Concerning which, and other ornaments, we shall speak in the following chapter.

[21] Psalm xxxiv (*Benedicam Dominum*), 8.
[22] Prov. xxxi, 18. Marg. reading. [23] Exodus xxiii, 15.
[24] S. Mark viii, 3. [25] Ecclesiasticus xxii, 2.
[26] Psalm ii (*Quare fremuerunt*), 12.

11. He buildeth this altar who adorneth his heart with true humility and other virtues. Whence Gregory: He who gathereth together virtues without humility, is as he who scattereth dust to the wind. For by the altar he understandeth our heart, as it shall be said when we treat of the dedication of the altar: it is in the middle of the body, as the altar is in the middle of the church.*

12. Concerning which altar the Lord commandeth in Leviticus : 'The fire shall always be burning upon Mine altar.'[27] The fire is charity. The altar is a clean heart. The fire shall always burn on the altar, because charity should always burn in our hearts. Whence Solomon in the Canticles: 'Many waters cannot extinguish charity,'[28] for that which ever burneth cannot be extinguished. Do thou, therefore, as the prophet commandeth, keep holy day and a solemn assembly, even to the horns of the altar: because the rest of thy thoughts will keep holy day. Concerning this the Apostle showeth 'unto us a more excellent way.'[29] He calleth charity a more excellent way, because she is above all virtues : and whoever possesseth her possesseth all virtues. This is the short word that the Lord speaketh over the earth: which is so short that it only saith, 'Have charity, and do whatsoever thou wilt. For from these two commandments hang all the law and the prophets.'[30]

13. Or by the altar we understand the soul of every man, which is by the Lord built up of various living stones, which are various and different virtues.

14. Furthermore, the white cloths wherewith the altar is covered signify the flesh of the Saviour, that is, His humanity: because it was made white with many toils, as also the flesh of Christ born of earth, that is, of Mary,

[27] Lev. vi, 9.   [28] Canticles viii, 7.
[29] 1 Corinth xii, 31.   [30] S. Matthew xxii, 40.   * See Appendix I.

which attained through many tribulations to the glory of the Resurrection, and the purity and joy of immortality. [Concerning which the Son exulteth, saying to the Father, 'Thou hast girded me with gladness, and exalted Me on every side.'[31] When, therefore, the altar is covered, it signifieth the joining of the soul to an immortal and incorruptible body.[32]] Again, the altar is covered with white and clean cloths, because the pure heart is adorned with good works. Whence the Apocalypse: 'And put on white garments, that the shame of thy nakedness do not appear.'[33] And Solomon: 'Let thy garments be always white,'[34] that is, let thy works be clean. [But it little profiteth him that approacheth to the altar to have high dignity, and a life sunk low in sins. Whence Benedict: It is a monstrous thing, exalted faith, and abandoned life. The highest step and the lowest state, is mighty authority joined with instability of soul.[35]] The silken coverings placed over the altar are the ornaments of divers virtues wherewith the soul is adorned. The hanging wherewith the altar is beautified setteth forth the saints, as below shall be said. [The beginning and the end of the Mass take place at the right side of the altar: the middle portion at the left: as shall be said when we treat of the changes of the priest. The ancients made their altars concave; as it is written in Ezekiel, that in the altar of God was a trench. And this, according to Gregory, lest the wind should scatter the sacrifices laid upon it. Also he saith in Ezekiel that the inner part of the altar was bent downwards in all its circumference.[36]

15. But the steps to the altar [spiritually set forth the

---

[31] Psalm lxxi (*Juste, Domine*), 21.
[32] This passage does not appear in the edition of Durandus published at Venice, in 1609.
[33] Apocalypse iii, 18.   [34] Ecclesiastes ix, 8.
[35] This passage also is not found in the Venetian edition.
[36] This passage also is not found in the Venetian edition.

apostles and martyrs of Christ, who for His love poured out their blood. The bride in the Canticles of Love calleth it a purple ascent. Also, the fifteen virtues are set forth by them: which were also typified by the fifteen steps by which they went up to the temple of Solomon:[37]] and by the prophet in fifteen Psalms of degrees, therein setting forth that he is blest who maketh ascents in his heart. This was the ladder that Jacob beheld: 'And his top reached to the heavens.' By these steps the ascent of virtues is sufficiently made manifest, by which we go up to the altar, that is, to Christ: according to that saying of the Psalmist, 'They go from virtue to virtue.'[38] And Job, 'I will seek him through all my steps.' Yet it is said in Exodus, 'Neither shalt thou go up by steps to my altar, that thy nakedness be not discovered thereon.'[39] For perhaps the ancients did not as yet use trousers. In the Council of Toledo, it is decreed that the priest, who for the sake of grief at the misfortune of another, strippeth the altar or any image of its garments, [or girdeth himself with a mourning vest, or with thorns,[40]] or extinguisheth the lights of the church, shall be deposed. But if his church be undeservedly spoiled, he is allowed to do this for grief: or, according to some, he may on the day of the Passion of our Lord make bare the altars as a sign of grief. Which is, however, reprobated by the Council of Lyons. Lastly, altars which have been built at the instigation of dreams, or the empty revelations of men, are altogether reprobated.

[37] This passage also is not found in the Venetian edition.
[38] Psalm lxxxiv (*Quam dilecta*), 7.   [39] Exodus xx, 26.
[40] This passage also is not found in the Venetian edition.

CHAPTER III

OF PICTURES, AND IMAGES, AND CURTAINS, AND THE ORNAMENTS OF CHURCHES

> Use of Pictures and Curtains—Objections against the Use, answered—Place of Pictures—The Saviour, how Represented—The Angels—The Evangelists—The Apostles—The Patriarchs—S. John Baptist—Martyrs — Confessors — Institution of Pictures—Of Crowns — Of Paradise—Of the General Ornament of Churches—Of Pyxes—Of Relicaries—Of Candlesticks—Of Cups—Of the Cross—Of Altar Cloths and Veils—The Treasures of the Church, when Displayed, and why—Of Ostrich Eggs—Of Vessels for the Holy Mysteries — Of Chalices — General Observations on the Respect due to Church Ornaments.

1. PICTURES and ornaments in churches are the lessons and the Scriptures of the laity. Whence Gregory: It is one thing to adore a picture, and another by means of a picture historically to learn what should be adored. For what writing supplieth to him which can read, that doth a picture supply to him which is unlearned, and can only look. Because they who are uninstructed thus see what they ought to follow: and *things* are read, though letters be unknown. True is it that the Chaldeans, which worship fire, compel others to do the same, and burn other idols. But Paynim adore images, as icons, and idols; which Saracens do not, who neither will possess nor look on images, grounding themselves on that saying, 'Thou shalt not make to thyself any graven image, nor the likeness of anything that is in heaven above, nor in the earth beneath, nor in the waters

under the earth,'[1] and on other the like authorities: these they follow incontinently, casting the same in our teeth. But we worship not images, nor account them to be gods, nor put any hope of salvation in them: for that were idolatry. Yet we adore them for the memory and remembrance of things done long agone.[2] Whence the verse,[3]

> What time thou passest by the rood, bow humbly evermore;
> Yet not the rood, but Him which there was crucified, adore.

And again:[4]

> That thing, which hath his being given, 'tis fond for God to own:
> A form material, carved out by cunning hands, in stone.

And again:[5]

> The form is neither God nor man, which here thou dost behold:
> He very God and Man, of whom thou by that form art told.

2. The Greeks, moreover, employ painted representations, painting, it is said, only from the navel upwards, that all occasion of vain thoughts may be removed. But they make no carved image, as it is written, 'Thou shalt not make a graven image.'[6] And again: 'Thou shalt not make an idol, nor a graven image.'[7] And again, 'Lest ye be deceived, and make a graven image.'[8] And again: 'Ye shall not make unto you gods of

---

[1] Exodus xx, 4.

[2] *Veneramur.*—We here use the word *adore* in the sense given to it by the great and good Bishop Montague, in his 'Just Treatise of Invocation': where he says, speaking of the Saints, 'I do admire, reverence, *adore* them in their kind.'

[3] Effigiem Christi, quum transis, pronus honora:
Non tamen effigiem, sed quem designat, adora.

[4] Esse Deum, ratione caret, cui consulit esse:
Materiale lapis, effigale manus.

[5] Nec Deus est, nec homo, quam præsens cernis imago;
Sed Deus est et Homo, quem sacra figurat imago.

The later editions add—
Nam Deus est, quod imago docet, sed non Deus ipse;
Hunc videas, sed mente colas, quod noscis in ipsa.

[6] Deut. v, 8.   [7] Lev. xxvi. 1.   [8] Deut. iv, 16.

silver:[9] neither shall ye make with Me gods of gold.' So also the Prophet, 'Their idols are silver and gold, the work of man's hand. They that make them are like unto them: and so are all they that put their trust in them.'[10] And again: 'Confounded be all they that worship graven images: and that put their glory in their idols.'[11]

3. Also, Moses saith to the children of Israel, 'Lest perchance thou shouldest be deceived, and shouldest worship that which the Lord thy God hath created.'[12] Hence also was it that Hezekiah King of Judah brake in pieces the brazen serpent which Moses set up: because the people, contrary to the precepts of the law, burnt incense to it.

4. From these forementioned and other authorities, the excessive use of images is forbidden. The Apostle saith also to the Corinthians, 'We know that an idol is nothing in the world: and there is no god but One.'[13] For they who are simple and infirm may easily by an excessive and indiscreet use of images, be perverted to idolatry. Whence he saith in Wisdom, 'There shall be no respect of the idols of the nations, which have made the creatures of God hateful, and temptations for the souls of men, and snares for the feet of the unwise.'[14][15] But blame there is none in a moderate use of pictures, to teach how ill is to be avoided, and good followed. Whence saith the Lord to Ezekiel, 'Go in, and behold the abominations which these men do. And he went in, and saw the likeness of reptiles and beasts, and the abominations, and all the idols of the

---

[9] Exodus xx, 20. [10] Psalm cxv, 4. [11] Psalm xcvii, 7.
[12] Deut. iv, 19. [13] 1 Corinth. viii, 4. [14] Wisdom xiv, 11.
[15] A more solemn protest against the sin of idolatry can hardly be found than the above passage: and they who brand every return to, and every wish for the restoration of, Catholic practices, by so hateful a name, would do well to bear it in mind.

house of Israel portrayed on the wall.'[16] Whence saith Pope Gregory in his Pastorale, When the forms of external objects are drawn into the heart, they are as it were painted there, because the thoughts of them are their images. Again, He saith to the same Ezekiel, 'Take a tile, and lay it before thee, and describe in it the city Jerusalem.'[17] But that which is said above, that pictures are the letters of the laity explaineth that saying in the Gospel, 'He saith, They have Moses and the prophets: let them hear them.'[18] Of this, more hereafter. The Agathensian[19] Council forbids pictures in churches: and also that that which is worshipped and adored should be painted on the walls. But Gregory saith, that pictures are not to be put away because they are not to be worshipped: for paintings appear to move the mind more than descriptions; for deeds are placed before the eyes in paintings, and so appear to be actually carrying on. But in description, the deed is done as it were by hearsay: which affecteth the mind less when recalled to memory. Hence, also, is it that in churches we pay less reverence to books than to images and pictures.

5. Of pictures and images some are above the church, as the cock and the eagle: some without the church, namely, in the air in front of the church, as the ox and the cow: others within, as images, and statues, and various kinds of painting and sculpture: and these be represented either in garments, or on walls, or in stained glass. Concerning some of which we have spoken in treating of the church: and how they are taken from the tabernacle of Moses and the temple of Solomon. For Moses made carved work, and Solomon made carved work, and pictures, and adorned the walls with paintings and frescoes.

[16] Ezekiel viii, 10. [17] Ezekiel iv, 1. [18] S. Luke xvi, 29. [19] A.D. 605.

6. The image of the Saviour is more commonly represented in churches three ways: as sitting on [20] His throne, or hanging on His cross, or lying on the bosom of His Mother. And because John Baptist pointed to Him, saying, 'Behold the Lamb of God,' [21] therefore some represented Christ under the form of a lamb. But because the light passeth away, and because Christ is very man, therefore, saith Adrian, Pope, He must be represented in the form of a man. A holy lamb must not be

---

[20] Durandus had doubtless in his mind the ancient mosaic over the apsides of the earliest churches in Rome. The extremely beautiful one in San Clemente represents our Lord as crucified. The frescoes with which the walls of our own churches were anciently adorned, seem usually to have represented the Saviour as seated on the Throne of His Majesty. In the chancel of Widford, Herts, is, or was till lately, a fresco of the Saviour seated on a rainbow, a sword proceeding from His mouth, His feet and His hands pierced. In Alfriston, Sussex, there was, we believe, before it was whitewashed over by Bishop Buckner's order, a painting of a similar kind. There is a singular, and, we believe, undescribed painting over the altar in Llandanwg church, Merion. The Saviour is seated in judgment, as before: at His side is His Blessed Mother in a kneeling posture: around Him are angels blowing trumpets, and S. Peter in eucharistical vestments. There is a representation of the souls under the altar. Below are devils torturing souls in cauldrons of brimstone. The evangelistic symbols are also represented.

In a fresco at Beverstone, Gloucestershire, our Saviour is represented on the Cross, with blood flowing from His side into a chalice. (See App. I.) There are remains also of a crucifixion in fresco, in the exquisite, but desecrated chapel of Prior Crauden, in the Deanery, Ely. On the Iconostasis of the Greco-Russian Church, all the three positions are to be found.

In stained glass, the Crucifixion generally supplies the place of any other representation of the Saviour. Brasses occasionally, as a very curious one in Cobham, Surrey, represent His nativity or epiphany: but most commonly the Crucifixion, or a Trinity.

There can be no doubt, that many of the most graphic pictures in our old poets owed their origin to the then undestroyed fresco paintings of churches. Some painting, like that above described, of hell, very probably suggested the noble lines of Spenser (1. ix. 50. 6):

He showed him painted in a table plaine,
The damned ghosts that doe in torments waile,
And thousand feends that doe them endless paine
With fire and brimstone, which for ever shall remaine.

Who can estimate the effect of such pictorial representations on the minds of our ancestors? or the good which might be the result, if our churches were again frescoed with similar subjects, wrought with the genius and Catholic feeling of an Overbeck or Cornelius?

[21] S. John i, 29.

depicted on the cross, as a principal object: but there is no let when Christ hath been represented as a man, to paint a lamb in a lower or less prominent part of the picture: since He is the true Lamb which 'taketh away the sins of the world.' In these and divers other manners is the image of the Saviour painted, on account of diversity of significations.

7. Represented in the cradle, the artist commemorateth His nativity: on the bosom of His Mother, His childhood: the painting or carving His cross signifieth His Passion (and sometimes the sun and moon are represented on the cross itself, as suffering an eclipse): when depicted on a flight of steps, His ascension is signified: when on a state or lofty throne, we be taught His present power: as if He said, 'All things are given to Me in heaven and in earth:' [22] according to that saying, 'I saw the Lord sitting upon His throne:' [23] that is, reigning over the angels: as the text, 'Which sitteth upon the cherubim.' [24] Sometimes He is represented as He was seen of Moses and Aaron, Nadab and Abihu, on the mountain: when 'under His feet was as it were a paved work of sapphire stones, and as the body of heaven in His clearness:' [25] and as 'they shall see,' as saith S. Luke, 'the Son of Man coming in the clouds with power and great glory.[26] Wherefore sometimes He is represented surrounded by the seven angels that serve Him, and stand by His throne, each being portrayed with six wings, according to the vision of Isaiah, 'And by it stood the seraphim: each one had six wings: with twain he covered his face, and with twain he covered his feet, and with twain he did fly.' [27]

8. The angels are also represented as in the flower of

---

[22] S. Matt. xxviii, 18.
[24] Psalm lxxx, 1.
[26] S. Matthew xxiv, 30.
[23] Isaiah vi, 1.
[25] Exodus xxiv, 10.
[27] Isaiah vi, 2.

youthful age: for they never grow old.[28] Sometimes S. Michael is represented trampling the dragon, according to that of John, 'There was war in heaven: Michael fought with the dragon.' Which was to represent the dissensions of the angels: the confirmation of them that were good, and the ruin of them that were bad: or the persecution of the faithful in the Church Militant. Sometimes the twenty-four elders are painted around the Saviour, according to the vision of the said John, with 'white garments, and they have on their heads crowns of gold.'[29] By which are signified the doctors of the Old and New Testament; which are twelve, on account of faith in the Holy Trinity preached through the *four* quarters of the world: or twenty-four, on account of good works, and the keeping of the gospels.[30] If the seven lamps be added, the gifts of the Holy Spirit are represented: if the sea of glass, baptism.[31]

9. Sometimes also representation is made of the four living creatures spoken of in the visions of Ezekiel and the aforesaid John: the face of a man and the face of a

---

[28] Many of our readers will call to mind the peculiar expression always given to the countenances of angels in Catholic illuminations or paintings, a conventional propriety uniformly neglected by modern artists. The same character was beautifully given in the relieved figures of angels upon the shrine of S. Henry lately exhibiting in London.

[29] Apocalypse xii, 7.   [30] Apocalypse iv, 4.

[31] This very obscure passage is an instance of the symbolism in the combination of numbers. It seems to mean that faith in the Holy Trinity preached through the four quarters of the world, may be represented by three multiplied into four or twelve: and again, this symbolical fact multiplied by general good works and keeping of the Gospels, may be set forth in twenty-four. It is to be remarked that the princeps edition alone gives *Evangeliorum:* the later have *Evangelistarum*, which with *observantia* is scarcely intelligible. Compare S. August, Expos. in Psalm lxxxvi. Non solum ergo illi duodecim (sc. Apostoli) et Apostolus Paulus, sed quotquot judicaturi sunt, propter significationem universitatis ad sedes duodenas pertinent... partes enim mundi quatuor sunt, Oriens, Occidens, Aquilo, et Meridies. Istæ quatuor partes assidue inveniuntur in Scripturis. Ab istis quatuor ventus, sicut dixit Dominus in Evangelio vocatur Ecclesia. Quomodo vocatur? Undique in Trinitate vocatur. Quatuor ergo ter ducta duodecim inveniuntur. See also S. Isidore, Alleg. in S. S. folio 353, C. D.

lion on the right,—the face of an ox on the left, and the face of an eagle above the four. These be the Four Evangelists. Whence they be painted with books by their feet, because by their words and writings they have instructed the minds of the faithful, and accomplished their own works. Matthew hath the figure of a man, Mark of a lion. These be painted on the right hand: because the nativity and the resurrection of Christ were the general joy of all: whence in the Psalms: 'And gladness at the morning.'[32] But Luke is the ox: because he beginneth from Zachary the priest, and treateth more specially of the Passion and Sacrifice of Christ: now the ox is an animal fitted for sacrifice. He is also compared to the ox, because of the two horns,— as containing the two testaments; and the four hoofs, as having the sentences of the four Evangelists.[33] By this also Christ is figured, who was the sacrifice for us: and therefore the ox is painted on the left side, because the death of Christ was the trouble of the apostles. Concerning this, and how blessed Mark[34] is depicted, in the seventh part. But John hath the figure of the eagle: because, soaring to the utmost height, he saith, ' In the beginning was the word.'[35] This also representeth

[32] Psalm xxx (*Exaltabo Te*), 5. These symbols, however, were not at first definitely settled, and as we are informed by S. Austin, the lion was sometimes given to S. Matthew and the angel and or man, to S. Mark. The reasons of the appropriation of the various symbols are beautifully expressed in a hymn quoted in the Camden's Society's 'Illustrations of Monumental Brasses,' Part I, p. 30.

[33] This passage is very obscure. Durandus's words are, *quasi quatuor evangelistorum sententias*. We cannot but think that the two sentences have been misplaced. The sense is then plain. Christ is also signified by the ox—as containing in Himself the Law and the Gospel—and accomplishing that which is written of Him by the four Evangelists, *e.g.* His promises of the descent of the Holy Ghost, of being always with His Church, etc. S. Peter Chrysologus, Sermo v. de Christo, Hic est *Vitulus*, qui in Epulam nostram quotidie, et jugiter immolatur.

[34] S. Mark is painted with a contracted brow, a large nose, fair eyes, bald, a long beard, fair complexion, of middle age, with a few grey hairs. Durand. vii, 44, 4.

[35] S. John i, 1.

Christ, 'Whose youth is renewed like the eagle's':[36] because, rising from the dead, He ascendeth into heaven. Here, however, it is not portrayed as by the side, but as above, since it denoteth the ascension, and the word pronounced of God. But how, since each of the living creatures hath four faces and four wings, they can be depicted, shall be said hereafter.[37]

10. Sometimes there are painted around, or rather beneath, the Apostles; who were His witnesses by deed and word to the ends of the earth: and they are portrayed with long hair, as Nazarenes, that is, holy persons. For the law of the Nazarenes was this: from the time of their separation from the ordinary life of man, no razor passed upon their heads. They are also sometimes painted under the form of twelve sheep: because they were slain like sheep for the Lord's sake: and sometimes the twelve tribes of Israel are so represented. When, however, more or less sheep than twelve are painted, then another thing is signified, according to that saying of Matthew, 'When the Son of Man shall come in His glory—then shall He sit on the throne of His glory: and before Him shall be gathered all nations, and He shall separate them one from the other, as a

---

[36] Psalm ciii (*Benedic, anima mea*), 5.

[37] Durandus, book vii, 44. 'S. Matthew is signified by a man, because his Gospel is principally occupied concerning the humanity of Christ: whence his history beginneth from his human pedigree. S. Mark by a lion, which roareth in the desert: for he chiefly describeth the Resurrection: whence his Gospel is read on Easter day. But the lion is said to rouse his whelps on the third day after their birth. His Gospel beginneth, 'The voice of one crying in the wilderness.' S. Luke by the ox, an animal fit for sacrifice: because he dwelleth on the Passion of Christ. S. John by the eagle, because he soareth to the Divinity of Christ, while the others walk with their Lord on earth. The Evangelists be likewise set forth by the four rivers of Paradise: John by Pison; Matthew by Gihon; Luke by Euphrates; Mark by Tigris:—as is clearly proved by Innocent III, in a certain sermon on the Evangelists.'—We may add, that the finest representation of the evangelistic symbols with which we are acquainted in this country, occurs in the chancel of Oxted church, Surrey.

shepherd divideth the sheep from the goats.'[38] How the Apostles Bartholomew and Andrew are to be painted, shall be said hereafter.[39]

11. And note that the patriarchs and prophets are painted with wheels in their hands. Some of the apostles with books and some with wheels: namely, because before the advent of Christ the faith was set forth under figures, and many things were not yet made clear; to represent this, the patriarchs and prophets are painted with wheels, to signify that imperfect knowledge. But because the apostles were perfectly taught of Christ, therefore the books, which are the emblems of this perfect knowledge, are open. But because some of them reduced their knowledge in writing, to the instruction of others, therefore fittingly they are represented with books in their hands like doctors. So Paul, and the Evangelists, Peter, James, and Jude. But others, who wrote nothing which has lasted, or been received into the canon by the Church, are not portrayed with books but with wheels, as a type of their preaching. Whence the Apostle to the Ephesians, ' And he gave some apostles, and some prophets, and some evangelists, and some pastors and teachers for the work of the ministry.'[40]

12. But the Divine Majesty is also portrayed with a closed book in the hands: ' which no man was found worthy to open but the Lion of the tribe of Juda.'[41] And sometimes with an open book: that in it every one may read that ' He is the Light of the world':[42]

---

[38] S. Matthew xxv, 41.

[39] S. Bartholomew is represented with black and grizzled hair, fair complexion, large eyes, straight nose, long beard, few grey hairs, moderate height, with a high white neck, clothed in purple, with a white pall, having purple gems at each angle. Durand. vii, 25, 2.

S. Andrew had a dark complexion, long beard, moderate height. This is therefore said, that ye may know how he ought to be painted: which should be known of the other apostles and saints. Durand. vii, 38, 1.

[40] Ephes. iv, 11.   [41] Apocalypse v, 2.   [42] S. John viii, 12.

'and the Way, the Truth, and the Life': [43] and the Book of Life [is also portrayed]. But why Paul is represented at the right, and Peter at the left of the Saviour, we shall show hereafter.

13. John Baptist is painted as a hermit.

14. Martyrs with the instruments of their torture: as S. Laurence with the gridiron: S. Stephen with stones: and sometimes with palms, which signify victory, according to that saying, 'The righteous shall flourish like a palm-tree: [44] as a palm-tree [45] flourishes, so his memory is preserved. Hence is it that palmers, they who come from Jerusalem, bear palms in their hands in token that they have been the soldiers of that King Who was gloriously received in the earthly Jerusalem with palms: and Who afterwards, having in the same city subdued the devil in battle, entered the palace of heaven in triumph with His angels, where the just shall flourish like a palm-tree, and shall shine like stars.

15. Confessors are painted with their insignia, as bishops with their mitres, abbots with their hoods: and some with lilies,[46] which denote chastity. Doctors with books in their hands: virgins, according to the Gospel,[47] with lamps.

16. Paul with a book and a sword: with a book, as a doctor, or with reference to his conversion: with a sword as [48] a soldier. Whence the verse:

---

[43] S. John xiv, 6.   [44] Psalm xcii, 12.

[45] This explanation differs from that usually received: namely, that the righteous flourishes best in adversity: as the palm-tree grows fasteth when loaded with weights.

[46] So in the beautiful hymn at Lauds in the commemoration of a virgin martyr, of the Parisian Breviary:
>Liliis Sponsus recubat, rosisque;
>Tu, tuo semper bene fida Sponso
>Et rosas Martyr, simul et dedisti
>   *Lilia Virgo.*

[47] S. Matthew xxv, 1.

[48] This is undoubtedly a mistake: the sword represents in this case, as in others, the instrument of martyrdom.

> The sword denotes the ire of Saul,
> The book, the power converting Paul.

17. Generally the effigies of the holy fathers are portrayed on the walls of the church, or on the back panels of the altar, or on vestments, or in other various places, so that we may meditate perpetually, not indiscreetly or uselessly, on their holiness. Whence in Exodus it is commanded by the divine law, that in the breast of Aaron, the breastplate of judgment should be bound [49] with strings: because fleeting thoughts should not occupy the mind of a priest, which should be girt by reason alone. In this breastplate also, according to Gregory, the names of the twelve patriarchs are commanded to be carefully inscribed.

18. To bear the fathers thus imprinted on the breast, is to meditate on the lives of ancient saints without intermission. But then doth the priest walk blamelessly when he gazeth continually on the example of the fathers which have gone before, when he considereth without ceasing the footsteps of the saints, and represseth unholy thoughts, lest he wander beyond the limits of right reason.

19. It is to be noted that the Saviour is always represented as crowned, as if he said, 'Come forth, children of Jerusalem, and behold King Solomon in the diadem with which his mother crowned him.'[50] But Christ was triply crowned. First by His Mother on the day of His conception, with crown of pity: which was a double crown: on account of what He had by nature, and what was given Him: therefore also it is called a diadem, which is a double crown. Secondly, by His step-mother in the day of His Passion, with the crown of misery. Thirdly, by His Father in the day of His Resurrection, with the crown of glory: whence it is written, 'O Lord,

---

[49] Exodus xxviii, 22. [50] Canticles iii, 11.

Thou hast crowned Him with glory and honour.'[51] Lastly, He shall be crowned by His whole family, in the last day of Revelation, with the crown of power. For He shall come with the judges of the earth to judge the world in righteousness. So also all saints are portrayed as crowned, as if they said: Ye children of Jerusalem, behold the martyrs with the golden crowns wherewith the Lord hath crowned them. And in the book of Wisdom: 'The just shall receive a kingdom of glory, and a beautiful diadem from the hand of their God.'[52]

20. But their crown is made in the fashion of a round shield: because the saints enjoy the divine protection. Whence they sing with joy: 'Lord, Thou hast crowned us with the shield of Thy favour.'[53] But the crown of Christ is represented under the figure of a cross:* and is thereby distinguished from that of the saints: because by the banner of His cross He gained for Himself the glorification of His humanity, and for us freedom from our captivity, and the enjoyment of everlasting life. But when any living [54] prelate or saint is portrayed, the glory is not fashioned in the shape of a shield, but four-square: that he may be shown to flourish in the four cardinal virtues: as it is contained in [55] the legend of blessed Gregory.

21. Again, sometimes Paradise is painted in churches, that it may attract the beholders to a following after its

---

[51] Psalm viii (*Domine Dominus*), 5.
[52] Wisdom v, 16. [53] Psalm v (*Verba mea*), 12. * See Appendix I.
[54] This does not appear to have prevailed in England. The nearest contemporary effigy of a saint which we have observed in stained glass, is that of S. Thomas, of Hereford, in the church of Cothelstone, Somersetshire. Here the glory is, as usual, of the circular form. As also in the fresco of the martyrdom of S. Thomas of Canterbury, in Preston church, Sussex, which is nearly contemporary. (See Appendix I.)
[55] This refers to the account given by Paulus Diaconus of the visible effulgence which surrounded the head of this great doctor when he was dictating his works.

rewards: sometimes hell, that it may terrify them by the fear of punishment.[56] Sometimes flowers [57] are portrayed, and trees: to represent the fruits of good works springing from the roots of virtues.

22. Now the variety of pictures denoteth the diversity of virtues. For 'to one is given by the Spirit the word of wisdom: to another the word of knowledge,' etc.[58] But virtues are represented under the forms of women: because they soothe and nourish. Again, by the ceilings or vaultings, which are for the beauty of the house, the more unlearned servants of Christ are set forth, who adorn the Church, not by their learning, but by their virtues alone.

The carved images which project from the walls, appear as it were to be coming out of it: because when by reiterated custom virtues so pertain to the faithful, that they seem naturally implanted in them, they are exercised in all their various operations. How a synagogue is depicted, shall be said hereafter: as also how the pall of the Roman Pontiff: and the year [59] and the zodiacal signs and its months. But the diverse histories of the

---

[56] 'A monk named Constantine set before the prince those judgments of God which are in all the world, and the retribution of the life to come: his discourse powerfully affected the heathen monarch (Vladimir, afterwards S. Vladimir); and this was particularly the case when the monk pointed out to him on an icon, which represented the Last Judgment, the different lot of the good and the wicked. "Good to those on the right hand—woe to those on the left," exclaimed Vladimir, deeply affected.'— Mouravieff's 'Hist. of the Russian Church,' p. 11. On which his translator, the Rev. R. W. Blackmore, sensibly remarks, 'Whatever may be the right view of the abstract question respecting icons, and the showing outward respect to them, the Russians at least cannot reasonably be blamed for revering a usage which was made the means, in part at least, of so blessed a result as the conversion of the great Prince Vladimir, the Constantine of their church and nation'

[57] This flower work is excessively common in Norman churches: that of S. Sepulchre's, at Cambridge, was a notable example of it.

[58] 1 Corinth. xii, 8.

[59] These are often to be found round Norman doors: as in that of S. Laurence, at York, and Egleton, Rutland.

Old and New Testaments may be represented after the fancy of the painter. For

> Pictoribus atque poetis
> Quod libet [60] addendi semper fuit æque potestas.

23. Furthermore, the ornaments of the church consist of three things :—the ornaments of the nave,[61] the choir, and the altar. The ornaments of the nave consist in dorsals, tapestry, mattings, and cushions of silk, purple, and the like. The ornaments of the choir consist in dorsals, tapestry, carpets, and cushions. Dorsals are hangings of cloth at the back of the clergy. Mattings, for their feet. Tapestry is likewise strewed under the feet, particularly under the feet of bishops, who ought to trample worldly things under their feet. Cushions are placed on the seats or benches of the choir.

24. But the ornament of the altar consists in portfolios, altar cloths, relicaries, candlesticks, crosses, an orfray, banners, missals, coverings, and curtains.

25. And notice, that the portfolio in which the consecrated host is kept, signifieth the frame of the blessed Virgin, concerning which it is said in the Psalms, 'Arise, O Lord into Thy resting place.'[62] Which sometimes is of wood: sometimes of white ivory: sometimes of silver: sometimes of gold: sometimes of crystal: and according to the different substances of which it is made, designateth the various dignities of the body of Christ. Again, the pyx which containeth the host, whether consecrated or not consecrated, typifieth the human memory. For a man ought to hold in remembrance continually the benefits of God, as well temporal, which are represented by the unconse-

---

[60] A false reading, of course ; yet not without its appropriate sense—the power of *adding* any ornamental circumstance to the main subject.

[61] *Ecclesiæ :* here undoubtedly the nave : as often *church* is so used in our prayer-book.   [62] Psalm cxxxii (*Domine, memento*), 8.

crated, as spiritual, which are set forth by the consecrated host. Which was also set forth by the urn in which God commanded that the manna should be deposited: which, albeit it was temporal, prefigured nevertheless this our spiritual sacrifice, when the Lord commanded that it should be laid up for an everlasting memorial unto future generations. But the pyx, being placed on the altar, which is Christ, signifieth apostles and martyrs. And the altar cloths and coverings are confessors and virgins, or all saints: of whom saith the Prophet to the Lord, 'Thou shalt be clothed with them as with a garment.' And of these we have spoken above.

26. Now there is a difference between *phylacterium* and *phylacteria*. *Phylacterium* is a scroll on which the ten commandments were written: and this kind of scroll the Pharisees used to wear on the front part of their garments, as a sign of devotion. Whence in the Gospel, 'They make broad their phylacteries.'[63] And the word is derived from *philare*, which is *to keep*, and *teras*, which is *law*. But *phylacteria* (a relicary) is a vessel of silver or gold, or crystal, or ivory, or some substance of the same kind, in which the ashes and relics of the saints are kept. For when Vigilantius called the faithful *Cinericii*,[64] because they preserved the ashes themselves, to testify contempt of his decision, it was ordered by the Church that they should be honourably preserved in precious vessels. And the name is derived from *philare*, which is to *preserve*, and *teron*, which is an extremity, because in them some

[63] S. Matthew xxiii, 5.
[64] Ais, Vigilantium, qui κατ' ἀντίφρασιν hoc vocatur nomine (nam Dormitantius rectius diceretur), os fœtidum rursum aperire, et putorem spurcissimum contra sanctorum martyrum proferre relliquias, et nos, qui eas suscepimus, appellare *cinerarios*.—S. Hieron, in Epp. See also the 'Church of the Fathers,' 2nd ed. chapter xv.

portion of the extremities of the bodies of saints is preserved: such as a tooth or a finger, or somewhat of the like kind. Over the altar in some churches also is placed a shrine: of which we have spoken in our section on the Altar.

27. At the horns of the altar [65] two candlesticks are placed to signify the joy of Jews and Gentiles at the nativity of Christ: which candlesticks, by means of a flint, have their wicks lighted. For the angel saith to the shepherds, 'I bring you good tidings of great joy, which shall be to all people: for to you is born this day the Saviour of the world.'[66] He is the true *Isaac*,[67] which being interpreted, is laughter. Now the light of the candlestick is the faith of the people. For to the Jewish people, saith the Prophet, 'Arise, shine, for thy light is come: and the glory of the Lord is risen upon thee.'[68] But to the Gentiles the Apostle saith, 'Ye were sometimes darkness, but are now light in the Lord.'[69] For before the birth of Christ a new star appeared to the wise men, according to the prophecy of Balaam. 'There shall rise,' saith he, 'a star out of Jacob, and a sceptre out of Israel.'[70] Concerning this we have also spoken in our section of the Altar.

28. The snuffers or scissors for trimming the lamps are the divine words by which men amputate the legal titles of the law, and reveal the shining spirit, according to that saying, 'Ye shall eat old store, and bring forth the old because of the new.'[71] The vessels in the which the wicks, when snuffed, are extinguished, are the hearts of the faithful, which admit the legal observance to the letter.

---

[65] This use of *two* candlesticks is very remarkable: as giving fresh authority to the custom of the English Church.
[66] S. Luke ii, 10. [67] Genesis xvii, 17, 19. [68] Isaiah lx, 1.
[69] Ephes. v, 8. [70] Numbers xxiv, 7. [71] Leviticus xxvi, 10.

29. Again, the tongs, by the double tooth of which the fire is arranged, are preachers; who instruct us by the accordant pages of both Testaments, and by their behaviour setting us right, inflame us to the practice of charity.

30. But the scuta, that is cups, of equal size at top and bottom, made for warming water, are those doctors who do not conceal the treasure of their hearts: but 'bring forth out of it things new and old':[72] as a 'candle which is not put under a bushel, but in a candlestick,'[73] that they who are in the house of the Lord may receive the light and the heat of the Holy Ghost.

31. The cross also is to be placed on the altar that the cross-bearers may thence raise it: in which action we commemorate how Simon the Cyrenian took the cross from the shoulders of Christ and bore it. Between the two candlesticks the cross is placed on the altar: because Christ standeth in the church, the Mediator between two peoples. For He is the Corner-stone, 'Who hath made both one':[74] to Whom the shepherds came from Judæa, and the wise men from the East. Concerning this we shall hereafter speak in another sense, when treating of the priest's approach to the altar.

32. Again, the front of the altar is ornamented with an orfray. As it is written: 'Thou shalt make Me an altar, and shalt make a crown in a circle about it of four fingers' breadth.'[75] The altar, ye know, sometimes signifieth the heart: in which the sacrifice of true faith must be offered by contrition: and then the orfray signifieth the taking in hand of a good occupation: wherewith we ought to adorn our foreheads, that we may give light to others. Sometimes the altar signifieth Christ: and then by the orfray the ornament of charity

[72] S. Matthew xiii, 52.   [73] S. Matthew v, 15.   [74] Ephesians ii, 14.
[75] Exodus xxvii, 4.

is fitly represented. For as gold hath the superiority over all metals, so hath charity over other virtues. Whence the Apostle, in the first to the Corinthians: 'But the greatest of these is charity.'[76] For our faith ought to be adorned with the orfray of charity, that we may be ready to lay down our lives for Christ's sake. Banners are also suspended above the altars: that in the church that triumph of Christ may evermore be held in mind, by which we also hope to triumph over our enemy.

33. The book of the Gospel is fixed on the altar, because the Gospel hath Christ for its author, and beareth witness to Him. Which book is therefore adorned on his outside, for the cause that we shall make mention of hereafter. Next, the vessels and utensils in the house of the Lord had their origin from Moses and Solomon: which in the Old Testament were many and diverse, as it is written in Exodus, and having divers significations, concerning which, for the sake of brevity, we will not in this place treat.

34. Now all things which pertain to the ornament of a church, must be removed or covered over in the season of Lent: which according to some taketh place on Passion Sunday, because after that time the Divinity of Christ was hidden and concealed in Him. For He gave Himself up to be betrayed and scourged, as if He were only man, and had not in Him the virtue of divinity: whence in the Gospel of this day it is written, 'But Jesus hid Himself, and went out of the temple.'[77] Then therefore the crosses are covered, that is, the virtue of His divinity is hidden. Others do this from the first Sunday of Lent: because after that time the Church beginneth to treat of His Passion. Whence in that time the cross must not be borne in procession

---

[76] 1 Corinth. xiii, 13.   [77] S. John viii, 59.

from the church, except it be covered; and, according to the use of some places, two coverings or curtains are then only retained: of which the one is hung all round the choir, the other is suspended between the altar and the choir: that those things which be within the Holy of Holies may not appear. In that the Sanctuary and Cross are then veiled, we be taught the letter of the Law, that is, its carnal observance, or that the understanding of Holy Scriptures before the Passion of Christ was veiled, hidden, and obscure: and that in that time there was a veil: that is, men had an obscurity before their eyes. It signifieth also the sword which was set before the gate of Paradise: because the carnal observance we have spoken of, and this obscurity, and the sword at the gate of Paradise, were removed by the Passion of Christ. Therefore the curtains and veils of this kind are removed on Good Friday. But in that in the Old Testament, there were beasts that chewed the cud, and cleft the hoof, as oxen used in ploughing, that is discerning and spiritually perceiving the mysteries of Scripture: therefore in Lent only a few priests, to whom 'it is given to know the mysteries of the Kingdom of God'[78] go behind the veil.

35. Concerning this it is to be noted that there be three kinds of veils which be hung in churches: that which concealeth the mysteries: that which divideth the sanctuary from the clergy: that which divideth the clergy from the laity. The first denoteth the law: the second denoteth our unworthiness, in that we are unworthy, nay unable to behold things celestial. The third is the coercion of our carnal pleasures. The first, namely, the curtain that is hung from each side of the altar, when the priest goeth into the holy place, is typified by that which is written in Exodus. 'Moses put a

---

[78] St. Matthew xiii, 11.

veil over his face, for the children of Israel could not sustain the brightness of His countenance.'[79] And as the Apostle saith, 'Even to this day is this veil over the hearts of the Jews.[80] The second, namely the curtain that in the office of the Mass during Lent is suspended before the altar, was set forth by the veil which was hung up in the tabernacle, and divided the Holy of Holies from the holy place, as shall be declared in the proeme to the fourth part : by which the ark was concealed from the people : and it was wrought cunningly, and adorned with a fair variety of devices. This was it that was rent in the Passion of the Lord : and after its pattern, the curtains at this day are cunningly wrought with divers patterns. Concerning the aforesaid veil, and of what sort the curtains ought to be, it is written in Exodus. The third kind of veil deriveth its origin from thence, that the *peribolus* in the primitive Church, or wall which encompasseth the choir, was only raised as far as the elevation of the choir ;[81] which even to this day is observed in some churches : which was done that the people

---

[79] Exodus xxxiv, 33.   [80] 2 Corinth. iii, 15.
[81] There is much difficulty in this passage. We conceive that Durandus while writing it had in his mind's eye the arrangement of many of the Basilican churches, in which the choir was raised over the crypt (called Confessio, or Martyrium), in which the ashes of the saints were laid, and was detached from the nave by two flights of steps, one on each side of the descent to this undercroft. In this case the *appodiatio* would mean the elevation of the choir, itself considered as a sufficient distinction from the nave. The usual representations of Basilican churches, however, always show some rails, or cancelli, besides this *appodiation*. The learned Father Thiers devotes the third section of his 'Dissertation sur la Clôture du Chœur des Eglises' to the consideration of this passage. 'Guillaume Durand, Evêque de Mande, assure que dans la Primitive Église, le chœur etait séparé de la Nef par une *muraille d'appui*, afin que le peuple voïant la Clergé chanter les louanges de Dieu en fût édifié. Mais comme il parle d'un fait beaucoup éloigné de son tems, et qui n'est attache par aucun ancien auteur, je ne pense pas que l'on doïve faire grande fonds sur son temoignage.' We suspect that Thiers is wrong in construing *appodiatio* by *muraille d'appui :* the latter would well express the real Basilican arrangement, with which the translator was probably acquainted. Durandus, therefore, is wrong in his fact ; and Thiers wrong in his understanding of Durandus, as well as in the theory stated in the next section, that 'Depuis

seeing the clergy singing psalms, might follow their good example. But at this time as it were a veil or wall is suspended or interposed between the clergy and the laity, that they may not be able to behold each other: as if to say, in very deed, 'turn away mine eyes, lest they behold vanity.'[82]

36. But on Holy Saturday all the curtains are taken away, because on the Passion of the Lord the veil of the temple was rent: and by that thing the spiritual intelligence of the Law was revealed unto us, which till that time lay hid, as is said afore: and the door of the kingdom of heaven is opened, and power was given unto us, that we cannot be overcome of our carnal concupiscence, unless we ourselves do yield. But the veil which separateth the sanctuary from the choir, is drawn or lifted up at vespers on every Saturday of Lent: when the office of the Sunday is begun, that the clergy may be able to look into the sanctuary: because the Sunday commemorateth the Resurrection.

37. This therefore is done on the six Sundays of Lent: because there was no age in which joy, and that joy eternal, was not made in some sort manifest, that joy which is concealed in heaven, as is signified by that veil. Thence is it that we fast not on the Sundays, and this on account of the glory of the Resurrection. For the first Sunday signifieth the joy which our parents enjoyed in the Paradise before the fall. The second Sunday signi-

Constantin le chœur de quelques Eglises etoit distingué de la Nef par des tapisseries ou des voiles.' For he grounds this chiefly on the next assertion of Durandus about the use curtains, 'hoc tempore. vers la fin du 13 siecle.' If we did not know from facts that before this time roodscreens were in ordinary use, the words of Durandus *velum aut murus* would show us that he means the *wall* to be taken metaphorically for a *veil*. And so Thiers may have seen, since he concludes his section thus—' Mais peut être que Theodoret parle des tapisseries et Durand des voiles qui convroient la Clôture du Chœur par le dedans, et que sous ces tapisseries et ces voiles il y avoit une veritable clôture de balustres, ou de murailles pleines.'

[82] Psalm cxix (*Beati immaculati*). 37.

fieth the joy of the few who were preserved in the ark of Noah, when all else were drowned in the deluge. The third, the gladness of the children of Israel, when in the time of Joseph others were afflicted with famine. The fourth, their joy when they lived with all peace under Solomon.[83] The fifth, their gladness when returning from the Babylonian captivity. The sixth, that of the disciples from the Resurrection to the Ascension: when the bridegroom was with them in presence.

38. In feasts likewise of nine lessons,[84] when they occur in Lent, the before-mentioned veil is raised and lifted up. But this is not of the institution of the earliest times, because then no feast was celebrated in Lent. But then on whatever day a feast occurred, commemoration was made of it on the Saturday and Sunday following, according to the canon of Pope Martin; and so in the xiiith book of Burchardus.[85] And all this on account of the sadness of that time. Afterwards the contrary use prevailed: that feasts of nine lessons occurring in Lent should be solemnly observed, and a fast nevertheless kept.

39. Again, on festivals curtains are hung up in churches, for the sake of the ornament they give; and that by visible, we may be led to invisible beauty. These curtains are sometimes tinctured with various hues, as is said afore: so that by the diversity of the colours themselves we may be taught that man, who is the temple of God, should be ordained by the variety and diversity of virtues. A white curtain signifieth

---

[83] 3 Kings iv, 20.

[84] For an explanation of the whole Catholic system of feasts, double, semi-double, and simple, the reader is referred to the *Tracts for the Times*, vol. iii.

[85] S. Burchardus of Worms flourished in 1025: and is not to be confounded with John Burchardus, who wrote an explanation of the Mass for the use of the Venetian Church, which was published in 1559.

pureness of living: a red, charity: a green, contemplation: a black, mortification of the flesh: a livid-coloured, tribulation. Besides this, over white curtains are sometimes suspended hangings of various colours: to signify that our hearts ought to be purged from vices: and that in them should be the curtains of virtues, and the hangings of good works.

40. Moreover, on the Feast of the Nativity of the Lord some churches exhibit no hangings: some poor, and some good. Those which have none, signify our shame; for even if we are filled with the greatest joy at the birth of a Saviour,[86] we ought not, however, to be without shame that such was our sin that the 'Son of God emptied Himself on our account, and took upon Him the form of a servant.'[87] And on that account also we solemnise His Passion not with joy, but with a severe fast; whereas when we celebrate the passion of other saints we do it with gladness, and indulge ourselves somewhat in meat and drink, as shall be said in the sixth book. But our Lord's Passion is a source of shame to us on account of our sins. The saints, on the other hand, died not for our sins, but suffered for Christ. Those churches which on the Nativity suspend curtains of poor texture thereby typify that Christ did then 'take upon Himself the form of a servant,'[88] and was clothed in miserable rags. Those which employ richer hangings, set forth by them the gladness arising from the Birth of a King: and teach what manner of persons we ought to be in our reception of so great a Guest.

41. In some churches the altar at Easter-tide is decked with precious hangings, and veils of three colours are placed over it: red, pale, and black, which

---

[86] In accordance with this feeling, the first Psalm at the second vespers of the nativity in the Benedictine Breviary is the *De profundis*.
[87] Philip. ii, 7.   [88] Philip. ii, 7.

denote three seasons. When the first lesson and its response are finished, the black veil is removed; which signifieth the time before the Law. When the second lesson and its response are finished, the pale veil is removed: which signifieth the time of the Law. The third being finished, the red is removed, which setteth forth the time of Grace: that is, that by the Passion of Christ an entrance is administered unto us to the Holy of Holies and to eternal glory. But concerning the coverings and cloths of the altars we have spoken in our sections on the same.

42. On high feasts, the treasures of the church are brought forth on three accounts. Firstly, by way of safeguard: that it may be made manifest that he who hath them in charge hath been careful in his care of them. Secondly, for the more reverence of the solemnity. Thirdly, for the memory of their oblation; namely, for the commemoration of them that bestowed them on the church.

But in that the church is gloriously adorned within and not without, it is thereby signified that 'all its glory is from within.'[89] For although its outward appearance be despicable, the soul which is the seat of God is illuminated from within: according to that saying, 'I am black but comely.'[90] And the Lord saith to the Prophet: 'I have a goodly heritage.'[91] Which the Prophet considering in his mind, saith, 'Lord, I have loved the beauty of Thine house':[92] which is spiritually adorned by Faith, Hope, and Charity. Sometimes the church, both material and spiritual, hath need to be cleansed: concerning which in the seventh book.

In some churches two eggs of ostriches and other

---

[89] Psalm xlv (*Eructavit*), 6.   [90] Cantic. i, 5.
[91] The bishop probably refers to Psalm xvi (*Conserva me*), 6. The words in reality spoken by David are understood by him as if spoken by the Almighty.   [92] Psalm xxvi (*Judica me*), 8.

things which cause admiration, and which are rarely seen, are accustomed to be suspended: that by their means the people may be drawn to church, and have their minds the more affected.

43. Again, some say that the ostrich, as being a forgetful bird, 'leaveth her eggs in the dust':[93] and at length, when she beholdeth a certain star, returneth unto them, and cheereth them by her presence. Therefore the eggs[94] of ostriches are hung in churches to signify that man, being left of God on account of his sins, if at length he be illuminated by the Divine Light, remembereth his faults and returneth to Him, Who by looking on him with His Mercy cherisheth him. As it is written in Luke that after Peter had denied Christ, the 'Lord turned and looked upon Peter.'[95] Therefore be the aforesaid eggs suspended in churches, this signifying, that man easily forgetteth God, unless being illuminated by a star, that is, by the Influence of the Holy Spirit, he is reminded to return to Him by good works.

44. Now in the Primitive Church, the sacrifice was

---

[93] Job xxxix, 14.
[94] Perhaps this custom was introduced by the Crusaders. 'As the ostrich is good for food, so, it seems, are its eggs: to say nothing of their being objects of attention, as being used much in the East by way of ornament; for they are hung up in their places of public worship, along with many lamps.' Harmer's 'Observations,' vol. iv, p. 336, who refers to Pococke's 'Travels,' vol. i, p. 31, and imagines that Dr Chandler, in his travels in Asia Minor, was mistaken when he supposed that the Turkish Mosque of Magnesia was ornamented with lamps pendent from the ceiling intermixed with balls of polished ivory, p. 267. Ostrich eggs might easily be mistaken for ivory balls. The following passage from De Moleon is curious: 'At the conclusion of matins,' he says, speaking of the rites of S. Maurice at Angers on Easter Day, 'two chaplains take their place behind the altar curtains. Two corbeliers (*Cubiculares*) in dalmatics, amices, and *mitellæ*, with gloves on their hands, present themselves before the altar. The chaplains chant, *Quem quæritis?* The corbeliers representing the Maries, reply, Jesum *Nazarenum Crucifixum.* The others answer, *Resurrexit, non est hic.* The corbeliers take from the altar *two* ostrich eggs wrapped in silk, and go forth, chanting, *Alleluia resurrexit* Dominus, *resurrexit Leo Fortis,* Christus, *Filius* Dei.'—*Voyag. Lit.* p. 98.
[95] S. Luke xxii, 61.

offered in vessels of wood, and common vests: for then were 'chalices of wood, and priests of gold': whereof the contrary is now. But Severinus, Pope, decreed that it should be offered in glass:[96] but because such vessels were easily broken, therefore, Urban, Pope, and the Council[97] of Rheims decreed that gold or silver vessels should be used: or on account of poverty, tin, which rusteth not: but not in wood nor in brass. Therefore it might not be in glass on account of the danger of effusion: nor of wood since being porous and spongy, it absorbeth the blood: nor of brass nor of bronze, the rust of which is unseemly.

45. And note that the name of chalice is derived from the Old Testament: whence Jeremiah, 'Babylon is a golden chalice that maketh drunk the nations.'[98] And David: 'In the hand of the Lord is a chalice, and the wine thereof is red':[99] and in another place, 'I will receive the chalice of salvation, and will call on the name of the Lord.'[100] Again, in the Gospel: 'Are ye able to drink the chalice that I shall drink?'[101] And again, 'When He had taken the chalice He gave thanks.'[102] A golden chalice signifieth the 'treasures of wisdom that be hid in Christ.'[103] A silver chalice denoteth purity from sin. A chalice of tin denoteh the similitude of sin and punishment. For tin is as it were halfway between silver and lead: and the Humanity of Christ, albeit it were not lead, that is, sinful, yet was it like to sinful flesh. And therefore not silver: and although impossible for His own sin, passible He was for ours: since 'He thus took our infirmities, and bare our sicknesses.'[104]

---

[96] See Martene, Tom. IV, ii, 9; the *Ducretum*, fol. 395.
[97] 'A.D. 874, Vid. Concil. Coll. Reg. Tom. I. p. 288.' See also P. Tunoc. iv, Ep. ad Otton. Carel. xiii *Hardouin* vii, 365.
[98] Jeremiah li, 7.   [99] Psalm lxxv (*Confitebimur*), 8.
[100] Psalm cxvi (*Dilexi*), 13.
[101] S. Matthew x, 22.   [102] S. Matthew xxvi, 27.   [103] Coloss. ii, 3.
[104] S. Matthew viii, 17.

Concerning the Chalice and the Paten we shall speak hereafter.

46. But if anyone, through cause of his little religion, should say that the Lord commanded Moses to make all the vessels of the Tabernacle for every use and ceremony whatever, of brass, as it is written in the eight and twentieth chapter of Exodus, and that precious vessels of this sort, 'could be sold for much, and given to the poor,'[105] he is like Judas, and acteth contrarywise to the woman which brought the alabaster box of ointment. This we reply to him: not that God is better pleased with gold than brazen ornaments: but that when men offer to God that which they value, by the worship of the Almighty they vanquish their own avarice. Moreover, these offices of divine piety be moral, and significative of future glory. Whence also under the old law the priest's garments were to be made of gold, and jacinth, and purple, and scarlet twice dyed, and woven linen, and other precious things: that thereby might be made manifest with how great diversity of virtues the priest ought to shine: and it was also commanded that the altar, and the mercy-seat, and the candlestick, and the other vessels and ornaments of the altar should be made of gold and silver. The Tabernacle also was to be made of divers precious materials, as is said in our section concerning the Church. Also the high priest under the Law used divers precious ornaments, as we have both noted, and shall hereafter note.

47. Moreover, it was forbidden in the Council of Orleans,[106] that the divine ornaments should be used for the adorning of nuptials, lest they should be polluted by the touch of the wicked, or by the pomp of secular luxury. By this doubtless it is shown that a chasuble, or any

---

[105] S. Matthew xxvi, 9.
[106] A.D. 535. Decret. viii. See also the Council of Tribur. A.D. 1036.

other ornament intended for the divine mysteries, must not be made out of a common person's vest.

48. Stephen, Pope, moreover, forbade that anyone should have the use of the vests of a church, or of those things which be touched by religious men alone, for other purposes: lest that vengeance come upon these transgressors which befel Belshazzar the King.[107]

49. Also Clement, Pope, forbade that the dead should be buried or wrapped or covered, they or their bones, with the altar cloth, or covering for the chalice, or napkin wherewith the priest washeth his hands before consecrating.

50. But when the palls, that is the corporals, and the veils, that is the ornaments of the altar, or the curtains hanging over it shall have become unclean, the deacons with their ministers shall wash them within the sanctuary, and not without. But when the veils, used in the service of the altar, be washed, let there be a new basin. And let the palls, that is the corporals, be washed in another basin. And let the veils for doors, that is, the curtains which are hung up in churches at high feasts, and in Lent, be washed in another. This is it that was decreed of the Council of Lerida:[108] that for washing the corporal, and the altar palls certain vessels be appropriated and kept within the church: in which nothing else ought to be washed. But according to the afore-mentioned Clement, if the altar pall or covering, or the covering of the seat where the priest sitteth, in his holy vests, or of the candlestick, or the veil, that is the cloth or curtains hanging over the altar be consumed by old age, let them be burnt; and their ashes cast in the baptistery, or on the wall, or in the drains, where there is no treading of passers by. And note that ecclesiastical ornaments be consecrated: as shall be said under the section of Consecrations and Unctions.

[107] Daniel v, 1.   [108] 'A.D. 524, Concil. Coll. Reg. Tom XI, p. 24.'

CHAPTER IV

OF BELLS

Bells, what and where first used—Why Blessed—Analogy between Bells and Trumpets—Mystical Signification—Of the Bell-Frame—Of the Bell-Ropes—Use of Bells at the Canonical Hours—Six kinds of Bells—Bells when Silent—Of the Passing Bell—Of the Prayer Bell—Of the Storm Bell.

1. BELLS are brazen vessels, and were first invented in Nola, a city of Campania: wherefore the larger bells are called *Campanæ*, from Campania the district, and the smaller *Nolæ*, from Nola the town.

2. The reason for consecrating and ringing bells is this: that by their sound the faithful may be mutually cheered on towards their reward; that the devotion of faith may be increased in them; that their fruits of the field, their minds and their bodies may be defended; that the hostile legions and all the snares of the Enemy may be repulsed; that the rattling hail, the whirlwinds, and the violence of tempests and lightning may be restrained; the deadly thunder and blasts of wind held off; the spirits of the storm and the powers of the air overthrown; and that such as hear them may flee for refuge to the bosom of our holy Mother the Church, bending every knee before the standard of the sacred rood. These several reasons are given in the office for the blessing of bells.[1]

---

[1] See the account of the consecration of several churches in the island of

3. You must know that bells, by the sound of which the people assembleth together to the church to hear, and the clergy to preach, 'in the morning the mercy of God and His power by night,[2] do signify the silver trumpets, by which under the Old Law the people were called together unto sacrifice. (Of these trumpets we shall speak in our sixth book.) For just as the watchmen in a camp rouse one another by trumpets, so do the ministers of the Church excite each other by the sound of bells to watch the livelong night against the plots of the devil. Wherefore our brazen bells are more sonorous than the trumpets of the Old Law, because then God was known in Judea only, but now in the whole earth. They be also more durable: for they signify that the preaching of the New Testament will be more lasting than the trumpets and sacrifices of the Old Law, namely, even unto the end of the world.

4. Again bells do signify preachers, who ought after the likeness of a bell to exhort the faithful unto faith: the which was typified in that the Lord commanded Moses to make a vestment for the high priest, having seventy-two bells to sound when the high priest entered into the Holy of Holies.[3] Also the cavity of the bell denoteth the mouth of the preacher, according to the saying of the Apostle, 'I am become as sounding brass or a tinkling cymbal.'[4]

5. The hardness of the metal signifieth fortitude in the mind of the preacher: whence saith the Lord, 'Behold I have made thy face strong against their faces.'[5] The clapper or iron, which by striking on either side maketh the sound, doth denote the tongue of the teacher, the

---

Guernsey, taken from the Black Book of the Diocese of Contances, in a paper by the Rev. W. C. Lukis, B.A., Trinity College, published in the First Part of the Transactions of the Cambridge Camden Society.

[2] Psalm xcii (*Bonum est confiteri*), 2

[3] Exodus xxviii, 35. [4] 1 Cor. xiii, 1. [5] Ezekiel iii, 8.

which with the adornment of learning doth cause both Testaments to resound.

6. Wherefore a prelate which hath not the skill of preaching will be like unto a bell without a clapper: according to that saying of Gregory, 'A priest, if he knoweth not how to preach nor what voice of exhortation he can deliver, is a dumb preacher, and also as a dumb dog which cannot bark.' The striking the bell denoteth that a preacher ought first of all to strike at the vices in himself for correction, and then advance to blame those of others: lest indeed, contrary to the teaching of the Apostle, 'when he hath preached to others, he himself should be a castaway.'[6] Which also the Psalm doth testify, 'But unto the ungodly, saith God: why dost thou preach my laws, and takest my covenant in thy mouth?'[7] Because truly by the example of his own suffering he often gaineth access to those whom by the learning of his discourse he cannot move. The link by which the clapper is joined or bound unto the bell is moderation: by which, namely, by the authority of Scripture, the tongue of the preacher who wisheth to draw men's hearts is ruled.[8]

7. The wood of the frame upon which the bell hangeth, doth signify the wood of our Lord's Cross: which is on this account suspended on high, because the Cross is preached by the ancient Fathers. The pegs by which the wooden frame is joined together or fastened, are the Oracles of the Prophets. The iron cramps by which the bell is joined with the frame, denote charity, by which the preacher being joined indissolubly unto the Cross, doth boast and say, 'God forbid that I should glory save in the Cross of our Lord Jesus Christ.'[9] The hammer

---

[6] 1 Corinthians ix, 27. [7] Psalm l (*Deus deorum*), 16.
[8] The passage is very unintelligible in the original, and is probably corrupted or transposed.
[9] Gal. vi, 14. *Cavilla* is thus explained by Belethus. Expl. Divin.

affixed to the frame by which the bell is struck, signifieth the right mind of the preacher, by which he himself, holding fast to the Divine commands, doth by frequent striking inculcate the same on the ears of the faithful.

8. The rope hanging from this, by which the bell is struck, is humility, or the life of the preacher: the same rope also showeth the measure of our own life. Besides these, since the rope hath its beginning from the wood upon which the bell hangeth, by which is understood our Lord's Cross, it doth thus rightly typify Holy Scripture which doth flow down from the wood of the Holy Cross. As also the rope is composed of three strands, so doth the Scripture consist of a Trinity: namely, of history, allegory, and morality. Whence, the rope coming down from the wooden frame into the hand of the priest is Scripture descending from the mystery of the Cross into the mouth of the preacher. Again, the rope reacheth unto the hands by which it is grasped, because Scripture ought to proceed unto good works. Also the raising and the lowering of the rope in ringing doth denote that Holy Scripture speaketh sometimes of high matters, sometimes of low: or that the preacher speaketh sometimes lofty things for the sake of some, and sometimes condescendeth for the sake of others: according to that saying of the Apostle: 'Whether we exalt ourselves it is for God, or whether we humble ourselves it is for you.'*
Again, the priest draweth the rope downwards, when he descendeth from contemplation unto active life: but is himself drawn upward when under the teaching of Scripture he is raised in contemplation. Also he draweth it downwards when he understandeth the Scripture according to the 'letter which killeth'; he is drawn up-

---

Off. xxiv. Cavilla, sic enim ferrum illud pensile vocat, quod Græci rectius ῥόπαλον nominant, cujus pulsu campana sonum reddit.

* This appears to be a reference to 2 Cor. v, 13.

wards when he expoundeth the same according to the Spirit. Again, according to Gregory, he is drawn downwards and upwards when he measureth himself in Scripture, namely, how much he still lieth in the depths and how much he advanceth in doing good.

Furthermore, when the bell doth sound from the pulling of its rope, the people are gathered in one for the exposition of Holy Scripture, the preacher is heard, and the people are united in the bond of faith and charity. Therefore when a priest acknowledgeth unto himself that he is a debtor unto preaching, he must not withdraw himself from calling men together by his bells, just as also the sons of Aaron did sound their silver trumpets. He therefore moveth the ropes who doth of his office call his brethren or the people together.

The ring (or pully) in the length of the rope, through which in many places the rope is drawn, is the crown of reward, or perseverance unto the end, or else is Holy Scripture itself. Moreover, Savinianus, Pope, hath commanded that the hours of the day should be struck in churches.

9. And note that bells are commonly rung for the Divine Offices [10] twelve times during the twelve hours of

---

[10] The reader will scarcely need reminding that the day is canonically divided into two parts of twelve hours each, beginning at six o'clock respectively. Prime therefore is at our six a.m., tierce at nine, sexts at twelve, nones at three p.m., vespers at six p.m., and compline at bedtime.

> Hæc sunt septenis propter quœ psallimus horis.
> *Matutina* ligat Christum, qui crimina purgat :
> *Prima* replet sputis ; causam dat *Tertia* Mortis :
> *Sexta* Cruci nectit : latus Ejus *Nona* bipertit :
> *Vespera* deponit : tumulo *Completa* reponit.

Which may thus be translated ;

> At *matins* bound : at *prime* revil'd : condemn'd to death at *tierce:*
> Nail'd to the cross at *sexts :* at *nones* His blessed side they pierce :
> They take him down at *vesper*-tide ; in grave at *compline* lay
> Who thenceforth bids His Church to keep her sevenfold hours alway.

The twelve hours of the night are divided into three nocturns, which the day : namely, once at prime, and in like manner once at the last hour, because all things come from one God, and God is One, All in All. At tierce they are rung three times, for the second, third, and fourth hours which are then chanted. In like manner three times at sexts, for the fifth, sixth, and seventh hours. Also three times at nones for the three hours. But at vespers, which is the twelfth hour, not one only but many times are they rung, because in the time of grace the preaching of the Apostles was multiplied. Also in the night for matins they are rung often, because we ought often to call out, 'Wake, thou that sleepest, and arise from the dead.'[11]

10. Commonly also they be rung three times at nocturns. First with a *squilla*[12] or hand-bell, which by its

may be supposed to be said at twelve, two, and four, and are immediately followed by lauds at five. Nocturns and lauds (together called matins), with the six hours above-mentioned, make the seven canonical hours. On this subject we can but refer our readers to the extremely beautiful fifth book of Durandus, and particularly his first chapter, in which all the pregnant symbolism of the canonical hours is set forth. Hugo de Sancto Victore has briefly touched upon the same in the third chapter of the *In Speculum Ecclesiæ*, but nearly the whole of his account is contained in Durandus. See also S. Isidore 'De Eccles. Offic.' lib. 1, cap. xix—xxiii; and Belethus whose account is valuable for its conciseness. 'Explic. Divin. Offic.' Caps. xxi—xxix.

The twelve ringings mentioned in the text as being in 'the twelve hours of the *day*' are thus to be made out. At prime, one ; at tierce, three ; at sexts, three ; at nones, three ; at vespers, one (the ringing 'many times' being only thus accounted) ; and at the last hour, one ; in whole twelve, Hugo de S. Victor has a passage almost identical with this. 'The bells be also rung twelve times. At prime, once, and again at the last hour once ; because all things be from One God, and the Same will be All in All. But at tierce, three times for the second, third, and fourth hours ; and so at sexts, for three hours, namely, the seventh, eighth, and ninth ; but at vespers many times, because in the time of grace the preaching of the Apostles was multiplied. Also at matins oftentimes, because we should often exclaim, 'Arise, thou that sleepest.' It will be observed that this passage is corrupt, nones being omitted, and its three hours given to sexts. Matins also, as in the text, are belonging to the twelve hours of the *night*.

[11] Eph. v, 14.

[12] *Squilla* is properly a *sea onion*. We conceive that the sort of a bell here meant is a kind of hand-bell, formed out of a hollow ball of metal, furnished with a slit for the sound, and with a loose pellet inside. This answers to the squilla in shape and utters a very shrill sound. We find

sharp sound signifieth Paul preaching acutely. The second ringing signifieth Barnabus joined to his company. The third intimateth that, when the 'Jews put from them the word of God, the Apostles turned themselves to the Gentiles,' whom also they instructed in the faith of the Trinity by the doctrine of the four Evangelists. Whence also some do use *four* peals.

11. And note that there be six kinds of bells which be used in the church; namely, the *squilla*, the *cymbalum*, the *nola*, the *nolula* (or double *campana*), the *signum* [and the *campana*]. The squilla is rung in the *triclinium*, that is, in the refectory; the cymbalum in the cloister; the nola in the choir; the nolula or double campana in the clock, the campana in the campanile, the signum in the tower. Either of these, however, may be called generally a bell. And these be known by diverse names, because the preachers signified thereby be necessary for diverse ends.

12. During the whole Septuagesima, in the which Quadragesima [or Lent] is contained, on common days the bells be not chanted, nor chimed, but tolled, that is rung singly, at the hours of the day, or at matins.[13] In well-ordered churches, they be struck twice at prime; first to call unto prayer, secondly to begin: three times at tierce, according to the number of hours then struck,

---

below that it was used chiefly in the refectory. So in a note to Martener vol iv, p. 32, we read 'ad gratiarum actionem Sacrista sciliam (the other form of squillam) pulsabat. Cons. S. Benigni, cap. 9. Fratribus exeuntibus de prandio sive de cœna scillam pulsare non negligat Hebdomadarius Sacrista.'

[13] It is to be remarked that throughout this chapter there is no allusion to ringing the bells by raising them and causing them to revolve on axes as practised in England. This and the beautiful science of bell-ringing consequent on it are peculiar to ourselves. The method of sounding the bells here understood is by a hammer acting on the rim, or by pulling the clapper, as is used with us for chimes, and where the bell frame is weak. This accounts for the much larger bells which are found abroad, and which were never meant to be poised and swung. Owing to the above difference between the Continental and English methods of bell-ringing, it is

as was said above; once to call to prayer, twice to assemble them together, thrice to begin. In like manner it is done at sexts and nones. But for matins the same bells are rung and in the same order. For a mass or for vespers only two bells be rung. But in smaller churches they simply ring the bells as aforesaid, and this on the common days. But on Sundays and holy days, they chime them, as at other times. For because preachers who be figured by bells, do the more abound in a season of grace, and 'are instant in season,' therefore on festivals which pertain to grace, the bells do sound more pressingly and are rung for a longer time, to arouse those 'that sleep and be drunken,' lest they sleep beyond measure. But what is signified by the ringing of bells when the Te Deum is chanted we shall speak hereafter.[14]

13. Moreover, the bells ought to be rung when anyone

not easy to express the difference between *simpulsare, compulsare,* and *depulsare.*

Depulsare is to ring by tying a rope to the *clapper* of a bell, and pulling the rope to and fro : we have accordingly translated it, *to chant a bell.*

Simpulsare is to ring by tying a rope to the hammer, and pulling it back ; this we have translated *to toll.* Tolling is of course performed by swinging the bell round : but as there is no English word which expresses *simpulsare*, we thought it better to use an old term in a new sense, than to coin a new one.

Compulsare is to do to several bells what *depulsare* is to do to one : and we have translated it to *chime.*

Pulsare we have translated *to ring.*

It may be worthy of remark, how completely the ringing of the bells is here considered a part of the priest's office.

[14] In Book V, chapter iii, '*of Nocturns,*' Durandus says, 'When the nocturns be finished, the bells be rung and the *Te Deum laudamus* is chanted with uplift voice, to denote that the Church doth openly and wonderfully laud God in the time of grace, and to show that if by good works we answer rightly to holy doctrine, we shall attain to singing heavenly praises in concert with the angels. The chant also is then made with a loud voice, to signify the joy of the woman at finding the lost 'piece of silver.' And the versicle *Day by day we magnify Thee,* and the following, be chanted still more loudly to set forth the gratulations of the neighbours over the finding of the piece of silver : and the ringing of the bells representeth the calling together of the neighbours. In some churches also the candles be lighted, because the woman also 'lighted a candle and sought diligently till she found it.' This also signifieth that the Church Catholic is drawn by Christ out of hell. And the hymn itself representeth

Of Bells

is dying, that the people hearing this may pray for him.[15] For a woman indeed they ring twice, because she first caused the bitterness of death: for she first alienated mankind from God; wherefore the second day had no benediction.[16] But for a man they ring three times, because the Trinity was first shown in man. For Adam was first formed from the earth, then the woman from Adam, afterwards was man created from both, and so there is therein a trinity. But if the dying man be an ecclesiastic, they toll so many times as he hath received orders. And at the last time they ought to chime, that so the

the future joy and gladness, which the Church resting from her labours shall attain in the day of judgment.' Hugo de S. Victore, and Belethus agree as to this ringing of the bells at matins: a practice of which perhaps we may find the shadow in our own use in many places of ringing the bells at eight o'clock on Sunday mornings, to which day our services are now chiefly confined.

[15] For an account of the 'passing-bell,' and the authority for its right use among ourselves, the reader is referred to Bp. Montague's 'Articles of Inquiry.' Camb. 1841, pp. 76, 116. It is to be observed that the bells are here said to be rung, not *tolled*, as is generally the case now. Many will remember a beautiful passage upon this custom in one of the Rev. F. E. Paget's 'Tales of the Village.' The practice of their distinguishing the sex of the dying person is still in most places retained.

[16] '*Wherefore the second day had no benediction.*' It will be observed that of this day only it is not said expressly that 'God saw that it was good.' We give a chapter of Hugo S. Victore upon this question

'But it is admirable wherefore God did not see the works of the second day that they were good: since in each other day He is said to have seen them, and that they were good. For either it was not His work, and so not good; or if it were His work, it was good. But if it was good, it was also His work: and then He saw it was good, Who could not be ignorant what it was, whether good or bad. Wherefore then is it not said here as elsewhere "God saw that it was good"? For if this be said elsewhere only because the work was made, why ought it not also to be said here since it was made? Perhaps because *dual* is the sign of division; since it first recedeth from *unity:* and so here we perceive some sacrament. Thus the works of the second day be not praised, not because they were not good, but because they were signs of evil. For God made His first works "and behold they were all very good:" in the which neither was corruption present, nor perfection absent. But afterwards cometh the devil and man, and they also made their works: and these second works came after the first; the evil after the good: and God was unwilling to behold these works because they were evil; but beholding them by His wisdom, He disapproved them by his judgment.' 'De Sacramentis,' Lib. i, Pars 1, cap. xx. S. Isodore (Sentent. I, xx de Mundo) does not allude to this, nor S. Augustin upon Genesis.

people may know for whom they have to pray. The bells ought also to be chimed when the corpse is brought to the church, and when carried out from the church to the grave.

14. Also bells be rung at processions, that the evil spirits may hear them and flee, as shall be said hereafter.[17] For they do fear when the trumpets of the Church Militant, that is the bells, be heard, like as a tyrant doth fear when he heareth on his own land the trumpets of any potent king his foe.

15. And this is the reason also why the Church, when she seeth a tempest to arise, doth ring the bells; namely, that the devils hearing the trumpets of the Eternal King, which be the bells, may flee away through fear and cease from raising the storm; and that the faithful also may be admonished at the ringing of the bells and be provoked to be urgent in prayer for the instant danger.[18]

But for three days before Easter the bells be silent, as shall be said hereafter.[19] Also the bells be silent in time of an interdict, because often for the fault of those put under them the tongue of the preachers is hindered; according to that of the Prophet, 'I will make thy tongue cleave to the roof of thy mouth, for they are a rebellious house'; [20] that is, for the people are disobedient.

The Church also hath organs, of which we shall speak hereafter.[21]

---

[17] 'The bells be rung in processions. For as an earthly monarch hath in his army royal insignia, namely trumpets and banners; so Christ the Eternal King hath in His Church Militant bells for trumpets, and crosses for banners. Thus the ringing of the bells doth signify the prophets, who foretold the advent of Christ.' Durandus, book iv, chapter 6. 'Of the priest's approach to the altars,' sec. 19. The same idea is applied by Belethus to the matin bells in his 24th chapter.

[18] See note 1 to this chapter. [19] See Appendix. [20] Ezekiel iii, 26.

[21] Durandus, in his fourth book, chapter xxxiv, '*Of the Sanctus,*' says, 'Moreover in this concert of angels and men, the organs do from time to time add their harmony: the which was introduced by David and Solomon, who did cause hymns to be sung at the sacrifice of the Lord, with the concert of organs and other instruments of music, and the people also to join in chorus.'

CHAPTER V

OF CEMETERIES AND OTHER PLACES, SACRED AND RELIGIOUS

Holiness of Places; its Origin—Difference between Sacred, Holy, and Religious—Different Names for Cemetery—First use of Cemeteries—Who are not to be Buried in the Church—Ancient Method of Burial—Who are to be Buried in a Cemetery.

1. Now we will speak of cemeteries and other sacred and religious places. Of consecrated places, some be appropriated to human necessity, others to prayers. Those of the first sort be a *xenodochium* or *xenostorium*, which is the same: a *vasochonium*, a *gerontocomium*, an *orphanotrophium*, a *brephotrophium*. For holy fathers and religious princes have founded places of this kind, where the poor, the pilgrims, old men, orphans, infants, men past work, the halt, the weak, and the wounded should be received and attended. And note that *geronta* in Greek is the same as *senex* in Latin.

But of places appropriated to prayer, there be that are *sacred*, there be that are *holy*, and there be that are *religious*.

2. *Sacred* be they which by the hands of the bishop have duly been sanctified and set apart to the Lord, and which be called by various names, as hath been said in the section on Churches. *Holy* be they which have

immunity or privilege: and be set apart for the servitors or ministers of the Church, concerning which, under threat of condign punishment, either by the canon law or by special privilege, it is ordained that no man shall presume to violate them. Such be the courts of churches, and in some places the cloisters, within which be the houses of the canons. To which when criminals of whatever kind betake themselves they have safety. And so according to the statutes of the civil law be the gates and theatres of cities.

3. *Religious* places be they where the entire body of a man, or at least the head is buried: because no man can have two sepulchres. But the body or any member without the head doth not make the place wherein it is buried religious. But according to the civil law the corpse of a Jew, or paynim, or unbaptised infant maketh the place of its sepulchre religious: yet by the Christian religion and the canonical doctrine the body of a Christian alone maketh it so. And note that whatever is *sacred* is *religious;* but the contrary holdeth not. But the afore-named religious place hath divers appellations: such be *cemetery, polyandrum*, or *andropolis* (which is the same thing), *sepulchrum, mausoleum* (which is also the same), *dormitorium, tumulus, monumentum, ergastulum, pyramid, sarcophagus, bustum, urna, spelunca.*

4. *Cemetery* hath its name from *cimen* which is *sweet*, and *sterion*, which is a *station:* for there the bones of the departed rest sweetly, and expect the advent of their Saviour. Or because there be therein *cimices*, that is reptiles of intolerable odour.

5. *Poliantrum*, from *pollutum antrum*, on account of the carcases of men therein buried. Or *poliantrum* signifieth a multitude of men, from *polus*, which is a *plurality*, and *andros*, which is a man; and therefore a cemetery is

so called on account of the number of men therein buried.'¹

. . . .

11. Cemeteries are said to have their beginning from Abraham, who bought a field from Hebron: in which was a double cave,² where he and Sarah were buried: there also Isaac and Jacob were buried: there also Adam and Eve.³ Therefore there was a double cave there: since they who buried therein were placed side by side, every man and his wife; or the men in the one, and their wives in the other: or because everyone there interred had a double cave, after the fashion of a chair. Whence saith Hierome, Three patriarchs are buried in the city Hebron, with their three wives. But they were buried as it were in a sitting posture: the upper part of the cave held the trunk from the loins: the lower the thighs and legs.

12. But all men ought not to be buried promiscuously

---

¹ It has been thought right to give a few of the bishop's derivations, lest his translators should be accused of concealing a circumstance which may weaken, with some, his testimony on other points (though, as we have before shown, most unjustly): it has not, however, been thought necessary to follow him through all his names of a cemetery: since to do so would be a mere waste of the reader's time.

² Genesis xxiii, 9 : 'We take this word Machpelah for a proper name, as many others do: but the Talmudists generally think it to have been a double cave, as the lxx also, with the vulgar Latin, understand it. Yet they cannot agree in what sense it was so: whether they went through one cave into another, or there was one above the other.'—Bishop Patrick, s.l.

³ One might almost have thought that this is a false reading for *Leah and Rebecca*. For the common tradition was that Adam and Eve were buried in Mount Calvary: so that where the first Adam fell before death, the second Adam triumphed over death. And the bishop speaks below of *three* patriarchs, and their *three* wives buried in Machpelah: which is at variance with the text as it stands: but would agree with the proposed emendation.

Yet S. Isidore says, ' De morte Abrahæ,' fol. 295 : ' Sepultusque est in spelunca duplici; in cujus interiore parte Adam esse positum traditio Hebræorum testatur.' S. Victor upon Spelunca duplex : ' Domus quædam fuit subterranea, in qua erat solarium, et multi fuerant sepulti, in ea et diversis foveis et subter et supra ;' and in another place, ' Spelunca in qua est sepulta spiritualem designat vitam, quæ est occulta : quæ recte duplex vocatur ; propter bonam actionem et contemplationem.'

in the church: for it seemeth that that place of sepulchre profiteth not. Lucifer was thrown down from Heaven, and Adam cast out of Paradise; and what places be better than these? Also Joab was slain in the Tabernacle, and Job triumphed in the dunghill. Nay rather, it is to his hurt if a man unworthy or a sinner be buried in a church. We read in the 'Dialogues' of Blessed Gregory, book the fourth, chapter the fifty-sixth, that when a certain man of notorious wickedness[4] had been buried in the church of S. Faustinus at Brescia, in the same night Blessed Faustinus appeared to the warden of the church, saying, Speak unto the bishop that he cast out the body; otherwise he shall die in thirty days. Now the warden feared to tell the thing to the bishop: and the bishop on the thirtieth day suddenly departed out of this life. It is also written in the same book, chapter the fifty-seventh, that another wicked man was buried in a church, and that afterwards his body was found outside the church, the cerecloths remaining in their own place. And Austin says, they who are guilty of notorious sins, if they be buried in the church by their own desire, shall be judged for their presumption; for the sacredness of the place doth not free those whom the accusation of temerity condemns.

No body, therefore, ought to be buried in a church, or near an altar, where the Body and Blood of our Lord are made, except the bodies of holy fathers, who be called patrons, that is defenders, who defend the whole country with their merits, and bishops, and abbots, and worthy presbyters, and laymen of eminent sanctity. But all ought to be buried about the church, or in the court of the cloisters, or in the porch: or in the exedræ and

---

[4] A similar story has been parodied in the 'Ingoldsby Legends'; a work which for irreverence and profanity has hardly an equal. Disgraceful as it would be to any author, it is trebly so, if (as it is said) that author is a clergyman.

apses which are joined to the church, or in the cemetery. Some also say that a space of thirty feet round the church ought to be set apart for that purpose. But others say that the space enclosed by the circuit which the bishop makes around the church must suffice for this. S. Augustine saith in his book 'On the Care of the Dead,' towards the end, that to be buried near the tombs of martyrs advantageth the dead in this, that by commending him to the guardianship of the martyrs, the earnestness of our supplication for him may be increased.

13. Of old time men were buried in their own houses: but on account of the stench thereby engendered, it was decreed that they should be buried without the city, and certain places should be set apart by sanctification for that purpose. But noblemen were buried in mountains, both in the middle of them and at the foot: and also under mounds raised of their own expense.[5] But if anyone be slain in besieging a town, where there is no cemetery, let him be buried where he can. But if a merchantman or pilgrim die by sea, and any inhabited land be near, let him be buried in it: but if no port be near, let him be buried in some island. If, however, land cannot be seen, let a little house of timbers (if they can be had) be made for him, and let him be cast into the sea.

14. In a Christian cemetery none may be buried but a baptised Christian: nor yet every such an one neither: one, namely, slain in the act of sin, if it be mortal sin, as if he were slain in adultery, or theft, or some forbidden amusement. And also where a man is found dead, there let him be buried, on account of the doubtful cause of his death. But if anyone dieth suddenly in games accustomably used, as the game of ball, he may be buried

---

[5] *Sub propriis podiis.* For some account of the curious word *podium*, whence *pew* or *pue* is derived, see the Cambridge Camden Society's 'History of Pews' (or the 'Supplement,' pp. 6, 7).

in the cemetery, because it was not his desire to injure anyone: but because he was occupied in worldly matters, some say that he ought to be buried without psalms and the other obsequies of the dead. But if anyone attacking another in a strife or tumult dieth impenitent, and hath not sought the priest, he ought not, as some say, to be buried in the cemetery: nor yet he who hath committed suicide. But if anyone dieth, not from any manifest cause, but from the visitation of God alone, he can be buried in a cemetery. For the just man, in what hour soever he dieth, is saved. The rather if he were following some lawful occupation. To defenders of justice and those who are engaged in a pious fight, the cemetery and the office of burial are freely conceded: yet they who come to a violent death are not borne into the church, lest the pavement be polluted with blood. But if anyone returning from any place of fornication be slain in the way, or be slain anywhere, where by unforeseen case, he hath tarried, he is not to be buried in the common cemetery; and this if it can be proved, by evidence sufficient for a court of law, that he had not confessed after the act of fornication nor was contrite: otherwise he ought to be buried.

15. Again, a woman who dieth in child-birth ought not to be carried into the church, as some say, but her obsequies must be said without the church, to which I agree not: otherwise it would be as if she died in fault. Whence she may allowably be borne into the church.

16. But stillborn and unbaptised children are to be buried without the cemetery. Some say, however, that they should be buried with the mother as being a part of her body.

17. A man and wife are to be buried in the same sepulchre, after the example of Abraham and Sarah (unless a wish be specially expressed to the contrary).

Whence also Tobias commanded his son, that when his mother had accomplished her days, he should bury her in the same grave with himself.[6] Also everyone is to be buried in the sepulchre of his fathers, unless from a principle of devotion he hath chosen another sepulchre. But it was decreed in the Moguntine Council, that they who have paid the extreme penalty for their crimes, if they have confessed, or have desired to confess and have communicated, may be buried in the cemetery, and the Mass and oblations may be offered for them. How the human body is to be buried, shall be said under the section of the Office for the Dead.

[6] Tobit xiv, 10

CHAPTER VI

OF THE DEDICATION OF A CHURCH

Rise of the Dedication of Churches—By whom Performed—Particulars of Consecration—The Twelve Crosses—Banners—Dedication—Re-consecration Considered—Reconciliation—In what Cases—Of Scandals—Reconciliation of Cemeteries.

1. TWICE in the former part of this treatise we have described the material church and the altar; it followeth that we must add something about their dedication: stating,

> I. Whence the consecration of churches hath its origin.
> II. At whose hands a church is consecrated.
> III. For what reason.
> IV. In what form; and what is signified, as well by the dedication itself, as by each of the ceremonies observed therein.
> Of the offices for the festival of the dedication of a church we shall speak in the seventh book.[1]

2. We have first to state whence the dedication of churches hath had its rise. Upon which, note that under the teaching of the Lord, Moses made the tabernacle, and consecrated it together with its table of show-bread, and altar, and brazen vessels, and utensils for performing

[1] Appendix H.

Of the Dedication of a Church

the divine worship. And these he not only consecrated with prayers to God, but also anointed, at the command of the Lord, with sacred oil. For[2] we read that the Lord taught Moses to prepare a chrism, with which to anoint the tabernacle and the ark of the testimony at the time of their dedication. Solomon also the son of David, at the command of the Lord, completed the temple and its altar, and consecrated what was still necessary for the performance of the divine worship; as it is written in the third book of Kings.[3] Nebuchadnezzar the king also summoned all his satraps, chief men, and governors to the dedication of the golden image which he had made.[4] The Jews therefore, as we read in Burchardus,[5] used to have the places in which they sacrificed to the Lord consecrated by divine petitions, nor used they to offer gifts to God in any places but such as were dedicated unto Him. If then they who were in bondage to the shadow of the Law used to do this, how much the more ought we, to whom the truth hath been made manifest—'grace and truth came by Jesus Christ'[6]—to build temples to the Lord, and adorn them as best we may, and devoutly and solemnly consecrate (according to the institution of Pope Felix III)[7] by divine prayers and holy unctions both them and their altars and vessels, and vestments also, and other utensils for fulfilling the divine service?

Again, when once in Syria, in the city of Baruth, the Jews had trampled underfoot an image of the Crucified,

---

[2] Exodus xxx, 23-34.   [3] 1 Kings iii, 6.   [4] Daniel iii, 2.
[5] Book iii, ch. 1.   [6] S. John i, 17.
[7] 'The solemnities of the consecration of churches and of priests ought to be celebrated year by year, after the example of our Lord Himself, Who at the feast of the Dedication of the Temple did set us a pattern of this in that He celebrated this festival with the rest of the people; as it is written in S. John, "And it was at Jerusalem the feast of the Dedication, and it was winter, and Jesus walked in the Temple in Solomon's porch." Felix Papa in 'Epist. ad Episc. per divers. provincias,' cap. i.

and had pierced its side, there soon came forth therefrom blood and water. But the Jews marvelled at this spectacle, and their sick when anointed with this blood were freed from all their infirmities: by reason of which all, having received the faith of Christ, were baptised, and proceeded to consecrate their synagogues into churches. And hence hath grown the custom that churches should be consecrated, whereas before this altars alone used to be consecrated. On account of this miracle also the Church ordained that a memorial of the Lord's Passion should be made on the fifth day before the Calends of December: and for the same reason the church was consecrated to the honour of the Saviour, in which a vessel containing some of the blood is preserved, and a solemn festival is celebrated on that day.[8]

3. Secondly, it is to be noted that a bishop alone can dedicate churches and altars: since he beareth the image and figure of the Chief Bishop, Christ, dedicating spiritually, without Whom we can do nothing stable in the Church: whence He hath Himself said, 'Without Me ye can do nothing';[9] and the Psalm saith, 'Unless the Lord build the house their labour is but lost that build it:[10] hence the Council of Carthage prohibiteth a priest from doing this, nor can this office be deputed to anyone of an inferior order.

4. Further, as the Sacred Canons instruct us, a church must not be dedicated, unless it be first endowed, and that from goods lawfully acquired. For we read how when a certain bishop was consecrating a church built out of the fruits of usury and pillage, he saw behind the altar the devil in a pontifical vestment, standing in the bishop's throne: who said unto the bishop, Cease from

---

[8] The editors have not been able to find any other account of this legend.
[9] S. John xvii, 5.   [10] Psalm cxxvii (*Nisi Dominus*), 1.

consecrating the church: for it pertaineth to my jurisdiction, since it is built from the fruits of usuries and robberies. Then the bishop and the clergy having fled thence in fear, immediately the devil destroyed that church, with a great noise.

5. Again, a church which hath been erected from the profit of avarice must not be consecrated; nor one for which a sufficient endowment hath not been assigned; nor one in which a paynim or an infidel hath been buried, until he shall have been cast forth thence, and the church reconciled, the walls and timbers having been first scraped. The case is the same also with respect to an excommunicate person. But if a woman with child be buried there, though she be not removed, the church may be consecrated, even if the child hath not been baptised.

Although certain learned authors have written otherwise the church may also be consecrated on ordinary days as well as on Sundays: and more bishops than one and more altars than one may be consecrated at the same time by the same person in one church.

6. Thirdly, we have to say for what reason a church is dedicated: and indeed there be five reasons. First, that the devil and his power may be entirely expelled from it. Gregory relateth in a dialogue, in his third book, that when a certain church of the Arians having been restored to the Orthodox was being consecrated, and relics of S. Sebastian and the Blessed Agatha had been conveyed thither, the people there assembled of a sudden perceived a swine to be running to and fro among their feet; the which regaining the doors of the church could be seen of none, and moved all to marvel. Which sign the Lord showed for this cause, that it might be manifest to all that the unclean inhabitant had gone forth from

that place. But in the following night a great noise was made on the roof of the same church, as if someone were running confusedly about upon it. The second night the uproar was much greater. On the third night also so vast a noise was heard as if the whole church had been overthrown from its foundations: but it immediately ceased and no further inquietude of the old enemy hath appeared in it. Secondly, that those who fly for refuge to it may be saved, as we read in the Canons of Gregory. And with this view Joab fled into the tabernacle and laid hold of the horns of the altar. Thirdly, that prayers may be heard there. Whence in the prayer of the Mass of Dedication it is said, 'Grant that all who shall meet together here to pray may obtain, whatsoever be their trials, the benefits of the consolation.' Thus also Solomon prayed at the dedication of the Temple, as we read in the eighth chapter of the third book of Kings.[11] Fourthly, that praises may there be offered to God, as has been already mentioned under the head of the Church. Fifthly, that there the sacraments of the Church may be administered. From which the church itself is called a tabernacle, as it were the hostelrie of God, in which the divine sacraments be contained and adminstered.[12]

7. Fourthly, we have to speak of the manner in which a church is consecrated. All being excluded from the church, a single deacon remaining shut up within, the bishop with his clergy before the doors of the church proceedeth to bless water mixed with salt. In the meanwhile within the building twelve lamps be burning before twelve crosses which be depicted on the walls of the church. Next, the bishop, the clergy and people following him and performing the circuit of the church, sprinkleth from a rod of hyssop the external walls with

---

[11] 1 Kings viii, 30. [12] See chapter i, 4.

holy water; and as he arriveth each time at the door of the church he striketh the threshold with his pastoral staff, saying, 'Lift up your heads, O ye gates,' etc. The deacon from within answereth, 'Who is the King of Glory?' To whom the Pontiff, 'The Lord of Hosts,' etc. But the third time, the door being thrown open, the bishop entereth the church with a few of his attendants, the clergy and people remaining without, and saith, 'Peace be to this house'; and then the Litanies. Next on the pavement of the church, let a cross be made of ashes and sand; upon which the whole alphabet is described in Greek and Latin characters.[13] And then he sanctifieth more water with salt and ashes and wine, and consecrateth the altar. Lastly, he anointeth with chrism the twelve crosses depicted on the wall.

8. In good truth whatsoever things be here done visibly, God by His invisible power worketh the same in the soul which is the temple of the true God: in which Faith layeth the foundation, Hope buildeth up, and Charity perfecteth. For the Catholic Church herself, made one out of many living stones, is the Temple of God, because many temples make one temple, of which the true God is one, and the Faith one. The house, therefore, must be dedicated; the soul sanctified.

9. And it is to be observed that consecration effecteth two things; for it appropriateth the material church itself to God, and doth insinuate our own betrothal, as well namely of the church as of the faithful soul. For a house not consecrated is as a damsel designed for some man, but not furnished with dowry or united in the commerce of wedlock. But in consecration it is endowed, and passeth into the proper spouse of Jesus Christ, which further to violate is sacrilege. For it ceaseth to be the resort of demons, as is evident in the

[13] See the Appendix on the 'Dedication of a Church.'

consecration of that temple, which used formerly to be called the Pantheon, or place of all demons.[14]

10. First, however, we have to speak of the benediction of water, concerning which the Lord saith, 'Unless a man be born again of water and of the Spirit, he cannot enter the Kingdom of Heaven.'[15] For water which is designed for washing the body, hath merited to receive from God so great a virtue, that as it washeth the body from impurities, so also it should cleanse the soul from sins. It is manifest indeed that this water, by the aspersion of which a church is consecrated, signifieth baptism, because in some sort the church itself is baptised; and the church itself assuredly denoteth that Church which is contained in it, namely, the multitude of the faithful. Whence also it is called a church because it contains the Church; the thing containing, namely, for the thing contained.

11. But we must inquire wherefore salt is to be mixed with this water, since our Saviour, speaking of baptism, made no mention of salt. For He saith not 'unless a man be born again of salt water or water mixed with salt,' or anything of this sort: but He said 'unless a man be born again of water and of the Holy Spirit,' etc. And the very same inquiry may be made concerning oil and chrism. But we must note that salt in the divine language is often put for wisdom; according to that saying, 'Let your speech be savoured with salt.' And the Lord saith to His disciples, 'Have salt in yourselves and have peace one with another.'[16] And again, 'Ye are the salt of the earth; but if the salt have lost its savour wherewithal shall it be salted?'[17] Hence also it is that

---

[14] 'Pope Boniface the Fourth did consecrate to the most Blessed Virgin and All Saints the famous monument of Agrippa, the *Pantheon*, having purified it from the base herd of vain gods.' Ciampini IV, vi, 55. This is now called Santa Maria Rotonda. Doard.

[15] S. John iii, 5.   [16] S. Mark ix, 50.   [17] S. Mark v, 13.

according to the law no victim was offered without salt, but salt was a part of every sacrifice. From all which passages it is clearly shown that salt is put for wisdom. And wisdom indeed is the seasoning of all virtues, as salt is of all meats. Hence therefore it is that no one is baptised before he hath tasted salt; and in order that even infants may have by the symbolical meaning of the sacrament that which they cannot have in fact, the water is not blessed without a mixture of salt. Of the second benediction of water we shall speak in the following treatise.

12. Again, the trine aspersion within and without with hyssop and holy water signifieth the threefold immersion in baptism. And it is done for three reasons. First, to drive away evil spirits. For holy water availeth from its own proper virtue to drive away demons. Whence in the Office for Exorcising the Water we say—'that this water may become exorcised in order to put to flight all the power of the enemy, and may avail to eradicate the enemy himself,' etc. Secondly, for the cleansing and expiation of the church itself. For all earthly things be corrupted and defiled by reason of sin. Hence it is also that in the Law almost everything was cleansed by water. Thirdly, to remove all malediction, and to bring in a blessing instead. For the earth from the beginning received the curse with all its fruits, because that the great deceit was made out of its fruit. But water hath not been under any curse. Hence it is that our Lord ate fish, but we do not read expressly that he ate flesh, unless of the Paschal Lamb; and this on account of the precept of the Law, as an example, namely, sometimes to abstain from lawful things, sometimes to eat the same. Again, the aspersion in going the circuit signifieth that the Lord having a care of His own, sendeth His angel round about them that fear Him.

13. But the three responses which be chanted in the meantime testify the joy of the three ages of men receiving the faith, namely, Noah, Daniel, and Job. And since at this invocation the grace of Faith, Hope, and Charity, is poured out as the sprinkling is directed to the foot and middle part, as well as to the upper part of the walls. We will now also speak of the interior aspersion. (Of the virtue of the hyssop, we will speak under the next head.)

14. But the trine circuit, which the bishop maketh while sprinkling, denoteth the thrice-repeated circuit which Christ made for the sanctification of the Church. The first was that by which He came down from heaven to the world: the second in which He descended into hell from the world: the third in which returning from hell and rising again He ascended into heaven. The trine circuit also showeth that that church is dedicated to the honour of the Trinity. It showeth also the three states of such as shall be saved in the Church, which be the virgins, the continent, the married: which also the arrangement of the material church itself showeth, as hath been said under the head of the Church.

15. Moreover, the trine striking on the lintel of the door signifieth the threefold right which Christ hath in His Church why it ought to be opened unto Him. For it hath from Him Creation, Redemption, and promise of Glorification. For the bishop representeth Christ, and the rod His power. Again, by the triple striking of the door with the pastoral staff, the preaching of the Gospel is understood. For what else is the pastoral rod than the divine Word? According to that of Esaias, 'He shall smite the earth with the rod,' *i.e.* the word, 'of His mouth,' etc.[18] Wherefore to strike the door with the rod is to strike the ears of the hearers by the word of

[18] Isaiah xi, 4.

preaching. For the ears are the gates by which we bring in the words of holy preachings to the hearts of the hearers. Whence in the Psalm, 'Who liftest me up from the gates of death that I may show all Thy praises within the ports of the daughter of Sion.'[19] For what are the gates of the daughter of Sion but the ears and hearing of the faithful? Thirdly, the trine striking with the staff, and the opening of the gates, signifieth that by the preaching of the pastors the unbelieving shall come to the agreement of the Faith. For by it the gates of justice be opened, and they that enter therein do confess the faith. Whence the Psalm, 'Open unto me the gates of righteousness: I will go into them and I will praise the Lord: this is the gate of the Lord, the righteous shall enter into it.'[20] Wherefore the bishop striketh the lintel, namely, of reason, saying, 'Lift up your heads, ye princes,' that is, ye evil spirits: or rather, 'Lift up, ye men,' that is, remove the gates, that is, your ignorances, namely, from your hearts.[21]

16. Again, the question of the deacon shut up within answering in the character of the people, 'Who is the King of glory?' is the ignorance of the people which knoweth not Who He is Who ought to enter.

17. The opening of the doors is the ejection of sin. Rightly, therefore, doth the bishop strike three times, because that number is most known and most sacred; and in any consecration the bishop ought to smite the doors three times, because without the invocation of the Trinity, there can be no sacrament in the Church.

18. The threefold proclamation, 'Lift up your heads,' etc., signifieth the threefold power of Christ, that, namely, which He hath in heaven, and in the earth, and in hell. Whence it is said in the hymn for the Ascension, 'That

---

[19] Ps. ix (*Confitebor tibi*), 13, 14.   [20] Ps. cxviii (*Confitemini Domino*), 19, 20.
[21] Ps. xxiv (*Domini est terra*), 'Attollite portas principes vestras.'

the threefold frame of things, whether heavenly, earthly, or infernal, may bow the head, having been subdued.[22]

19. Next the bishop entereth by the open door to denote that if he duly exercise his office, nothing can resist him; according to that saying, 'Lord, who shall resist Thy power?' And he entereth, accompanied by two or three, that in the mouth of two or three witnesses every word of the consecration may stand sure. Or else because the Lord in His Transfiguration, in the presence of a few, prayed for the Church. And the bishop as he entereth saith, 'Peace be to this house and to all them that dwell therein'; because Christ entering the world made peace between God and man; for He came that He might reconcile us to God the Father.

20. After this while the Litany is being said the bishop prostrateth himself and prayeth for the sanctification of the house. For Christ also humbling Himself before His Passion prayed for His disciples and 'them that should believe through His word,' saying, 'Father, sanctify them in Thy name.'[23] But after he hath risen up he prayeth without benediction, since he saith not 'The Lord be with you'; because the Church is not yet as it were baptised, and because Catechumens only are not worthy that this mark of approval should be given to them, since they are not yet sanctified: but nevertheless prayer is to be made for them.

21. The clergy praying and chanting the Litany representeth the Apostles who intercede with God for the sanctification of the Church and of souls.

The alphabet is written on the pavement of the church in this manner. A cross made with ashes and sand is described athwart the church, upon which cross of dust

---

[22] This hymn, by S. Gregory, is used in the office of matins in the Roman Breviary.

[23] S. John xvii.

the alphabet is written in the shape of a cross in letters of Greek and Latin, but not of Hebrew, because the Jews have departed from the faith; and it is written with the pastoral staff.

22. This alphabet written upon the cross representeth three things. First, the writing made in Greek and Latin characters in the shape of a cross representeth the conjunction or union in faith of both people, namely, the Jews and the Greeks, which is made through the Cross of Christ: according to the saying that Jacob blessed his sons with his hands crossed. But the cross itself or the legend that is described in a direction athwart the church, namely, the one arm from the left corner of the east to the right of the west, and the other from the right of the east to the left of the west,[24] signifieth that that people, which was before on the right is now made on the left, and that which was first is now made last, and the converse: and this owing to the power of the Cross. For Christ passing from the east, left the Jews on His left hand, because they were unbelieving, and came to the Gentiles, to whom, though they had been in the west, He grants to be on the right hand: and at length returning from the Gentiles, who are situated at the right hand of the east, He visited the Jews in the left corner of the west; who it is evident are worse than He before found the Gentiles. But on this account the characters are written obliquely and in the shape of a cross, and not in a straight line, because such an one as doth not receive the mystery of the Cross and doth not believe that he must be saved by the Passion of Christ, is not able to attain to this holy wisdom. Wisdom will not enter into the evil-disposed mind, and where

---

[21] We understand this to mean that the cross described in the church is a saltire, or S. Andrew's Cross, and not a plain one. Upon this again consult the Appendix.

Christ is not the foundation, no edifice can be built upon it.

23. Secondly, the writing of the alphabet representeth the page of both Testaments, because they be fulfilled by the Cross of Christ. For the veil of the temple was rent asunder at His Passion, because then the Scriptures were opened, and the Holy of Holies revealed. Whence He Himself said when dying, 'IT IS FINISHED.' In these few letters also all knowledge is contained; and the alphabet is written crosswise, because one Testament is contained in the other. For there was a wheel within a wheel.

24. Thirdly, it representeth the articles of faith; for the pavement of the church is the foundation of our faith. The elements written thereon, are the articles of faith, in which ignorant men and neophytes from both peoples be instructed in the Church; who indeed ought to esteem themselves dust and ashes. Just as Abraham saith in the xviii chapter of Genesis, 'Shall I speak to my Lord, who am but dust and ashes?' Wherefore the writing of the alphabet on the pavement is the simple teaching of faith in the human heart.

25. The *sambuca* or staff, with which the alphabet is written, showeth the doctrine of the apostles, or the mystery of the teachers, by which the conversion of the Gentiles hath been effected, and the perfidy of the Jews. Afterwards approaching the altar the bishop standeth, and beginneth by saying, 'O God, make speed to save us;' because he is then beginning the principal part of office. And the versicle, 'Glory be to the Father,' etc., is then said.

26. Because this benediction is used to set forth the glory of the Trinity, Alleluia is not then uttered, as will be set forth in the next chapter. Then the bishop consecrateth the altar, for which he blesseth other water, as

shall also be declared in the next chapter. With which water also, after that the altar hath been sprinkled seven times, the whole interior of the church is sprinkled three times, as at first without any distinction between greater and smaller stones, since 'there is no respect of persons with God.' For this reason is the interior sprinkled, to signify that an external ablution profiteth nothing without an internal charity. And for this reason *three* times, because, as hath been premised, that aspersion signifieth the aspersion and cleansing of baptism, which is conferred through the invocation of the Trinity, according to the saying, 'Go ye and teach all nations, baptising them in the name of the Father, and of the Son, and of the Holy Ghost:'[25] for since a church cannot be immersed in water as a man in baptism is immersed, it is on this account sprinkled three times with water, as if in the place of a threefold immersion.

27. Again, the bishop performeth the aspersion proceeding from the east to the west and once through the middle in the form of the cross; because Christ gave instructions to baptise the whole of Judea and all nations in the name of the Trinity, to which baptism He gave efficacy in the ministry of His Passion, beginning from the Jews, from whom He had His birth. And what remains of the water is poured away at the foot of the altar, as shall be mentioned in the next chapter. Some, however, do not bless any fresh water, but perform the whole office with that which was blessed at first. In the meanwhile, however, the choir is chanting the Psalm *Exsurgat Deus* ('let God arise and let His enemies be scattered,' etc.), and the *Qui habitat* ('whoso dwelleth,' etc.), in which mention is made of the church and its consecration, as is plain in that verse, 'He is the God

---

[25] S. Matt. xxviii, 19.

that maketh men to be of one mind in an house.'[26] But the bishop saith, 'My house shall be called an house of prayer,' because it is his duty to cause that the church should be a house of God, not of merchandise.

28. Next, when the altar hath been anointed with chrism, the twelve crosses painted on the walls of the church are also anointed. But the crosses themselves be painted; first, as a terror to evil spirits, that they, having been driven forth thence, may be terrified when they see the sign of the cross, and may not presume to enter therein again; secondly, as a mark of triumph. For crosses be the banners of Christ, and the signs of his triumph.[27] Crosses therefore are with reason painted there that it may be made manifest that that place hath been subdued to the dominion of Christ.

29. For even in the pomp of an earthly sovereign it is customary when any city hath been yielded, for the imperial standard to be set up within it. And to represent the same thing, Jacob is said to have set up the stone, which he had placed under his head, as a historical, traditional, and triumphal monument.[28]

30. Thirdly, that such as look on them may call to mind the Passion of Christ, by which he hath consecrated His Church, and their belief in His Passion. Whence it is said in the Canticles, 'place me as a signet upon thy arm,' etc.[29] The twelve lights placed before these crosses signify the twelve Apostles who have illumined the whole world by the faith of the Crucified, and whose teaching hath dispersed the darkness: whence Bernard saith, 'All prophecy is verified in the faith of the crucified One;' and the Apostle, 'I determined not to know anything among you except Jesus Christ and Him cruci-

[26] Psalm lxviii (*Exsurgat Deus*), v, 5.
[27] Compare the hymn, *Vexilla Regis prodeunt*.   [28] Genesis xxviii.
[29] Cant. viii, 6.

fied.'[30] Wherefore the crosses on the four walls of the church are lighted up and anointed with chrism, because the apostles preaching the mystery of the cross have by the faith of Christ illumined the four quarters of the earth unto knowledge, have lighted them up unto love, have anointed them unto purity of conscience—which is signified by the oil; and unto the savour of a good reputation—which is signified by the balsam. In addition to this, after the anointing of the altar, the altar itself and the church are ornamented; the lamps lighted up; a Mass is said, in which the priest useth different vestments from those which he hath used in the aspersion, as shall be explained in the sequel.

31. Lastly, it is to be noted that a church is said to be consecrated in the blood of someone; whence, according to Pelagius and Pope Nicholas, the Roman Church was consecrated in the martyrdom of the Apostles, Peter and Paul.[31] A church therefore is consecrated in the way just described; and an altar, as will be set forth in the next chapter; and a cemetery and other things, as is declared under the head of its consecration. And although we read in the Old Testament that the Temple was consecrated three times: first, in the month of September; secondly, in March under Darius; thirdly, in December by Judas Maccabæus.

32. Yet a church once consecrated, is not to be consecrated again unless it shall have been profaned, which happeneth in three ways. First, if it hath been burnt so as that all the walls or the greater part of them be destroyed. But if only the roof or some part of it hath been burnt, the walls remaining entire, or at least only

---

[30] 1 Cor. ii, 2.
[31] This passage is obscure. A confession or martyrium was built over the place of S. Peter's martyrdom in the earliest times, and is now covered by the Vatican. See Ciampini de Vaticana Basilica. The expression probably means, in honour of the martyrdom.

partially destroyed, it need not be reconsecrated. Secondly, if the whole church or the greater part of it hath fallen to the ground at the same time, and hath been repaired entirely or not with the original stones. For the consecration of a church consisteth mainly in the exterior anointings, and in the conjunction and arrangement of the stones. If, however, all the walls shall have fallen in, not at the same time, but in succession, and shall have been repaired, the church is to be considered the same. And so it need not be reconsecrated, but only exorcised with water and reconciled by the solemnisation of a Mass: however, some learned authors have said that it ought to be reconsecrated. Thirdly, a church must be reconsecrated, if it be doubtful whether it ever hath been consecrated, should there remain no writing or painting or inscription to that effect, nor even a single eye-witness, nor yet an ear-witness, who (as some say) would be sufficient.

33. An altar also which hath been once consecrated must not be consecrated again unless it should happen that it become profaned. Which taketh place first if the table, that is the upper surface on which the principal part of the consecration is bestowed, be moved or changed in its form, or broken beyond measure, for instance above a half. However, a disproportion of this sort may rightly be referred to the decision of the bishop. The same also is especially the case, if the whole structure of the altar hath been moved and repaired. Nevertheless, the church is not to be reconsecrated on account of either the movement or the breaking of the structure of the altar: because the consecration of an altar and of a church be two different things. So conversely if when the church is entirely destroyed the altar be not injured, the church only is to be repaired, and the altar not reconsecrated:

although in such case it is fitting that it be washed with exorcised water.

34. Further, when the chief altar hath been consecrated the inferior altars are not the less to be consecrated : although some have said that it is sufficient for the rest to be pointed out with the finger while the former is under consecration.

35. If, however, the altar hath suffered a trifling injury, it is not on this account to be reconsecrated.

Secondly, an altar is reconsecrated, if the *seal* of the altar—that is the little stone by which the sepulchre or cavity in which the relics be deposited is closed or sealed—be moved or broken. And the cavity itself is made sometimes on the top part of the block, and sometimes no other seal is put over it, but the *table*, being placed over it, is considered as the seal. But sometimes it is placed in the hinder part, and sometimes in the front: and in the same cavity the bishop's letters of consecration be generally carefully deposited in testimony of the consecration : containing his own name and that of the other bishops present at the consecration : and declaring in honour of what saint the altar is consecrated, and also the church itself, when both be consecrated at the same time, and the year also and day of consecration.

Thirdly, an altar is reconsecrated, if the junction of the seal to the cavity, or of the *table* to the block, where there is no other seal than this slab, be disturbed ; or if any of the stones of the junction or the block, which toucheth either the table or the seal, be either disturbed or broken. For in the conjunction of the seal and cavity, and of the table and block or inferior structure, the consecration is most especially perceived.

Fourthly, an altar is reconsecrated, if to it or to the conjunction of the table with the under structure so great an enlargement be made as that it loseth its original form, since the form giveth the existence to the thing. Yet it doth not become profaned on account of a trifling enlargement: but in that case the sacred part draweth over to itself the part not sanctified: so long as the conjunction of the top slab and under structure be not greatly changed.

Fifthly, an altar, just as a church, is reconsecrated in cases of doubt.

Sixthly, a travelling altar, if the stone be removed from the wood in which it is inserted, which in some sort representeth its *seal*, and be replaced again in the same or in other wood, some think should be reconsecrated, but others only reconciled. But although it be often by the command of the bishop transferred from place to place, and carried on a journey (on which account it is called a portable or a travelling altar) yet it is not reconsecrated in consequence of this, nor yet reconciled.

36. But if a consecrated chalice be regilt, is it therefore to be reconsecrated? It seemeth so, since it appeareth to become a new chalice. For he who doth renew the old fashion of a work seemeth to make a new work: and he doth remake, who doth mend a thing already made. And assuredly consecration doth pertain to the outer surface. And hence it is that I have said above that a church, if its walls be stripped of their outer coat, must be reconsecrated.

37. The converse is nevertheless true, that neither on account of whitewashing or painting the walls, nor of any small addition to them, is a church to be reconsecrated; as I have already said. Wherefore, if the shape of the chalice be not changed, it remaineth the same chalice, and is not to be reconsecrated; just as also a church being repaired, since it remaineth the same church, is not to be reconsecrated, as aforesaid. But if

the former shape be changed, the case were otherwise, since, as I have said, the shape giveth existence to the thing. Nevertheless, it is decent, as well by reason of its contact with unclean hands as also of the increment of unconsecrated matter, that a chalice, being regilded, should be washed with exorcised water before that the most Holy Body and Blood of the Lord be sacrificed therein. Let us now say something about Reconciliation.

38. Upon this head it is to be noted that the spiritual temple, which is man, is ofttimes polluted. Whence we do read in the twentieth of Leviticus what men be polluted, and how they may not enter the church until they be washed with water and cleansed : as also in the nineteenth of Numbers, ' He that toucheth the dead body of a man shall be unclean .... wherefore he shall purify himself and wash his clothes and bathe himself in water and shall be clean.' And the Prophet saith, ' Thou shalt purge me with hyssop and I shall be clean.'[32]

39. The material temple also, which as Pope Gregory doth testify, is the church, is sometimes polluted, as we do read in Leviticus.[33] Whence saith the Prophet, ' Thy holy temple have they defiled and made Jerusalem an heap of stones.'[34] And the material temple is also washed with water in order to be reconciled.[35] Reconciliation is also effected by the celebration of a Mass, and the aspersion of water duly consecrated with salt, wine, and ashes. For by the salt, is signified discretion; by the water, the people ; by the wine, the Divinity ; by the ashes, the remembrance of the Passion of Christ ; by the wine mixed with water, the union of Godhead and Manhood. These things, therefore, be put together to denote

[32] Psalm li (*Miserere mei*), 7.   [33] Levit. xv, 31.
[34] Psalm lxxix (*Deus, venerunt*), 1.
[35] Some of our readers may not know that *reconciliation* is the technical term for the restoring a desecrated church to a state fit for the performance of the divine offices.

that the people, being cleansed by a discerning remembrance of the Passion of Christ, are made one with Him. Also if the church hath once been consecrated, the reconciliation can be made by a bishop only. And albeit he might devolve upon a fellow-bishop the whole office, namely, both the blessing of the water and the reconciliation; or the benediction of the water only; or even the reconciliation alone with water blessed beforehand by himself; yet can neither be devolved upon a mere priest, unless perchance this be competent to him by a special privilege. But if the church hath not been consecrated, it ought, according to the Constitution of Gregory, to be washed forthwith with exorcised water: the which washing some do affirm may be done by a mere priest, though at the bidding of the bishop: since it hath to be done by exorcised water, which every priest may use. Yet some skilful men of the highest authority have written that it is safer for this also to be done by none but a bishop, and that this may not be devolved by him to a priest; for certain canons do call exorcised water that which is solemnly blessed with wine and ashes :—and this is true indeed in regard of a church which although not consecrated hath been dedicated unto God. For it is otherwise with a mere oratory, which is neither a holy nor a religious place, inasmuch as any man doth order it at his will—at least for prayers, albeit perchance not for celebration without the license of the diocesan—and at his will assigneth the same place to another use.

40. A church then is to be reconsecrated in the aforesaid case: and also if any uncleanness be committed therein, whether by clerk, layman, heretic, or paynim. But albeit some wise men have thought otherwise, we opine that the case is different in regard of unintentional pollution.[36]

---

[36] The editors have ventured to make a few omissions in this and some of the following sections.

41. A church also must be reconciled on account of any homicide, in any way intentionally committed therein, whether with or without the shedding of blood: and also, besides homicide, for any violence or injurious shedding of human blood, whether from a wound or not, or from the nose or the mouth. For we read in the Old Testament, in the fourteenth and fifteenth of Leviticus, how that any man shedding blood, or polluted in divers ways, may not enter the temple. If, however, without violence or injury blood should flow in any natural way whatsoever within the church; or if any animal should be slain therein, or if anyone should die suddenly, or be killed by a falling stone or timber, or by lightning; for these and the like occasions the church is not reconciled. Nor again, if anyone, having been wounded elsewhere, should flee to a church and die there even with great effusion of blood: since then the homicide is not committed in the church. But conversely, if anyone having been wounded in a church dieth without, or even if blood flow from the wound away from the church, the case is otherwise, even if the blood did not flow at all within the church: since the law regardeth the blow which causeth the wound. But and if blood be shed or other pollutions be caused on the roof of a church, no reconciliation is made, because the deed is committed without the church.

42. But if theft and rapine be committed in a church, it is reconciled by the custom which usually obtaineth in such matters. And some do affirm that the same ought to be done in any case of violence committed therein without the shedding of blood; for example, if anyone having taken refuge therein should be drawn forth with violence. Also if anyone should break into the church or any quarrel should be tumultuously carried on, though without shedding of blood: or if anyone should be grievously beaten therein, so as his bones should be

broken, or he be covered with weals and bruises, though without blood; or again, if anyone, being condemned while present in a church either to death or mutilation, be led forth to go to the place of execution. But since these cases be not expressed in the law, it is not necessary for the church to be solemnly reconciled by the bishop. Yet we think it is decent for it to be washed by the priest with exorcised water at the command of the bishop: and the same is to be said, if the church being a long time without roof or doors, should have been open to all impurities, to animals and the natural use of men, as if a common inn: nor perchance would it be amiss for it in such case to be solemnly reconciled by the bishop. Again, if anyone, slain without the church, be shortly borne into the church, and there the murderer or anyone else thinking he will not die should inflict on his yet warm body a blow causing blood to flow, then the church must be reconciled, as well by reason of the horror and abomination, as of the violence and intention of sinning: for though a dead man be not a man, yet is his human blood shed there by violence; and to the corpse itself is violence, horror, and injury offered. But the case is otherwise if anyone, having died a natural death, be, through respect of, and honour to his body, dismembered in the church or disembowelled, that perhaps one part may be buried in one place, and another in another.

43. A church must also be reconciled, in which an infidel, or one publicly excommunicated be buried; and then the walls are to be scraped.

In the aforesaid cases, however, in which a church is to be reconciled, it is requisite that the fact causing the reconciliation should be known at least by report.

44. For this is a scandal to the church, the horror and abomination of baseness and sin and violence committed in a sacred place, or in a church: wherein the pardon for

offences is besought, wherein there ought to be a refuge of defence, wherein is offered the saving sacrifice for sins, wherein also those that flee for refuge be saved, and praises be rendered unto God. Furthermore, the intention and design of sinning mortally therein do cause a church to be reconciled. But if this design be hidden, reconciliation is not necessary, since the church itself, being holy, cannot be polluted; nay, the holiness of the place itself doth do away with the infamy: albeit some do think the contrary of this, as that it ought to be reconciled at least privately, so that the delinquents be not exposed.

45. For reconcillation is performed for an example and warning, that all who behold the church, which hath in no wise sinned, washed and purified for the delict of another, may reflect how they themselves must work out the expiation of their own sins.

46. Also a cemetery, in which a paynim, or an infidel or one excommunicate be buried, is to be reconciled; the bones, however, of the paynim, if they can be distinguished from those of the faithful, being interred elsewhere. A cemetery also is reconciled in the above-mentioned cases, in which a church is to be reconciled: for a cemetery enjoyeth the same privileges as doth a church, as we shall say in the chapter of Sacred Unctions; for it is a holy place from the time of its benediction; and it is reconciled by the bishop, just as a church, by the aspersion of water, blessed with wine and ashes.

47. But this is to be noted, that in whatsoever part of the church or the cemetery the violence or pollution be committed, both the church and the cemetery, and also the several parts of either, by reason of their contiguity, are understood to be violated. This first hath of late been set straight by Pope Boniface. For albeit the consecrations of the church, the altar, and the cemetery be

diverse, yet is the immunity of them one and the same and is not to be restricted to any one of them separately, nor to any individual part of either. This indeed is true if the church and cemetery be adjacent: but if the one be at a distance from the other, one may well be violated without the other. If therefore when one is violated or polluted, the other be also violated and polluted; by the like reason, if one only be reconciled the other is also taken to be reconciled: since nothing is more natural than that everything should be loosed in the same method as it is bound, and that the relation of binding and loosing should be the same. Wherefore when the cemetery is violated or polluted, it sufficeth that the church be reconciled. There be nevertheless some who do affirm simply that by the pollution of the one, the other is in no wise polluted, and by consequence that each should be reconciled separately. Yet these doth the authority of the Pontifical oppose, in which is found a special form for the reconciliation of a cemetery. Lastly, if a church or a cemetery, or any such thing, be consecrated or blessed by a bishop under excommunication, these, some affirm, do not require reconciliation, since sacraments administered by such in the form of the Church be valid. But since (as aforesaid) one or more excommunicate persons do profane a cemetery or church, much more indeed do the external sacraments and benedictions, which proceed from the hands and mouth of an excommunicate person, appear so far as pertaineth to their own merits to be contaminated and to stink before God. Wherefore it is decent that we should reconcile them before the faithful use these sacraments; as in truth the reading of the sacred canons doth evidently teach. For the Lord saith by the Prophet, 'I will curse your blessings.' [37]

[37] Malachi ii, 2.

CHAPTER VII

OF THE CONSECRATION OF AN ALTAR

Rise of the Consecration of Altars—Manner of the Same—The Benediction of Water—The Aspersions—The Hyssop—Consideration of Relics—The Altar must be of Stone—The Incense—The Benediction of Church Ornaments.

1. NOT only is a church consecrated, but also the altar: and this for three reasons. First, with regard to the sacrament thereon to be offered to God. Noah[1] built an altar to the Lord, and offered a sacrifice upon it, taking some of all clean birds and beasts. But this sacrament is the Body and Blood of Christ which is sacrificed in remembrance of the Lord's Passion, according to the command, 'This do in commemoration of Me.'[2]

2. Secondly, with regard to the invocation in that place of the name of God: whence[3] Abraham built an altar to God who appeared unto him, and called there upon the name of the Lord. But this invocation, which takes place over the altar, is properly called the *Mass*.

3. Thirdly, with regard to chanting: 'He gave him patience against his enemies, and caused singers also to stand before the altar, that by their voices they might make sweet melody.'[4]

4. The consecration of an altar is performed in this

---

[1] Genesis viii. [2] S. Luke xxii, 19. [3] Genesis xii. [4] Eccles. xlvii, 9.

method and order. The bishop beginneth, 'O God, make speed to save us.' Afterwards he blesseth the water, and then at the four horns[5] of the altar he describeth four crosses with the consecrated water. Next, he goeth round the altar seven times, and sprinkleth the *table*[6] of the altar seven times with holy water, by means of an aspersory of hyssop. The church also is again sprinkled, and the remainder of the water is poured at the foot of the altar: and then four crosses be made with chrism at the four corners of the sepulchre in which the relics are to be deposited; and the relics themselves be placed in a case, together with three grains of frankincense, and so be buried in the sepulchre. Then is placed upon the sepulchre its cover,[7] strengthened in the middle by the sign of the cross: afterwards the stone, which is called the table, is fitted to the top of the altar, and when fitted is anointed with oil in five places, and in the same way is further anointed afterwards with chrism, as hath been said when speaking about oil. The altar also is confirmed in front by the chrism applied in the form of the cross, and incense is burnt upon it in the five places. After this the altar is covered up, and is spread with clean cloths, and then at length the sacrifice is celebrated upon it. Now let us follow out each of the above-mentioned ceremonies in succession.

5. First, then, it is to be noted, that an altar is consecrated by the unction of chrism and act of blessing intervening, and that it is only and entirely of stone. The

---

[5] The word *horn* appears to be used simply for *corner*, evidently with reference to the altar of the temple, which had raised projections, or horns at its angles.

[6] We shall use the word *table* to denote the *mensa* or upper surface of the altar, on which the chief part of the ceremonies of consecration were performed.

[7] This passage is obscure, and receives no light from other ritualists who have not spoken much on the consecration of altars. From the 25 of the chapter we apprehend that this slab, or cover of the sepulchre, was marked with a cross of chrism before it was fitted on to the cavity.

bishop standing up beginneth, 'O God, make speed to save us,' because the Lord Himself saith, 'Without Me ye can do nothing.'[8]

6. And because this dedication signifieth that those must be baptised, who, after receiving the faith, are preparing themselves to fight, and who are still situated amongst the sighs and struggles of this world; on this account the Alleluia is omitted, since those who be not baptised be not worthy to join in the praises of angels: whence it is written in Tobit, 'And all her streets shall say Alleluia.'[9] But after that the consecration of the church or of the altar is completed, the Alleluia is chanted, because the delusions of devils having been expelled, God shall be praised thereupon. For Christ even when approaching to the altar of the cross in order to manifest the glory of His Eternity, paid the penalty of death: not until after His resurrection sang He Alleluia.

7. Secondly, with respect to the blessing of water, it is to be noted that this kind of exorcising water is performed in order to expel the enemy from it. In which blessing four things be necessary; namely, water, wine, salt, and ashes. And this for three reasons.

8. (i) Because there be four things which expel the enemy. The first is the outpouring of tears, which is denoted by the water: the second is the exultation of the soul, which is denoted by the wine: the third is natural discretion, which by the salt; the fourth, a profound humility, which is signified by the ashes. Wherefore the water is penitence, the wine exaltation of mind, the salt wisdom (as was shown in the preceding chapter), the ashes the humility of penitence. Whence it is said of the Ninevites that their 'king rose up from his throne, and clothed himself with sackcloth, and sat in

[8] S. John xv, 5.   [9] Tobit xiii, 18.

ashes.'[10] Hence also David saith, 'For I have eaten ashes as it were bread.'[11] Hence also Abraham saith, 'Shall I speak to my Lord, who am but dust and ashes?'[12]

9. (ii) In a second sense water is the people or mankind, because many waters are many peoples; wine is the Deity; salt, the teaching of the divine law which is the salt of the covenant; ashes, that which preserveth the remembrance of the Lord's Passion. Wine mixed with water, is Christ, God and Man. For by means of faith in the Lord's Passion (*ashes*), which is had through the teaching of the Divine Law (*salt*), the people, denoted by the water, is joined through the union of faith, to its Head, God and Man.

10. (iii) In a third method we may say also that this consecrated water signifieth the Holy Spirit, without Whose influence nothing ever is sanctified, and without Whose grace there is no remission of sins. That the Holy Spirit is called water, truth itself showeth when He saith, 'Whosoever believeth in Me, out of his belly shall flow rivers of living water':[13] which the Evangelist explaining saith, 'This He spake of the Holy Ghost which they should receive who believed upon Him.'

11. And note the order of the sacrament; the church is consecrated outwardly by water, inwardly by the Spirit. For this is what the Lord saith, 'Unless a man shall be born again of water and of the Holy Ghost,' etc.[14] Here is the water: here the Holy Spirit. For in the sacrament of baptism, neither is the water without the Spirit, nor the Spirit without the water: which element indeed the Spirit Himself did sanctify, when in the first creation of the world 'He moved upon the face

---

[10] Jonah iii, 6.
[11] Psalm cii (*Domine exaudi*), 9.
[12] Genesis xviii, 27.
[13] S. John vii, 38, 39.
[14] S. John iii, 5.

of the waters.'[15] With this water therefore, both the altar itself and the whole interior of the church is sprinkled, when both it and the altar are dedicated on the same occasion.

12. Although therefore the Spirit and water would suffice for the perfect operation of baptism and the consecration of a church, yet the holy fathers who have made this constitution, wished to satisfy us not only in those particulars which pertain to the efficacy of the sacraments, but in those also which relate to its greater sanctification: and on this account they have added salt, wine, oil, ashes, and chrism. (For Philip, when he baptised the eunuch, had neither oil nor chrism.) Therefore not one of these ingredients ought to be wanting; and they ought all to be mixed together, because the people of God, which is the Church, is neither sanctified nor released from sins without the union of these qualities. On this I shall treat also in the chapter upon consecrations. With respect to water indeed the case is evident, because 'unless a man be born again,' etc.

13. With respect to the salt also; because without the seasoning of faith, which is typified by the salt, no one shall ever be saved, albeit he be sprinkled by the water of baptism. Also with respect to wine, by means of which the spiritual intelligence of the divine law is denoted. Whence the Lord at the marriage in Cana turned the water into wine. But if anyone shall not have been sprinkled with this, that is, shall not have drunk of this or have believed those who offered it to him to drink, he shall not attain to the blessedness of eternal life. The aspersion of ashes also, by which the humility of penitence is understood, is so necessary, that without it there is no remission of sins in adults; for through it they come to baptism, and it is the sole refuge for such as have sinned

---

[15] Genesis i, 2.

after baptism. Whence not without reason is baptism called from it: the Lord speaking in the gospel concerning John Baptist 'that he came into the whole region of Galilee, preaching the baptism of repentance for the remission of sins.'[16] Note also that there be four kinds of consecrated water, of which we shall speak in the fourth book, and at the head of 'The aspersion of holy water.'[17]

14. When all these ingredients have been mixed, the bishop maketh four crosses with this water at the four horns of the altar, and one in the middle;[18] the four crosses represent the fourfold charity which they ought to have who approach the altar, viz., love for God, themselves, their friends, and their enemies. Of which four corners of charity it is said in Genesis, 'Thou shalt spread into the east, and the west, and the north, and the south': and for this reason be the four crosses made at the four corners to show that Christ, by His Cross, hath saved the four quarters of the world. Secondly, they be made to point out that we ought to bear the cross of the Lord in four ways; namely, in our heart by meditation, in our mouth by confession, in our body by mortification of the flesh, in our face by constant impression. The cross in the middle of the altar signifieth the Passion which Christ underwent in the middle of the earth, by which He worked out salvation in the middle of the earth; that is, in Jerusalem.

[16] S. Mark i, 4.

[17] There be four kinds of holy water, one, by the which is made the judgment of expurgation, which is no longer used; a second, which doth sanctify in the consecration of a church or an altar; a third, with which aspersions be made in the church; and a fourth, the water of baptism.'—Durandus, Lib. IV, iv, 10.

[18] The *tables*, or upper slabs of the altar, were inscribed with five crosses, one at each corner and one in the middle: as are also the altar stones which are found in the middle of the frightful wooden altars abroad at this day. See an interesting list of altar slabs in the 'Few Hints' of the Cambridge Camden Society.

15. Next, the bishop goeth seven times round the altar. (i) Firstly, to signify that he ought to exercise care for all, and to keep himself vigilant, which is denoted by the act of going round. Whence at that time they chant, 'The watchmen that went about the city found me.'[19] For a bishop ought to watch anxiously over the flocks committed to him: for as Gilbert saith, 'A ridiculous thing it is, a blind watchman, a lame leader, a negligent prelate, an untaught teacher, and a dumb preacher.'

16. (ii) Secondly, the seven circuits of the altar do signify the seven meditations which we ought to entertain respecting the sevenfold virtue of the humility of Christ, and of which we ought to make frequent circuits in our minds. The first virtue is, that from being rich He became poor; the second, that He was laid in a manger: the third, that he was subject to His parents; the fourth, that He bowed His Head under the hand of a slave; the fifth, that He bore with a thief and a betrayer as a disciple; the sixth, that He stood gentle before an unrighteous judge; the seventh, that He mercifully prayed for them that crucified Him.

17. (iii) Thirdly, by the seven circuits be indicated the seven journeys of Christ. The first was from heaven to the Virgin's womb; the second, thence into the manger; the third, from the manger into the world; the fourth, from the world to the cross; the fifth, from the cross to the sepulchre; the sixth, from the sepulchre to the place of spirits; the seventh, from the place of spirits to heaven.

18. After this, the bishop sprinkleth the altar. But what the altar signifieth in a temple, the Apostle telleth us: 'For the Temple of God is holy, which temple ye are.'[20] Wherefore, if we be the Temple of God, 'we

[19] Cant. v, 7.   [20] 2 Cor. vi, 16.

have an altar.'[21]   Our altar is our heart: for the heart is in a man what the altar is in a temple. On this altar is made the sacrifice of praise and joy, according to the saying of the Psalmist: 'The sacrifices of God are a broken spirit,' etc.[22]   On this altar is made the commemoration of the Body and Blood of Christ. From it do prayers rise to heaven, because God looketh to the heart. This altar, therefore, is sprinkled with water when the hearts of men, by means of the preaching of the gospel, are cleansed from sin. For preaching is water, according to that saying: 'All ye that thirst, come to the waters.'[23]   By this water, therefore, that is, by the preaching of the gospel and the sanctification of the Holy Ghost, both the altar of the heart and the whole man are cleansed and sanctified. For the altar of the heart is consecrated by the conception of fear, inviting to good, and by the affection of love, confirming to the better. 'For the fear of the Lord is the beginning of wisdom.'[24]

19. But the altar is sprinkled seven times with water to notify that in baptism the seven gifts of the Holy Spirit be conferred. By this also it is set forth that we ought to have a remembrance of the Lord's Passion. For the seven aspersions of water be the seven outpourings of the Blood of Christ. The first whereof was at circumcision; the second in prayer, when His sweat was as drops of blood; the third, at the scourging; the fourth, from the crown of thorns; the fifth, from His pierced hands; the sixth, when His feet were nailed to the cross; the seventh, when His side was opened. Some, however, sprinkle three times, because we baptise in the name of the Holy Trinity; or because the church is cleansed from sins of thought, word, and deed; whence also at that time the *Miserere mei* is said.

[21] Heb. xiii, 10.
[23] Isaiah lv, 1.
[22] Ps. li (*Miserere mei Deus*), 17.
[24] Ps. cxi (*Confitebor tibi*), 10.

20. Moreover, these aspersions be made with an aspersory made of hyssop, by which herb, because it is lowly, the lowliness of Christ is conveniently represented : since the above-mentioned effusions of blood were accompanied by the hyssop, of the humility and inextinguishable love of Christ by which the Catholic Church being sprinkled is purified. This herb also groweth naturally upon rock : and lowliness of disposition hath grown upon Christ the rock. For according to the Apostle, ' That rock was Christ.' [25] It is also of a warm nature ; and the humility of Christ inflameth cold hearts to the practice of works of love. Its roots also penetrate the rocks ; and humility breaketh through the hardest of obstinacy. It availeth for diseases of the breast and against swelling : so doth humility heal the swelling of pride. The former also is born from, and rooted in, the earth : whence by it the whole multitude of the faithful may be understood ; and those especially be figured by the hyssop, who, rooted and grounded in Christ, cannot be plucked up or separated from His love. By whom what can we understand better than the bishops and presbyters, because the more dignity they obtain in the Church, the more firmly ought they to cleave to the faith of Christ. By these assuredly is the water aspersed ; by and through these be the faithful of Christ baptised ; to these is it given to perfect the sacrament of baptism.

21. But whilst the altar is being sprinkled with water the bishop chanteth, ' My house shall be called an house of Prayer,' etc.,[26] and again, ' I will tell out thy name to my brethren.' [27] And because without God no work is perfectly consummated, he prayeth that those who enter therein to seek for blessings may be heard.

Afterwards, when the church and altar are consecrated

---

[25] 1 Corinthians x, 4.   [26] S. Matthew xxi, 13.
[27] Psalm xxii (*Deus Deus meus*), 22.

at the same time, the whole church is sprinkled with that water, as was discussed in the preceding chapter, which being done, the bishop approacheth the altar repeating Psalms, and what remains of the water is poured away at the foot of the altar, as in the old Testament[28] what remained of the blood was poured away at the bottom of the altar; by which it is signified that the remainder in so great a sacrament, which is beyond human power, is given over unto God, Who is the Chief High Priest, Whose part it is to supply the defect of other priests. But the sepulchre or cavity in which relics ought to be deposited, signifieth the golden pot full of manna, which was placed in the ark of the testimony, as hath been explained under the head of the Altar.

22. A sepulchre of this sort, which by some is termed a *confession*, is our heart; and it is consecrated by four crosses made with chrism, because there be four virtues described in the book of wisdom—namely, Prudence, Fortitude, Temperance, and Justice—with which our heart is, as it were, anointed, when it is prepared by the gift of the Holy Spirit to receive the mysteries of the heavenly secrets. But this sepulchre is made sometimes at the upper part of the altar, sometimes in the front side of it.

23. Without the relics of saints, or, where they cannot be had, without the body of Christ,[29] there is no consecration of a fixed altar: but there may be of a travelling or portable one. Relics in truth are, after the example of both Testaments, evidences of the suffering of martyrs and lives of confessors; which things be left to us as examples. These we enclose in a case, because we retain them, in order to imitate them in our heart: but if we hear and understand and do no works,

---

[28] Exodus xxix, 12.   [29] See chapter ii.

it tendeth rather to damnation than to salvation ; because 'not the hearers of the law are just before God, but the doers only';[30] whence the Apostle saith, 'Be ye imitators of me as I am also of Christ.'[31]

24. But the solemn carrying of relics is in imitation of what is read in the xxv chapter of Exodus. In the ark of the testament there were two golden rings, going through the whole thickness of the wood, and through these were put the staves of shittim wood overlaid with gold, by which the ark was borne. And before the bishop entereth the church he goeth round it with the relics in order that they may be protectors of that church. We read also in the viii chapter of the third book of Kings that at the dedication of the temple 'there were assembled together all the elders of Israel, with the chiefs of the tribes, and the heads of families to King Solomon in Jerusalem, to carry the ark of the covenant of the Lord ; and there came all the elders of Israel, and the priests brought in the ark of the covenant of the Lord into his place, into the oracle of the house, to the most holy place, even under the wings of the cherubims. For the cherubims spread forth their two wings over the place of the ark, and the cherubims covered the ark and the staves thereof above. And King Solomon, and all the congregation of Israel that were assembled unto him, marched with him before the ark.'[32] In remembrance of this event, the prelates, great men, and people * of the province meet together, even at this day, for the dedication of churches, and follow in procession him that consecrateth : and relics are solemnly carried by priests under a pavilion or canopy. Afterwards the bishop, before he entereth the church with these, addresseth the people. For Solomon also, after the ark had been

---

[30] Romans ii, 13.   [31] 1 Corinthians xi, 1.   [32] 1 Kings viii, 2, 6, 7.
* The Venice edition of 1609 reads *Apostoli* here.

carried, 'turned his face about, and blessed all the congregation of Israel,' and prayed for such as should pray in the church. 'For all the congregation of Israel stood, and Solomon said, Blessed be the Lord God of Israel,' etc., as is read in the same place.[33]

25. But the relics of saints are enclosed in a case together with three grains of frankincense, because we ought to retain in our recollection the examples of the saints, together with faith in the Trinity, that is, in the Father, Son, and Holy Ghost. For we ought to believe one God, one faith, one baptism, because 'the just liveth by faith,'[34] without which, as the Apostle hath said, 'It is impossible to please God.'[35] There is placed upon and fitted to the sepulchre itself a certain board fortified by the sign of the cross made with chrism.[36] For by chrism is understood the gift of the Holy Spirit, with which this board, that is charity, is anointed; because our heart is fortified by the grace of the Holy Spirit to observance of the heavenly mysteries. The board therefore fortified by this sign is placed over the relics, because by the example of the saints is inflamed charity, 'which covereth a multitude of sins,'[37] just as also the board covereth the relics. Whence saith the Apostle, 'The love of God is spread abroad in our hearts by the Holy Spirit which is given unto us.'[38] But this slab or stone containeth, or is called, the *seal* of the sepulchre; as saith Pope Alexander III.

After this, however, the stone, which is called the *table* of the altar, is fitted to the top of the altar; by which we may understand the perfection and solidity of the knowledge of God; and it ought to be of stone, not because of the hardness, but the solidity of faith. Just

---

[33] 1 Kings, viii. [34] Romans i, 17. [35] Hebrews xi 6.
[36] See above, section 4, note 7. [37] 1 S. Peter iv, 8.
[38] Romans v, 5.

as the Lord said unto Peter, 'Thou art Peter, and upon this rock'—that is, upon this firmness of faith—'I will build My Church.' [39]

26. For as this *table* is the completion and finishing of the altar, so is the knowledge of God the confirmation and perfection of all good gifts. Whence in the book of Wisdom it is said unto the Lord, 'For to know Thee is perfect wisdom, and to know Thy justice and Thy virtue is the root of immortality.' [40] The Lord saith by Jeremiah, 'Let him that glorieth glory in this, that he understandeth and knoweth Me.' [41]

27. Or, again, by this stone itself is understood Christ, of Whom the Apostle saith, 'Jesus Christ Himself being the chief corner-stone.' [42] By the stone indeed the humanity of Christ is denoted. Concerning which we read in Daniel that a stone was cut out of the rock without hands—because Christ was born of the Blessed Virgin (who for the excellency of her virtues is called a Mountain), without human agency—and, becoming a huge mountain, filled the whole earth. Concerning which it is said also by the Psalmist, 'The stone which the builders refused hath become the head stone of the corner:' [43] since Christ—Whom the builders, that is the Jews, refused, saying, 'We will not have this man to reign over us' [44]—hath been made the head of the corner. Because as saith the Apostle, 'God hath exalted Him, and given Him,' [45] etc. Or else by this stone, which ought to be great and wide, charity is understood, as was stated before; since the command of charity is wide, extending even unto our enemies; according to that precept of our Lord, 'Love your enemies.' [46]

28. Altars therefore, unless they be of stone, are not

---

[39] S Matthew xvi, 18. [40] Wisdom xv, 3. [41] Jeremiah ix, 24.
[42] Ephesians ii, 20. [43] Psalm cxviii (*Confitemini Domino*), 22.
[44] S. Luke xix, 14. [45] Philippians ii, 10. [46] S. Matthew v, 44.

anointed, because Christ signified by the altar is the Stone growing into a mountain: as it is said, The mountain itself is fat, 'being anointed with the oil of gladness, above his fellows.'[47] Nevertheless we read in Exodus that the Lord ordered the altars to be made of shittim wood, which does not decay[48]; and the Latern altar is of wood. Solomon also made an altar of gold, as we read in the eighth chapter of the third book of Kings: but these things were done for a type.* And in the county of Province, in the castle of S. Mary by the Sea, there is also an altar of earth, which Mary Magdalene, and Martha and Mary the mother of James, and Mary the mother of Salome, made there.[49] After this, the altar having been sprinkled and baptised with water, it remaineth for it to be anointed with oil and chrism. The bishop then poureth over it oil and chrism, and chanteth, 'Jacob set up the stone for a memorial, and poured oil upon it.'[50] For that church hath been the memorial of other churches; 'For the law hath gone out from Sion, and the word of the Lord from Jerusalem.'[51]

29. But first he maketh upon it the five crosses, with the oil of the sick, according to the Roman order; but according to the use of some other Churches, with both sorts of oil; one cross in the middle, and four at the

---

[47] Psalm xlv (*Eructavit cor meum*), 8.   [48] Exodus xxvii, 1, etc.

* The same examples are briefly adduced in the notes to the Decretal. Ciampini describes the wooden altar of the Lateran, and mentions its numerous escapes from fire. It was made of firewood, because 'abies non cedit vermibus unquam, nec putret facile.' See also Stephen Durantus, *De Rit. Ecc. Cathol.* Lib. I, xxv, 3, quoting from De Turrecremata, about the Lateran altar, and generally about the subject of this chapter.

[49] According to the Golden Legend, S. Mary Magdalene, with other saints, amongst whom was S. Lazarus, were placed by the Jews in a ship which was borne by the sea to Marseilles. The country was converted, and S. Lazarus became the first bishop. The people of Vezelay, in Burgundy, also claimed the honour of possessing the relics of S. Mary Magdalene. Durandus, a native of Provence, gives it to the latter country. This curious passage of our author seems to have been overlooked by some who have attempted to adjust the dispute.

[50] Genesis xxviii, 18.   [51] Isaiah ii, 3.

corners: afterwards, he maketh the same number of crosses in the same way with chrism. By the oil assuredly is understood the grace of the Holy Ghost, of which saith Esaias the Prophet, 'The yoke shall be destroyed because of the anointing.'[52] For as the bishop poureth oil upon the altar, so Christ, who is the Chief High Priest, poureth His grace upon our altar, which is our heart: for He is the distributor of all graces through the Holy Ghost, as saith the Apostle, 'To one is given the word of wisdom, to another the word of knowledge, to another faith, to another the gift of healing,' etc.[53] And just as the bishop, by means of oil, cleanseth the *table* of the altar, so also doth the Holy Ghost purify our heart from all vices and sins.

30. Christ also was anointed with oil, not with visible oil indeed, but with invisible; that is with the grace of the Holy Ghost. Whence David, 'The Lord thy God hath anointed thee with the oil of gladness above thy fellows';[54] that is above all the saints who have been partakers of His Grace, that is, Christ. Whence unction more expressedly agreeth with Christ (the Anointed One) than with others, because God hath anointed Him above all others to have the fulness of good things, and therefore his name is interpreted 'The Anointed.' Unction also with oil signifieth mercy, according to that saying of the Evangelist, 'Anoint thy head with oil, and wash thy face':[55] because as oil is among fluids, so is mercy superior among good works. For whatever liquid you pour upon oil, yet it always swimmeth at the top. Of mercy it is written, 'The Lord is loving unto every man, and His mercy is over all His works,'[56] and 'Mercy rejoiceth against judgment.'* With this oil, therefore, is the

---

[52] Isaiah x, 27.
[54] Psalm xlv (*Eructavit cor meum*), 8.
[56] Psalm cxlv (*Exaltabo te Deus*), 9.
[53] 1 Corinthians xii, 8.
[55] S. Matthew vi, 17.
* S. James ii, 13.

altar of our heart anointed, that being always mindful of mercy, we may never lose the effect of the aspersion of water, and of regeneration and of baptism.

31. The five crosses made with the oil signify that we ought always to have a remembrance of the five wounds of Christ, which He suffered for our sakes upon the Cross. For He suffered five wounds; namely, in His hands, His feet, and in His side.

32. They denote further the five feelings of pity which be necessary for us. For it is necessary for a man to pity Christ, by sympathising in His Passion: whence Job, in the person of Christ, saith, 'Pity me, pity me,' etc.[57] A man must also pity his neighbours whose calamities he seeth; whence in Ecclesiasticus, 'The pity of a man towards his neighbour.'[58] And a man must pity himself: and this in three ways; namely, for the sins of commission, by bewailing them; whence Jeremiah, 'There is no one who hath penitence for his sin, saying, What have I done?'[59]—for his sins of omission: whence Isaiah, 'Woe is me, for I have held my peace,'[60] that is, for I have not spoken; as if he should say, For I have omitted the good that I might have done:—and for good deeds done for less pure motives; whence S. Luke saith, 'When we have done all good deeds, we must say that we are unprofitable servants,' etc.;[61] as if we should say, We have done good, but not well, not purely, and therefore we have done it unprofitably; just as anyone giving alms for vain glory doth good indeed, but not well and not purely. Of this threefold compassion it is said in Ecclesiasticus, 'Have pity on thy soul and please God;'[62] because true compassion of mind ought to co-exist with the exhibition of good works. Wherefore the

---

[57] Job xix, 21.   [58] Eccles. xviii, 12—*Vulgate*.   [59] Jeremiah viii, 6.
[60] Isaiah vi, 5—*Vulgate*.   [61] S. Luke xvii, 10.
[26] Eccles. xxx, 24—*Vulgate*.

crosses be twice made; the first time of oil, the second of chrism : whence the Psalm, 'A good man is merciful and lendeth';[63] that is, pitieth in mind, and lendeth in deed. And since it sufficeth not to have compassion in mind together with the exhibition of good deeds, without the savour of a good report, according to that saying of the gospel, 'Let your light so shine before men that they may glorify God';[64] therefore the crosses be made with chrism, which consisteth of balsam and oil.

33. Balsam indeed, on account of its good odour, signifieth good report; oil, on account of its brightness, signifieth the clearness of conscience which we ought to have : according to the saying of the Apostle, 'Our rejoicing is this, the testimony of our conscience.'[65] Again, balsam is properly conjoined with oil, because good report is added to mercifulness.

34. Again, by the five crosses made of oil and of chrism the five senses of our body be understood, which are doubled and made into ten, because by properly using the senses of our body, we both keep ourselves, and confirm others by our example and teaching in welldoing. Whence that good trader boasted, saying, 'Behold I have gained five more talents.'[66] But whilst these anointings are going on, they chant, 'The Lord thy God hath anointed thee,'[67] which was said of Christ.

The altar therefore is anointed three times; twice with oil, and once with chrism; because the Church is marked by Faith, Hope, and Charity, which last is greater than the others. And while the chrism is used they chant, 'See the smell of my son is as the smell of a field.'[68] This field is the Church, which is verdant with flowers, which shineth in virtues, which is fragrant with good

---

[63] Psalm cxii (*Beatus vir*), 5.
[65] 2 Corinthians i, 12.
[67] Hebrews i, 9.
[64] S. Matthew v. 16.
[66] S. Matthew xxv, 20.
[68] Genesis xxvii, 27.

works; and wherein be the roses of martyrs, the lilies of virgins, the violets of confessors, and the verdure of beginners in the faith. After the unction there is incense burnt, which signifieth the devotion of prayer. For he that hath the seven gifts of the Holy Ghost, and is made like unto God, is able to offer unto Him devout prayer, of which he hath this similitude.

35. It is burnt in five places, namely, at the four corners and in the middle, because we ought so to exercise the five senses of the body that the report of our good works may extend to our neighbours. Of which saith the Apostle, 'We are the sweet savour of Christ in every place.'[69] And in the Gospel, 'Let your light so shine before men,' etc. Besides this, the frequent use of incense is the continual mediation of Christ the Priest, and our High Priest, for us unto God the Father.

36. To describe a cross with the incense, is to exhibit His Passion to the Father and Him interceding for us. The burning incense plenteously in the middle and at the corners is to multiply prayers through Jerusalem and in the Catholic Church.

37. Next to this the bishop confirmeth the altar with the sign of the cross, saying, 'Confirm this altar, O Lord,' etc. And this confirmation performed by the bishop with chrism on the front of the stone, signifieth the confirmation which is performed daily by the Holy Spirit, through charity, upon the altar of the heart, so that no tribulation should avail to separate our heart from the love of God: whence saith the Apostle, 'Who shall separate us from the love of Christ? shall tribulation?' etc.[70] Then there is added the *Gloria Patri* in praise of the Trinity.

38. The last benediction of the altar signifieth that final benediction when it shall be said, 'Come, ye blessed

---

[69] 2 Corinthians, ii, 15.   [70] Romans viii, 35.

of my Father,' etc. [71] Afterwards the altar is wiped over with a white linen cloth, to notify that we ought to cleanse our heart by chastity of life. Then the vessels, vestments, and linen cloths, devoted to the divine worship are blessed. For Moses also during the forty days was instructed by the Lord to provide linen cloths and the ornaments necessary for the Temple.

39. Assuredly, thus to bless the utensils is to refer all our works unto the Lord. After this, the altar is covered with white and clean cloths: concerning which ceremony we have spoken under the head of the Altar. Lastly, the church is ornamented and the lamps are lighted: for then shall the works of the just shine forth, 'Then shall the just shine, as sparks run swiftly among the stubble.' [72] And then upon the altar, consecrated after this order, the Mass is celebrated and the sacrifice offered unto the Most Highest: that sacrifice, namely, of which the Prophet speaketh, 'The sacrifices of God are a broken spirit; a broken and a contrite heart, O God, Thou wilt not despise': [73] as shall be declared in the introduction to the fourth book.[74] For consecration ought not to be performed without a Mass, according to Pope Gelasius,* because then there is revealed a sacra-

---

[71] S. Matthew xx, 34. [72] Wisdom iii, 7.
[73] Psalm li (*Miserere mei Deus*), 17.
[74] The blessed Bernard saith, My brethren, let us in sacrificing add the sacrifice of praise unto our words, let us add sense to sense, affection unto affection, exaltation unto exaltation, maturity unto maturity, and humility unto humility. Wherefore, he that is about to celebrate must offer unto the Highest that sacrifice of which the Psalmist speaketh, 'The sacrifices of God are a troubled spirit.' And again, 'Offer unto God the sacrifice of thanksgiving.' And the Apostle, 'Present your bodies a living sacrifice holy acceptable unto God which is your reasonable service. mortifying upon the altar of your heart your members which are upon the earth; fornication, uncleanness, inordinate affection, evil concupiscence, and covetousness, which is idolatry'; in order to sacrifice yourselves with a pure heart and chaste body unto God.—Proem. lib. iv, 17.

* Quoted also in the Decretal *De Consecrat. Distinct. I.*

ment, which hath been hidden from the angels even from the beginning.

And observe, that in the aspersion of the church the bishop useth only the linen and inferior vestments: but at the Mass he is adorned with pontifical and precious vestments, because the high priest in the law used to expiate the sanctuary in a linen ephod, and afterwards used to offer the ram for the burnt offering being washed and arrayed in the high priest's vestments. But because he used to send forth the scapegoat after the expiation being clothed in the same linen ephod, on this account some, in the consecration of fonts and immersion of the catechumens where their sins are transferred, do use the simple linen vestments.

CHAPTER VIII

OF CONSECRATIONS AND UNCTIONS

Of Chrism—Of the name Christ, and of Christians—The Heresy of the Arnaldistæ—The Anointing of Priests—Of Bishops—Of Kings—Of the Consecration of Chalices and Patens—Of Extreme Unction—Of the Benediction of Church Ornaments.

1. We read that the Lord commanded Moses[1] to make a chrism, with which unguent to anoint the tabernacle at the time of the dedication, and the ark of the testimony, and the table, together with the vessels; and with which also the priests and kings should be anointed. Yet Moses himself is not said to have been anointed, except with a spiritual unction, as also was Christ.

2. Christ hath willed that we should be anointed with a material unction in order that we may by it obtain the spiritual unction: and on this account our loving Mother, the Church, provideth different sorts of unction. Upon which let us here touch lightly, saying—

    I. What unctions of this sort signify.
    II. Of what they be made.
    III. Of the unction before baptism.
    IV. Of the unction after baptism, which is performed by the bishop on the forehead.
    V. Of the unction in ordination.

[1] Exodus xxx, 22.

VI. Of the unction in consecrating bishops and princes.
VII. Of the unction of a church, altar, chalice, and other ecclesiastical instruments.
VIII. Of extreme unction.
IX. Of the consecration and benediction of a cemetery, vestments, and other ecclesiastical ornaments.
X. Of the consecration and benediction of virgins.

3. Firstly; with respect to the first, then, it is to be noted that there be two kinds of unction: an *external*, which is material or corporeal, and visible; and an *internal*, which is spiritual and invisible. The body is anointed visibly with the external unction; the heart invisibly by the internal. Of the first, the Apostle S. James saith, 'Is any sick among you? Let him call for the elders of the Church; and let them pray over him, anointing him with oil in the name of the Lord; and the prayer of faith shall save the sick.'[2] Of the second the Apostle S. John saith, 'But the anointing which ye have received of Him abideth in you, and ye need not that any man teach you: but the same anointing teacheth you of all things.'[3] The external unction is a sign of the internal. But the internal is not only a sign, that is a thing signified, but a sacrament also; because if it be worthily received, it either effecteth, or without doubt increaseth, that which it doth signify—for instance, healing: according to the saying, 'They shall lay their hands upon the sick, and they shall be healed.'[4]

Secondly; with respect to the second point, you must know that in making use of the external and visible unction, two sorts of oil are consecrated: namely, holy oil, or the oil of the catechumens, with which catechumens are anointed; and the oil of the sick, with which the sick are anointed. Of which kind of unction the authority of

[2] S. James v, 14.   [3] 1 S. John ii, 27.   [4] See Acts xxviii, 8.

S. James quoted above doth speak, ' Is any sick among you,' etc.

But in what way the benediction of these two sorts of oil and of chrism is performed will be declared in the sixth book in the chapter upon the Fifth Day of the Holy Week.[5]

4. But is it asked why the sick and the catechumens are anointed with oil? I answer, in order that the invisible benefits may be more easily received through the visible signs: for as oil by expelling weakness refresheth the wearied limbs, and as it from its own natural qualities affordeth light, so it is to be believed that unction with consecrated oil, the which is a type of faith expelling sin, doth impart health to the soul and doth afford it light. Herein the visible oil is in the outward sign, the invisible oil in the inward sacrament; and the spiritual oil is within. For the oil of the sick we have received authority from the apostles; for the oil of the catechumens from apostolical men.

5. And although God can grant the spiritual oil without the material, yet because the apostles have used this rite in the case of the sick, and apostolical men in the case of catechumens, this practice which their authority hath consecrated cannot be omitted without sin (as hath been said in the chapter upon the Altar): just as anciently the just pleased God without circumcision; but after it had been enjoined them to be circumcised, such as omitted this rite were subjected to sin.

Thirdly; we have to speak of the unction before baptism. And indeed in the New Testament not only kings and priests be anointed, as hath been already said, but also— (because Christ by His Blood hath made us kings and priests, that is, royal priests, unto our God, as the

---

[5] It has not been thought necessary to translate the passages referred to.

Apostle S. Peter saith,[6] 'Ye are a chosen generation,' that is, chosen out from the tribes of men, 'a royal priesthood,' that is, governing yourselves well)—also, I say, all Christians be anointed twice before their baptism with consecrated oil—first, on the breast: secondly, between the shoulders: and twice after their baptism, with holy chrism—first, on the crown of the head; and secondly, by the bishop on the forehead.

6. And, according to Augustine, the first three unctions have been introduced rather by use than by any written authority. The candidate for baptism is anointed with oil—first, on the breast, in which is the locality of the heart; first, in order that by the gift of the Holy Ghost he may cast away error and ignorance and embrace a right faith; because 'the just liveth by faith,'[7] and 'with the heart we believe unto justification.'[8] But he is anointed between the shoulders, in order that he may, by the grace of the Holy Ghost, shake off indifference and sloth, and practise good works (because 'faith without works is dead'),[9] so that by means of sacraments of faith there may result a purity of thoughts. On the breast, again, that by the practising of good works there may arise a boldness of labour: between the shoulders, to the end that 'faith (according to the Apostle) may work by love.'[10] The oil therefore is carried over from the heart to the shoulders, since faith, which is conceived in the mind, is perfected in works (because, that is, faith consisteth in making our *deeds* like our *words*).* But the person after baptism is anointed by the priest on the head with chrism, that 'he may be ready always to give an answer to every man that asketh him a reason for the faith that is in him,'[11] because by

---

[6] 1 S. Peter ii, 9.   [7] Habakkuk ii, 4.   [8] Romans x, 10.   [9] S. James ii, 26.
[10] Gal. v, 6.   * This clause does not occur in the *Princeps* Edition.
[11] 1 S. Peter iii, 15.

the head is understood the mind: as it is written, 'The eyes,' that is the understanding, 'of the wise are in his head,'[12] that is, his mind; of which mind, the superior part is reason and the inferior sensuality. Hence, by the crown, which is the upper part of the head, is well represented reason, which is the superior part of the mind. Of this we shall speak in the sixth book also, under the head of Easter Eve, in which confirmation is treated of.[13] But this is the reason that before baptism one is anointed with consecrated oil, and after baptism with holy chrism; because chrism is competent to a Christian alone.

7. For Christ is so named from *chrism*, or rather *chrism* is so called from Christ, not according to the form of the name only, but according to the rational order of faith. For *Christians* are called from Christ, as *the anointed* would be derived from the Anointed One, namely, Christ; so that all may unite in the odour of that unguent, namely, Christ, Whose name is as oil poured out: but according to the power of the word, *Christians* are called so from *chrism*, according to Isidorus.[14] This subject is treated in the introduction to the second book.[15]

[12] Ecclesiasticus ii, 14.
[13] The passage referred to speaks of the diverse graces conferred by the several unctions, and does not illustrate our more particular object.
[14] 'For Christ is named of *chrism*, and meaneth the Anointed One. For it was commanded the Jews to make a holy unguent for such as were called unto the priesthood or the kingdom: and as now the vestment of purple is unto kings the mark of kingly power, so upon these did the unction with sacred unguent bestow the name and kingly power: and hence were they called *Christi*, from *chrism*, which is unction. For *chrisma* in Greek is *unctio* in Latin. And this unction did aptly give this name unto our Lord, because He was anointed of the Father by the Spirit, as is said in the Acts of the Apostles, "Against Thy Holy Child Jesus, Whom Thou hast anointed, were they gathered together": not, that is, with visible oil, but with the gift of grace, which is denoted by the visible oil.' S. Isidore of Seville, *Orig.* vii, 2. See also *Orig.* vii, 4, and *De Off. Ecc.* i, 1.
[15] 'Christians be named from Christ, and Christ from *chrism*, being *anointed*. For He was anointed by God from the beginning "with the oil of gladness above His fellows." In the Old Testament priests and kings be called *Christs* (or Anointed), because they were anointed with a tem-

8. Again, according to Augustine, the first unction with oil showeth us to be prepared fully to hear the faith, and called to the sweet odour of Christ, and warned to renounce the devil. The second unction, according to Rabanus, is upon the breast and between the shoulders, that we may be fortified on both sides by faith, and confirmed by the grace of God for the performance of good works. For by the breast is rightly understood the virtue of faith: but by the shoulders—upon which any burden is borne—the strength and working of a man: according to that saying, 'They bind heavy burdens and lay them on the shoulders of men,' etc.[16] A man is anointed therefore on the breast and between the shoulders, that both in thought and deed he may relinquish the works of the devil, and become capable of understanding the Word of God, and strong enough to bear its yoke and the burden of the law.

9. But the unction upon the crown, that is the top part of the head over the brain, is performed according to the same authority in order that he who is so anointed may become a partaker of the heavenly kingdom: and because the soul of the baptised person is espoused unto the Head, that is Christ, therefore this unction is made with chrism, compounded of oil and balsam, in order that we may know that the Holy Ghost, Who worketh invisibly, is given unto him: for oil, as we said above, cherisheth the wearied limbs and affordeth light. But balsam giveth

poral unction. As it is written, "Touch not my Christs" (*i.e.* mine anointed). Wherefore, Christ is not a peculiar name of our Saviour, but is a common appellation of dignity. But the name Jesus is peculiar to the person of our Saviour alone, and was given Him, as the Evangelist doth testify by the angel, Gabriel, at the Conception, and by men at His Circumcision.'—Durand. *loco cit.* This will explain the reason, to many persons so puzzling, why it is only to the name of Jesus that our Church, after the Apostle, commands due obeisance to be made: and will reprove the erroneous, though pious, zeal which makes so many of the poor even now bow at the other names of our Blessed Lord.

[16] S. Matthew xxiii, 4.

it a sweet odour. If so be the limbs of the soul be wearied, when it repenteth of having acted in opposition to God, the Holy Ghost cometh to it, giving light to its understanding and showing it that its sins are, or may be, forgiven, and bestowing on it good works which breathe out a sweet odour amongst others: all which is denoted by the fragrant balsam. Also because the seat of high-mindedness, which according to the name is always seeking higher things, appears to exist in the head, therefore the unction on this part is rightly performed in the form of the cross and in token of humility.

10. Pope Sylvester appointed that this unction might be administered by priests upon occasion of death: whence it is likely that before his time [17] the anointing both of the crown of the head and of the forehead was reserved for the bishop. For when the bosom of the Church was extended, and bishops could no longer be at hand for each individual in confirmation, he then ordered, lest any should perish without the unction of chrism, that all should be anointed on the crown of the head over the brain, which is the seat of wisdom, at the hands of a priest, for the increasing of strength and grace. Whence if afterwards they should have died, saith Richard (of Cremona), they shall receive an increase of grace and glory.

11. Yet nevertheless we believe that a man may be saved by baptism alone even without the unction, and that the Holy Ghost is given without the laying on of hands to such as God may will, as we read in the Acts of the Apostles.

12. Yet the faithless heretics, the Arnaldistæ,[18] assert

---

[17] S. Sylvester was the contemporary of Constantine. *Circa* A.D. 325.

[18] Our author mentions another heresy of the Arnaldistæ in the 19th section of the proem of book iv. These heretics were the followers of Arnaldus de Brixio (of Bresse), a disciple of Abelard. His opinions were condemned in the second General Lateran Council, 1139.—*Baron. Sub. Anno.* tom. xviii. See also S. Bernard, *Epist.* 195.

that men never receive the Holy Ghost through the baptism of water; and that Samaritans who were baptised did not receive Him until they received the laying on of hands. Both these unctions are administered, according to Rabanus, in the form of the cross, that the devil, whose vessel the person is, recognising the sign of his own discomfiture, the sign of the Holy Cross, may know that from that moment the vessel is Another's, being alienated from him.

13. According to the same writer the unction on the breast is afterwards administered with invocation of the Trinity, in order that no remains of the hidden enemy may abide therein, but the mind be comforted in the faith of the Holy Trinity, and receive and understand the commandments of God. Therefore each of the faithful is anointed first twice with oil, next in like manner twice with chrism. First in baptism on the crown of the head: secondly after baptism, namely at confirmation, on his forehead: because to the apostles also was the Holy Ghost twice given, as will be set forth in the sixth book on Holy Saturday.[19]

Fourthly; in the fourth place we were to speak of the unction which is administered by the bishop on the forehead of such as have been baptised: but of this we shall speak in the same place.[20]

14. Fifthly; in the fifth place, with respect to the unction of ordination, it is to be noted that the hands of the priest are anointed by the bishop, that he may know that he in this sacrament doth receive by the Holy Ghost the power and grace of consecrating. Whence the bishop, whilst anointing them, saith: 'Deign, O Lord, by means of this unction and our benediction to consecrate and sanctify these hands, that whatsoever they con-

---

[19,20] It has not been judged necessary to translate the passages referred to, for the same reason as stated above in note 13.

secrate may be consecrated, and whatsoever they bless may be blessed in the name of the Lord.' And for this cause devout men kiss the hands of priests immediately after their ordination, believing by this to become partakers of their prayers and blessings. And the anointing is with holy oil, because they ought to work with their hands the works of mercy with all their might towards all men: for the works are denoted by the hands; mercy by the oil. Whence the good Samaritan coming near to the wounded man poured wine and oil into his wounds. The hands are anointed with oil also that they may be supple for offering the host unto God for the sins of men, and that they may be open to all acts of piety and not be kept dry and clenched. For both these things, namely the grace of healing and the charity of loving, are denoted by the oil. Wherefore further the laying on of hands, together with oil upon the heads of such as be ordained, is done because by the hands the operation, by the fingers the gifts, of the Holy Ghost, and by the head the mind, be understood. The hand then is laid on because it is sent forth imbued with the gifts of the Holy Ghost to perform the works of Christ.

15. Sixthly, with respect to the unction of bishops and of temporal princes, it is to be known that the former hath derived its origin from the Old Testament. For in the 21st chapter of Leviticus the high priest is said to be he 'upon whose head the anointing oil is poured,'[21] and whose hands were consecrated in priesthood. A bishop, however, is anointed with chrism, which (as we said before) is composed of oil and balsam; and he is anointed therewith both outwardly, and inwardly in his heart, in order that by the inward oil he have a clear conscience towards God, and by the outward oil may have the odour of good report towards his neighbour: which is

[21] Leviticus xxi, 10.

denoted by the balsam. The Apostle saith of a clear conscience, 'For our rejoicing is this the testimony of our conscience.'[22] 'For the king's daughter is all glorious within,'[23] that is, her glory proceedeth from within. Concerning the odour of a good report the same Apostle saith, 'For in every place we are unto God a sweet savour of Christ,' that is, an example and imitation, and, 'to some we are the savour of life unto life,' etc.,[24] as if he had said, we are an example of love and a good opinion leading unto eternal life, 'and to others a savour of death unto death,' that is, of hatred and evil opinion leading unto eternal death.

16. For a bishop ought to have in himself 'a good report' both of them which are within and 'them which are without';[25] so that one curtain, that is, the faithful, may draw on the other curtain, that is, the unbeliever, namely, unto belief;[26] and 'he that heareth,' namely, by learning and believing, 'say, come,'[27] namely, by preaching and teaching. With this unguent be the head and hands of a bishop consecrated: for by the head is understood the mind, as the gospel saith, 'anoint,'[28] that is, humble, 'thy head and wash thy face,' that is, thy conscience, namely, with tears: by the hands be denoted good works, as is said in the Canticles, 'my hands,' that is, my good works, 'dropped with myrrh,' that is, gave to others a good example.[29]

17. The head, therefore, is anointed with the balsam of charity. (i) That the bishop may love God with his whole heart and with his whole mind and whole soul, and also, after the example of Christ, 'love his neighbours as,' that is, as much as, 'himself.' For according to

[22] 2 Corinthians i, 12.   [23] Psalm xlv (*Eructavit cor meum*), 14.
[24] 2 Corinthians ii, 15.   [25] 1 Timothy iii, 7.
[26] There appears to be here some mystical reference to the coupling of the curtains of the tabernacle. See Exod. xxvi.
[27] Apocalypse xxii, 17.   [28] S. Matthew vi, 17.   [29] Canticles v, 5.

Gregory, oil on the head is charity in the soul. (ii) Secondly, the head is anointed by reason of authority and dignity; since not only bishops but also kings are consecrated. (iii) Thirdly, to show that a bishop representeth the person of Christ, as being his vicar, of whom it is said by the Prophet, 'it is like the precious ointment upon the head.'[30] For the head of man is Christ, the head of Christ is God: Who saith of Himself, 'the Spirit of the Lord is upon Me, because He hath anointed Me to preach the gospel to the poor.'[31] For Christ, our Head, was anointed with the invisible oil. He intercedeth for the Church Universal, a bishop for that Church committed unto him.

18. But his *hands* also are anointed, on account of his mystery and office; and for the anointing of these, which do signify works, is employed *oil*, that is, the chrism of piety and mercy. (i) First, in order that the bishop may 'do good unto all men, and especially unto them that are of the household of faith,'[32] his hands should be closed to none, but be open to all; according to the saying, 'He hath opened his hands to the poor, and extended his arm to the destitute.'[33] A hand that is dried up, that is avaricious, that is tenaciously held clenched, cannot be opened: therefore his hands are anointed, in order that they may be healed and opened, and may bestow alms on the indigent. (ii) Secondly, to show that he hath received the power of blessing and consecrating. Whence the consecrating bishop, when he anointeth them, saith, 'Deign, O Lord, to consecrate and sanctify these hands,' and so forth, as we quoted above. (iii) That they may be clean for offering sacrifices for sins. And note, that although a bishop's hands were anointed with oil beforehand when he was ordained a priest, yet

---

[30] Psalm cxxxiii (*Ecce quam bonum*), 2.
[31] Isaiah lxi, 1.
[32] Galatians vi, 10.
[33] Proverbs xxxi, 20.

they be again anointed with chrism when he is consecrated a bishop. Herein by the hands are typified good works; by the oil, the abundance of the Holy Ghost of grace; by the balsam, which is mixed with the oil in making the chrism, the savour of good report; as in Ecclesiasticus, 'My sweet odour is as myrrh unmixed.'[34] Wherefore because in the works of bishops and other superiors there ought to appear more than in their inferiors the gifts of the Holy Ghost and the savour of good report; according to that saying, 'For we are unto God a sweet savour of Christ';[35] for even in the heavenly hierarchy the superior angels excel the inferior in blessings and grace; hence, therefore, at their consecration as bishops their hands, already anointed with oil, are with reason again anointed with chrism.

19. The thumb also is fortified with chrism, that the laying on of the thumb may profit all men for salvation.

20. Further, in the Old Testament, not only was a priest anointed, but also a king and prophet: as we find in the books of Kings. Whence the Lord enjoined Elias, 'Go return on thy way to the wilderness of Damascus: and when thou comest, anoint Hazael to be king over Syria; and Jehu the son of Nimshi shalt thou anoint to be king over Israel; and Elisha the son of Shaphat of Abel-Meholah shalt thou anoint to be prophet in thy room.'[36] Samuel also anointed David to be king. But after that Jesus of Nazareth, 'Whom (as we read in the Acts of the Apostles) God anointed with the Holy Ghost, was anointed with oil above his fellows,'[37] Who is (according to the Apostle) 'the Head of the Church, which is also His body';[38] after this the anointing of a sovereign was transferred from the head to the arm: whence princes since the time of Christ are not

---

[31] Ecclesiasticus xxiv, 15. [35] 2 Corinthians ii, 15. [36] 1 Kings xix, 15.
[37] See Acts iv, 27, and Hebrews i, 9. [38] Ephesians v, 23.

anointed on the head but on the arm, or on the shoulder; by which parts of the body kingly power is aptly represented, as we read, 'and the government was laid upon his shoulder':[39] to signify the same, Samuel caused the shoulder to be laid before Saul, when he placed him at the head of the table before those who had been bidden.[40] But in the case of a bishop the sacramental anointing is applied to the *head*, because in his episcopal office he representeth the Head of the Church, that is, Christ.

21. There is this difference, then, between the anointing of a bishop and a prince, that the head of the bishop is consecrated with chrism, while the arm of the prince is anointed with oil: to show, namely, how great a difference there is between the authority of a bishop and the power of a prince. And observe that, as we read in the gospel,[41] a certain man called his servants and gave unto them ten talents. Herein the calling of a servant is the canonical election of a bishop, which taketh place according to the calling of the Lord Who called Aaron. A talent is given to him, when he who hath laid his hands upon him giveth him the text of the gospel, saying, 'Go and preach.' And the bishop himself, according to the use of some churches, when first he entereth his see, carrieth the gospels in his bosom, showing his talent as if to trade with it. In some churches also when the archbishop giveth the bishop his pastoral staff, he saith, 'Go and preach,' and he immediately blesseth the people: by which is represented that Moses was sent into Egypt with a rod.

22. Furthermore, bishops on the day of their consecration have been wont to ride on horses covered with white robes; to represent that which we read in the Apocalypse, 'The armies which are in heaven follow him riding on

---

[39] Isaiah ix, 6.　　[40] 1 Samuel x, 24.　　[41] S. Matthew xxv.

white horses.'[42] The armies which are in heaven are good and just men and prelates, who as these heavenly riders do daily follow God in all good works: who for this reason are said to be in heaven, because they love and seek after heavenly things alone; whence the Apostle saith, 'Our conversation is in heaven.'[43] These armies, that is good and just men and prelates, follow Jesus, whensoever they vanquish vices in themselves by discipline, in their neighbours by admonition. Whence S. James saith, 'He which converteth the sinner from the error of his way shall save a soul from death, and shall hide a multitude of sins.'[44] These armies have white horses and chaste bodies.

23. The bodies of good men are also called horses, because, just as horses are governed by the will of the rider, so are the bodies of the just ruled according to the will of Christ. These horses ought to be white, or covered with white trappings: that is, the bodies of just men and prelates ought to be chaste and pure. For if they be not pure they cannot follow Christ. And S. Peter saith, 'Christ also suffered for us, leaving us an example that we should follow His steps, who did not sin, neither was guile found in his mouth.'[45] Further, the clergy of the holy Roman Church, by the grant of the Emperor Constantine, do ride upon horses adorned with trappings of the most snowy white. On what day a bishop ought to be consecrated, and why a copy of the gospels is put upon his shoulders in consecration, shall be declared in the second book, under the chapter upon Bishops.[46] Seventhly, we have to speak of the unction

---

[42] Apocalypse xix, 14.   [43] Philippians iii, 20.
[44] S. James v, 20.   [45] 1 S. Peter ii, 21.
[46] The consecration of a bishop, in the which the Holy Ghost is present unto such as receive it worthily, is administered always on the Lord's day, and at the third hour. For bishops do obtain the office of apostles, unto whom the Holy Ghost was given on the Day of Pentecost and at the third

of altars, chalices, and other instruments of the church; which according to the rule are anointed at their dedication; and this not only from the command of the divine law, but also because Moses 'sprinkled with blood the tabernacle and all the vessels of the ministry, and almost all things are by the law cleansed with blood;'[47] and also again after the example of S. Sylvester, who when he consecrated an altar used to anoint it with chrism. For the Lord commanded Moses to make oil of unction with which to anoint the tabernacle of the testimony, the table, the ark of the covenant, the candlestick, and other furniture as aforesaid. Which unctions are performed on things that have not been anointed, to show greater reverence to them and to bestow more grace upon them. And of these unctions we have spoken and shall again speak in their right places. But the sacrament of unction hath indeed some further effect and meaning both in the Old and New Testament: whence the Church doth not Judaize, when she observeth the unctions in her sacraments, as some old writers, who know neither the Scripture nor the power of God, do falsely say. Of the unctions of the church and altar we have spoken under their own heads.

24. Further the paten is consecrated and anointed for the administration of the body of Christ, who willed to be sacrificed upon the altar of the cross for the salvation

hour. When a bishop is to be ordained, the suffragans of the province should assemble with their metropolitan, and two bishops place and hold a volume of the gospels above his head and neck, or upon his shoulders, one shedding the benediction over him, and the rest, such as are present, touching his head with their hands. This book is held above his head; first, that the Lord may confirm the gospel in his heart; secondly, that he may understand by this, unto what burthen and labour he is subjected: because everyone that is pre-eminent, that is, a prelate, is more troubled with griefs than rejoiced with honours; thirdly, to denote that he ought not to be backward to carry with him everywhere the burthen of the preaching of the gospel; fourthly, to admonish him to submit himself more than ever to the yoke, and to obey the gospel.—*Rationale*, Book II, c. xi, 6.

[47] Hebrews ix, 2.

of all men. 'Almighty God also did order the flour to be brought to His Altar scattered on golden and silver patens. The chalice also is consecrated and anointed, that by the grace of the Holy Ghost it may be made a new sepulchre of the body and blood of Christ, and then He, Himself, may deign to make it overflow with his virtue, as He made the cup of Melchizedech, His servant, to flow over.

25. Eighthly; in the eighth place we have to speak of extreme unction, which from the institution of Pope Felix the Fourth, and from the command of the Apostle S. James, is administered unto such as are at the point to die. Concerning which some say that it is not so properly a sacrament as the anointing of the forehead or any other part with chrism, because (as they assert) it may be repeated and since there is offered a prayer over the man; a circumstance which is not a condition of a sacrament. This unction also may be administered by a single priest if more cannot be present: and by it venial sins are remitted, according to S. James, 'If any rich among you,' etc., as before, 'and if he have committed sins they shall be forgiven him.'[48] And this unction is applied to divers parts of the body or the limbs, for reasons which may be gathered from the prayers then used; and especially on those parts in which the five senses chiefly reside, that whatever sins the rich man may have committed by means of these may be abolished by virtue of this unction. Concerning some other rules we ordinarily read, that the party to be anointed must be at the least eighteen years of age, and that he ought to be anointed in sickness once only during a year, though he may be sick many times, and that no one must be anointed, unless, being in his senses, he shall have first demanded it either by words or signs :—

[48] S. James v, 24.

and besides this, that the shoulders ought not to be anointed, because they were anointed in baptism, and that a confirmed person ought not to be anointed on his forehead but on his temples, and a priest's hands ought to be anointed on the backs and not inside, because they were anointed on the inside at his ordination :—and that one who hath been once anointed by a bishop ought not in respect to him to be further anointed by a priest :— and that if a sick man who hath been anointed should recover, the anointed places should be washed, and the water used be thrown into the fire; but should he depart, his body ought not to be washed because of the recent unction. But if the sick man be at the point of death, he should be immediately anointed lest he die without the unction. Besides this, some penitents, and dying men, put on sackcloth and lay themselves down on ashes as we shall explain in the sixth book, when we speak of Ash Wednesday.[49]

26. Ninthly, a cemetery, which enjoyeth the same privileges as a church, is also consecrated and blessed; just as the Lord blessed by the hands of his servants Abraham, Isaac, and Jacob, the land bought for a burial

---

[49] 'On this day also ashes are blessed, and scattered over the head in token of humiliation. "Dust thou art, and unto dust thou shalt return," was said unto Adam (Gen. iv). And Job "repented in dust and ashes" (Job xlii, 6). And the Lord saith, "In the house of Aphrah (marg. read dust) roll thyself in the dust" (Mic. i 10). Also in Judith we read, "The children of Israel humbled themselves in fasting, and dust on their heads" (Chronicles iv). And Abraham saith, "Shall I speak unto the Lord, who am but dust and ashes?" (Gen. 18). And "Mordecai put on sackcloth with ashes" (Esther iv, 1). And "the daughters of Zion have cast ashes on their heads" (Samuel iii). Hence, we read in the Pontifical, penitents and the dying, in token of repentance and humility and that they are dust and ashes, do prostrate themselves in ashes and put on sackcloth—an use drawn from the Old Testament. For we read in Isaiah the fifty-eighth, that penitents do lie in sackcloth and ashes. And Hieremiah saith the same in the twenty-fifth chapter, "Wallow yourselves in the ashes, for the days are acccomplished." Also in the third of Jonah, "The king of Ninevah put on sackcloth and sat in ashes." Also in the Lamentations, "The virgins of Jerusalem are clothed in sackcloth."'—*Rationale* vi, 28, 18.

ground from the sons of Ephron. It is blessed also in order that it may cease from that time forward to be the abode of unclean spirits, and that the bodies of the faithful may therein rest in peace until the day of judgment; unless the bodies of paynims or infidels, or even of excommunicate persons should be buried there, until they shall be cast out thence.

27. This also is to be noted, that the palls of the altar, the priestly vestments, and ecclesiastical ornaments of this kind are to be blessed. For we have already read that Moses, by command of the Lord, consecrated the tabernacle with divine prayers, together with the table and altar, and vessels and utensils for performing the divine worship. If therefore the Jews, who served the 'shadow of the Law and of good things to come,'[50] did this, how much the more ought we to do it to whom the truth hath been made known by Christ! Whence we read in the last chapter but one of Exodus, 'Moses blessed all the vessels of the ministry.'[51] And should an additional piece or a fringe be attached to it, it is proved by the testimony of right that the blessing need not on this account be repeated. But the reason why these things and other like things are consecrated is evidently gathered from the forms of blessing them. Of the sacred vestments we shall speak in the introduction to the third book.[52] And observe: That the blessing or consecration of a church, and of vestments, and of ecclesiastical ornaments is not performed as if they were capable of receiving grace, for they are inanimate: but this practice is introduced, because as men are, so also are these things, by the act of blessing and consecration rendered suitable and fit for divine worship, and are

---

[50] Hebrews x, 1.   [51] Exodus xxxix.
[52] The history, use, and symbolism of the sacred vestments would themselves require a volume to be fully illustrated.

made of greater holiness. Whereas on *persons* greater grace is bestowed by unction and benediction. But some in the benediction of ornaments, let fall their hands, of which we shall speak in the second book under the head of the Deacon.[53]

Tenthly, we were to speak of the consecration of Virgins, but of this we shall treat in the preface to the second book.[54]

[53] 'Observe that when a person in confirmation is blessed on the forehead, and when salt, and water, and palls, and vestments, and the like be consecrated, the hands are held over them, because there is a certain virtue in consecrated hands, which is as it were stirred up when benediction is poured out over anything with the hands suspended in this way. Whence the Apostle admonishing his disciple Timothy, saith, "I put thee in remembrance that thou stir up the gift of God, which is in thee, by the laying on of my hands." So that devotion may be stirred up in the body by the suspension of hands, just as in the heart by the effect. For virtue existeth not only in animate things, but also in inanimate. Whence some do affirm that by the virtue of a church, if anyone entereth therein from devotion, his venial sins be forgiven. Again, the hands are thus held in cases of exorcism especially, as if the priest by the bodily act would put to flight and threaten the devil by the virtue of the consecration of his hands.' —Durandus ii, 9, 16.

[54] This point is not sufficiently connected with our subject to need illustration.

CHAPTER IX

OF THE SACRAMENTS OF THE CHURCH

Difference between a Sacrament and a Mystery—Distinction of Sacraments—Of Matrimony—Of the Ring—Of Second Marriages—Why Sacraments were Instituted.

1. WITH respect to the sacraments of the Church, it is to be noted that, according to Gregory, there is a *sacrament* in any celebration when an outward act is so performed as that we receive inwardly some degree of the thing signified; the which is to be received holily and worthily. Also a *mystery* is that which the Holy Ghost worketh secretly, and invisibly, so as to sanctify by His operation, and bless by His sanctification. A mystery is said to exist in sacraments; a ministry only in ornaments.

2. But, according to Augustine, a sacrament is a visible sign of an invisible grace. Again, a sacrifice is visible; a sacrament invisible. Again, the same sign is a thing which bringeth under cognisance some thing different from itself over and above the outward appearance which it presenteth to the senses.

3. A sacrament is said also to be a sign of a sacred thing, or a sacred concealment of a thing. Of this we shall further speak in the fourth book, under the seventh part of the Canon of the Mass, upon the word

'the mystery of faith,' and under the head of the Oblation.¹

4. Some of the sacraments be of necessity only ; some of dignity and necessity; some of order and necessity ; some of dignity and choice ; and some of choice only. The sacrament of necessity only is baptism, which when administered by anyone, so it be in the form of the Church, in the greatest extremity profiteth unto salvation. And it is said to be 'of necessity,' because without it no one can be saved, if it be neglected through contempt. Of this sacrament we shall speak in the sixth book, under the head of Holy Saturday.² The sacrament of dignity and necessity is confirmation: of dignity, because it is conferred by the bishop alone ; of necessity, because he who neglecteth it through contempt of it, cannot be saved. Of this also we shall speak under the head just specified.

5. The sacraments of order and dignity are Penance, the Eucharist, and Extreme Unction. Of order ; because they ought only to be administered by such as are rightly ordained according to the Church's power of the keys ; except in necessity, in which one may *confess* even unto a layman : of necessity ; since such as neglect them through contempt of them cannot be saved. About penance, see the sixth book, upon the fifth day of Holy Week, the *Cœna Domini*:³ about the Eucharist, we shall

---

¹ The seventh part of the Canon of the Mass is, 'Likewise after supper He took the cup into His holy and venerated hands; and when He had given thanks, He blessed it and gave it to His disciples, saying, Take and drink ye all of this ; for this is the chalice of My blood, of the New and Everlasting Testament, *the mystery of faith*, which is shed for you and for many for the remission of sins : Do this as oft as ye shall drink it in remembrance of me.'—See *Rationale* iv. 42, 20.

² The chapter referred to treats of holy baptism doctrinally, and does not therefore fall within the province of this volume.

³ What we call *Maunday Thursday*, from *Mandatum novum* ('A new commandment I give unto you,' etc.), which the Church of England retains as a Lesson for the day, is more properly called *The Cœna Domini*,

speak in the fourth book, upon the Canon;[4] about Extreme Unction we have spoken in the preceding chapter.

6. But the sacrament of dignity and choice is Orders: of dignity; because conferred by bishops alone, and because no one is admitted thereunto save a worthy person and in a worthy way: of choice; because anyone may be saved without it. Of this we shall speak in the preface to the second book.[5]

7. The sacrament of choice only is matrimony; and it is said to be of choice, because anyone may be saved without it. Indeed a man seeking to marry is not inclined to tend towards the kingdom of heaven.

With respect to this it is to be remarked that, according to the canons, the solemnity of marriage ought not to be celebrated from Septuagesima Sunday, because it is a season of sorrow, until the octave of Easter, nor in the three weeks before the Feast of S. John.[6] But according to the custom of the Catholic Church, marriages may be solemnised in the church from the morrow of Low Sunday, namely, from the octave of Easter, until the first Rogation Day. And from the morning of the first Rogation Day this rite is prohibited until the octave of Whitsuntide inclusively: and so saith Pope Clement in his Decretal. Again, marriages ought not to be celebrated

---

or *Lord's Supper*, in remembrance (as Bishop Andrewes says) *of the mighty mystery of Thy holy body and precious blood, instituted on the evening of this day.*—See S. Isidore, *De Offic. Eccles.* i, 28. The chapter referred to (73 of the sixth book), shows that penitents were restored to communion on this day, and with what ceremonies.

[4,5] These, besides their great length, are not required for the explication of our more immediate subject.

[6] Bp. Cosins says that marriages are not to be solemnised from Advent Sunday, until eight days after (or the octave of) the Epiphany; from Septuagesima Sunday until eight days after Easter; and from Rogation Sunday until Trinity Sunday. Some of these being times of solemn fasting and abstinence, some of holy festivity and joy, both fit to be spent in such holy exercises, without other avocations. See his 'Devotions,' republished by Messrs Rivington.

from the First Sunday in Advent until the Epiphany : nor would they have been allowed until the octave of the Epiphany had not the Lord honoured a marriage with His presence, and even with a miracle.[7] Whence they then chant, ' To-day the Church is united to her Heavenly Spouse.' Some, however, say that it is more holy to extend this prohibition unto the octave of the Epiphany.

In the aforesaid times, therefore, marriages are not to be contracted ; because these seasons are set apart for prayer.

8.[8] But although the solemnising of marriages is prohibited in these intervals, yet a contract of marriage holds good at whatever time it may have been duly made. But in that it is ordered by the canons that weddings should not be celebrated in the three weeks before the Festival of S. John Baptist, the rule was made that men might be more at leisure for prayer. For the Church had formerly appointed two periods of forty days, besides the great one of Lent :—the one preceding the nativity, usually called S. Martin's, and lasting from his day to the nativity ;[9] the other, forty days before the Feast of S. John Baptist :—in which men should give especial heed unto prayers, alms, and fastings. But in regard of the frailty of man, these two seasons have been

---

[7] We are accustomed to celebrate only the manifestation of Christ to the Gentiles, on the Epiphany. But S. Isidore (*De Off. Ecc.* i, 26) gives two other objects of commemoration upon this day : viz. the baptism of our Lord, and his first miracle at the marriage in Cana. And so the hymn in the Breviary :

Ibant Magi, quam viderant,	Stellam sequentes præviam ;
Lumen requirunt lumine,	Deum fatentur munere.
Lavacra puri gurgitis	Cœlestis Agnus attigit ;
Peccata quæ non detulit,	Nos abluendo sustulit.
Novum genus potentiæ !	Aquæ rubescunt hydriæ,
Vinumque jussa fundere	Nutavit unda originem.

Our own Church, however, retains the old Gospel for the second Sunday after the Epiphany.

[8] A few passages have been omitted in the course of this chapter.

[9] Martinmas is the 11th November. The forty days are not exactly made out between this and the Nativity.

reduced to one, and that one again divided into the three weeks of advent, and three before the nativity of S. John: at which times men ought to fast and abstain from marriage.

9. According to S. Isidore (of Seville), women wear veils, when they are married, so that they may know that they must always be subject to their husbands: and because Rebecca, when she saw Isaac, veiled herself. The same saith also that married persons after the benediction are coupled by a fillet, to show that they must not break the tie, that is the fidelity, of conjugal unity. And the same fillet is both white and purple mixed; because the white signifieth purity of life, and purple their lawful raising of offspring: so that by this symbol, their continuance and mutual 'defrauding one another for a time is signified, as well as their coming together again'[10] and return afterwards to conjugal duties.

10. Also in that at the beginning of the ceremony the husband giveth a ring to the bride, this is done as a sign of mutual love, or rather in order that their hearts may be united by the same pledge. And the same ring is put on the fourth finger, because (as some say) a certain vein runneth through it which reacheth to the heart. Also one Protheus is said to have first made a ring of iron as a pledge of love, and to have enclosed an adamant therein: and from this he founded the custom of betrothing brides, because as iron subdueth all things, so doth love conquer all things, since nothing is more violent than its ardour.

11. And as an adamant cannot be broken, so love can-

---

[10] See S. Paul 1 Corinthians vii, 5. The whole of this passage is quoted from S. Isidore, who is, however, more circumstantial than Durandus, and much more elegant and intelligible in his language. The extreme corruption of the printed copies of our author may be exemplified by referring the reader to the original in S. Isidore.—*De Off. Eccles.* ii, 19. See also Hugo de S. Victore, *Exercit. Theol. Summ. Sent.*, Tract vii.

not be overcome: for love is as strong as death. Therefore also he founded the custom of putting the ring on the ring-finger through which a vein passeth to the heart. Afterwards, however, golden rings were substituted for iron, and were set with gems, instead of adamant, because as gold excelleth other metals, so doth love excel all other blessings. And as gold is set off by the gems, so is conjugal love by other virtues. But the word *nuptials* (marriage) is so called according to Ambrose, *a nubendo* (from covering the head). For brides are wont to veil the head and abstain from speaking. Whence also Rebecca, when she saw Isaac to whom she was about to be espoused, began to veil her face. For bashfulness ought to precede marriage, inasmuch as bashfulness more highly commendeth wedlock itself: and the bride should appear rather to be sought by the husband, than herself to have sought after him. . . .

12. We have further to note that a threefold spiritual sacrament is signified by the consummation of marriage. The first sacrament is the spiritual union of the soul to God, through faith, love, and charity; or the union of will, namely charity which consisteth in the spirit, between God and a just soul. Whence saith the Apostle, 'but he that is joined unto the Lord is one spirit.'[11] This sacrament is signified by the union of soul which takes place at the first betrothal in carnal matrimony. The second is the union of the human nature with the divine, which took place in the incarnation of the Word of God; or the conformity of nature, which existeth in the flesh, between Christ and His Holy Church. To which that saying referreth, 'The Word was made flesh, and dwelt among us.'[12] The third sacrament is the unity of the Church, gathered out of all nations and subjected to one spouse, namely Christ. This sacrament is typified in

[11] 1 Corinthians vi, 17.   [12] S. John i, 14.

the case of such as, having had one wife and her a virgin, have afterwards been admitted into holy orders.

13. But when anyone yieldeth to a second marriage, he giveth up this unity, and the signification of this third sacrament does not hold in his case: wherefore marriage should not advance beyond *one*, because such advance cannot signify unity. Besides, by a second marriage he departeth from the union of his former marriage: but the Church ever since she hath united herself to Christ, hath never departed from Him, neither hath Christ ever departed from her. Wherefore one who hath twice married cannot signify such an unity. Whence also deservedly from the defect of this sacramental signification marriage cannot be repeated.

14. Note also this, that according to the statute of the Council of Carthage the bridegroom and bride are to be presented by the parents or bridesmen unto the priest in order to be blessed. And having received the blessing, out of reverence to it, they do not consummate the marriage till the next day.

15. Again by the appointment of Pope Evaristus marriages are to be blessed by the priest not without prayers and offerings. However, a man and woman who contract a second marriage must not be blessed by the priest, since, they having been already blessed, the ceremony may not be repeated. Nor ought marriages to be blessed unless both parties are still unmarried, for the reason given in the preface to the second book.[13]

---

[13] It is laid down that a *widow* on taking the vows is not veiled by the bishop, as is the case with a virgin. 'A priest,' Durandus continues, 'is prohibited from taking a part in second marriages and from giving the benediction to such as are twice married. But a widow taking the vows is married as it were twice, first to her late husband, and secondly unto Christ in her profession, wherefore the veil of consecration, or even of profession, is not given unto her, but she herself takes it from the altar. . . . Yet in the Pontifical, according to the Roman Order, we find the benediction of a widow professing continence, and also of her veil. For the Lord also com-

And any priest who shall have given the blessing in such a second marriage is to be suspended from his office and benefice and to be sent to the apostolical see; a custom this, introduced as an incitement to continence. According to the custom of some places, if anyone contracts a second marriage with an unmarried woman the benediction is repeated: but this does not avail unless our Lord the Pope know of it and approve it. Some also say that if any unmarried persons were not blessed when they contracted marriages, they may when marrying a second time receive the benediction; but if they were blessed at first, it cannot be repeated at a second marriage even though the first were never consummated. Of the benediction of virgins we shall speak in the preface and the second book.[14]

16. But it is to be noted that one sacrament may be more worthy than another in four ways: namely, in efficacy, as baptism; in sanctity, as the eucharist; in significancy, as marriage (though some do not admit this way); in the dignity of the administrator, as confirmation and orders.

17. But is it asked why sacraments are appointed, when without them God could have given eternal life and His Grace unto mankind? I answer, for three reasons. First, for our humiliation; in order that when man reverently humbleth himself by the command of God unto insensible and inferior things, he may from this obedience become more acceptable unto Him. Secondly, for our instruction; that by that which is seen objectively in a visible form, our mind may be instructed in that invisible virtue, which is to be perceived within. Thirdly,

---

forted the widow of Serepta by the hand of Elias the prophet. And I have myself seen in the city (Rome, of course) the [Cardinal] Bishop of Ostia bless two widows among the virgins who took the vows' (Proem. II, c. 47).

[14] See chap. viii, note 57.

for our exercising : in order that, since man ought not to be idle, there may be set before him a useful and healthy exercise in the sacraments ; so that he may avoid vain and hurtful occupation. According to that saying, 'Always be doing some good work, that the devil may find you occupied.' Wherefore, as we said in the foregoing chapter, they must never be neglected.

END OF THE FIRST BOOK

EPILOGUE TO THE WHOLE WORK*

LET none imagine that in the foregoing work the divine offices be sufficiently set forth, lest by extolling that which is human, he rashly depreciate that which is divine. For in the divine offices of the Mass, so many and so great be the mysteries involved, that none, unless he be taught of the spirit, is sufficient to explain them. 'For who knoweth the ordinances of heaven, or can explain the reasons of them upon earth?[1] For he that prieth into their Majesty is overwhelmed by their glory. But I, who cannot from the weakness of mine eyes behold the sun in his brightness, have looked on these mysteries, as through a glass, darkly: and, not penetrating into the interior of the palace, but sitting at the door, have done diligently, as I could, not sufficiently, as I would. For on account of the innumerable and inevitable business of the Apostolic See,[2] pressing on me daily, like a flood, and holding down the mind of him that would diligently rise to a contemplation of heavenly things: I, perplexed as it were, and entangled in the knots of various employments, could not have the leisure that I wished for, and could scarcely either dictate what I had composed, or compose what I had conceived. For the

[1] Job xxxviii, 31.   See the Proeme towards the beginning.
[2] See the Preface.   * Book viii, chap. 14.

mind that is divided in several trains of thought hath less power in each. Wherefore I not only ask pardon of the courteous reader, but implore the assistance of a friendly corrector. For I cannot deny that many things are inserted in this book which may be blamed, and that justly and without temerity. But if anything worthy be found in it, let the praise thereof be ascribed entirely to Divine Grace: for 'every good gift, and every perfect gift is from above, and cometh down from the Father of Light.'[3] But let that which is unworthy, be set down to human insufficiency, 'for the corruptible body presseth down the soul, and the earthly tabernacle weigheth down the mind that museth upon many things.'[4] That which is worthy hath been taken from the sayings of others, whose words I have introduced, rather by way of recital[5] after than of approval. I have collected from diverse books, the manner of the honey making bee, not without profit, of those things which divine grace hath held forth to me: and this doctrine, flowing with sweetness like the honeycomb, I offer, trusting in God's help, to those who desire to meditate on the divine offices: expecting this reward alone of my great toil among men, that they will pray earnestly to the merciful Judge for the pardon of my transgressions.

GULIELMI DURANDI, *Epi Mimatensis Liber de ecclesiis et ornamentis ecclesiasticis explicit feliciter.*

[3] S. James i, 17.   [4] Wisdom ix, 17.
[5] The passage seems corrupt: but the sense appears to be, ' reciting them, as testimonies in my favour, and not presuming to add my testimony to their worth.

SUPPLEMENT

[For the avoiding continual reference, for the extreme beauty of the treatise itself, for its value as an older document than the 'Rationale,' and for the advantage of comparison with the latter in subject, sentiment, style, and often language, the Editors have subjoined a translation of the first and second chapters of the 'Mystical Mirror of the Church' of Hugo de Sancto Victore.]

(Folio Edition, 237 E)

A PROLOGUE to the 'Mystical Mirror of the Church,' made by Master Hugh of S. Victor.

Your love hath asked of me to treat of the sacraments of the Church, and to set forth unto you their mystical sweetness. But since with the more willingness, because with the more ease and boldness I do evolve (after my custom) points of logic rather than of theology; I began to doubt whether to withstand your admonition or the rather to write. But when I presently remembered how that every good thing when shared with others becometh more bright and beautiful when it is shared, I incontinently betook myself to my pen, having invoked the aid of 'Him Who openeth and no man shutteth, and shutteth and no man openeth.'[1] Wherefore I have put into the lips of your understanding the tractate which you did desire, flowing within with nectar like the honeycomb:

[1] Apocalypse iii, 7.

and the same, because therein ye may see as in a mirror what every thing in the church doth mystically denote, I have called 'The Mystical Mirror of a Church.'

CHAPTER I

OF A CHURCH

The material church in which the people cometh together to praise God, signifieth the Holy Catholic Church, which is builded in the heavens of living stones. This is the Lord's house which is firmly builded. The 'chief corner-stone is Christ.' *Upon* this, not *besides* this, is the 'foundation of the apostles and prophets'; as it is written, 'Her foundations are upon the holy hills.'[2] The walls builded thereon, be the Jews and Gentiles coming from the four quarters of the world unto Christ. All the stones be polished and squared; that is, all the saints be pure and firm: the which also be placed so as to last for ever by the hands of the Chief Workman. Of these some be borne and do not bear, as the more simple folk in the Church; some be borne and do also bear, as the middling sort; others do only bear, and be not borne, save by Christ alone, Who is the single Cornerstone. And in this house by how much anyone doth differ from and excel others, by so much being the more humble doth he hold up more of the building. One charity doth join all together after the fashion of cement: and the living stones be bound together by the bond of peace. The towers be the preachers and the prelates of the Church: who are her wards and defence. Whence saith the bridegroom unto his spouse in the Song of

[2] Psalm lxxx (*Fundamenta ejus*), 1.

Songs: 'Thy neck is like the tower of David builded for an armoury.'[3] The cock which is placed thereon representeth preachers. For the cock in the deep watches of the night divideth the hours thereof with his song: he arouseth the sleepers; he foretelleth the approach of day; but first he stirreth up himself to crow by the striking of his wings. Behold ye these things mystically: for not one is there without meaning. The sleepers be the children of this world, lying in sins. The cock is the company of preachers, which do preach sharply, do stir up the sleepers to cast away the works of darkness, crying, 'Woe to the sleepers: awake thou that sleepest'; which also do foretell the coming of the light, when they preach of the day of judgment and future glory. But wisely before they preach unto others do they rouse themselves by virtues from the sleep of sin, and do chasten their bodies. Whence saith the Apostle, 'I keep under my body and bring it into subjection.'[4] The same also do turn themselves to meet the wind when they bravely do contend against and resist the rebellious by admonition and argument, lest they should seem to flee when the wolf cometh. The iron rod upon which the cock sitteth, showeth the straightforward speech of the preacher; that he doth not speak from the spirit of man, but according to the scriptures of God: as it is said, 'If any man speak, let him speak as the oracles of God.'[5] In that this rod is placed above the cross, it is shown that the words of Scripture be consummated and confirmed by the cross: whence our Lord said in His Passion, 'It is finished.'[6] And His title was indelibly written over Him. The ball (*tholus*) upon which the cross is placed doth signify perfection by its roundness: since the Catholic faith is to be preached and

---

[3] Cant. iv, 4.   [4] 1 Corinthians ix, 27.   [5] 1 S. Peter iv, 2.
[6] S. John xix.

held perfectly and inviolably: 'Which faith, except a man do keep whole and undefiled, without doubt he shall perish everlastingly.' Or else the ball doth signify the world redeemed by the price of the Cross: on which account the cross is placed over it. The cock being set over the cross signifieth that the preacher ought to make sure this point, that Christ redeemed the world by His Cross. The pinnacle and turret show the mind or life of a prelate who tendeth unto things above. The bells, by the voice of which the people are called together unto the church, typify also preachers: the which being necessary for many uses, are called by many names. The clapper, which causeth the sound from the two sides of the bell, is the tongue of the preacher which causeth both Testaments to resound. The wooden frame, whence the bell hangeth, signifieth the Cross; the cramps, charity; by which charity the preacher, being fast bound to the Cross, boasteth, saying, 'God forbid that I should glory save in the Cross of our Lord Jesus Christ.'[7] The rope is the life and humility of the preacher. Whence the Apostle saith, 'He condescendeth towards others. Whether we exalt ourselves it is for God; whether we abase ourselves it is for you.'[8] The rings on the rope are perseverance and the crown of reward. The glazed windows of the church be the Holy Scriptures, which do ward off the wind and the rain, that is, do repel all hurtful things; and when they do transmit the brightness of the True Sun by day into the church, they do give light to them that be therein. These be wider within than without, because the sense mystical is more ample and more pre-eminent than the sense literal. These be frequented of preachers, 'who do fly as a cloud and as the doves to the windows.'[9] Also by the windows the

---

[7] Galatians vi, 14. [8] 2 Corinthians v, 13. Vulgate. [9] Isaiah lx, 8.

five senses of the body be signified: which ought to be narrow without, lest they should take in vanities, but should be wide within to receive spiritual good. The door is Christ: whence the Lord saith in the Evangele, 'I am the door.'[10] The pillars be doctors; who do hold up spiritually the temple of God by their doctrine, as do the evangelists also the throne of God. These, for the harmony of divine eloquence, be called silver columns: according to that of the Song of Songs, 'He made the pillars thereof of silver.'[11] The stalls do denote the contemplative: in whom God doth rest without offence. These, for that they do contemplate the highest divinity and glory of the eternal life, be compared unto gold: whence in the aforesaid Song of Songs it is said, 'He made a golden bed.'[12] The beams be such as spiritually sustain the Church: the ceilings such as adorn it and strengthen it; of the which (because they be not corrupted by vices) the bride glorieth in the same Canticles, saying, 'The beams of our house are cedar and our rafters of fir.'[13] For God hath built His Church of living stones and imperishable wood: according to that, 'Solomon made himself a litter of the wood of Lebanon;[14] that is Christ of His saints made white by chastity. The chancel, when lower than the body of the church, showeth mystically how great humility ought to be in the clergy: according to the saying, 'The greater thou art the more humble thyself.'[15] The altar signifieth Christ, without Whom no acceptable gift is offered unto the Father. Whence the Church uttereth her prayers unto the Father *through* Christ. The vestments with which the altar is adorned be the saints of whom the Prophet speaketh unto God, saying, 'Thou shalt surely clothe Thee with them all as with an ornament.'[16] The

[10] S. John x. [11] Cant. iii, 10. [12] Cant. iii, 10. [13] Cant. i, 17.
[14] Cant. iii, 9. [15] Eccles. iii, 13. [16] Isaiah xlix, 18.

steps by which we ascend unto the altar do spiritually denote the apostles and martyrs of Christ who have shed their blood for the love of Him. The bride in the Canticles saith, 'The ascent unto it is purple, the midst thereof being paved with love.'[17] Furthermore, the fifteen virtues be expressed by the fifteen steps with which they went up unto the temple of Solomon: and the same be shown by the prophet in the fifteen continuous Psalms, which the righteous man hath disposed as steps or degrees in his heart.[18] This is the ladder which Jacob saw, the top of which touched the heavens. The lights of the church be they by whose doctrine the Church shineth as the sun and the moon; unto whom it is said by our Lord's voice,[19] 'Ye are the light of the world.' They be also the examples of good works: whence He saith in His admonitions, 'Let your light so shine before men.'[20] In that the church is adorned joyfully within but not without, is shown morally that its 'Glory is all from within.'[21] For although it be contemptible externally, yet doth it shine within in the soul, which is the abode of God: whence the Church saith, 'I am black but comely.'[22] And again, 'Yea, I have a goodly heritage.'[23] Which the Prophet considering, saith, 'Lord, I have loved the habitation of Thy house: and the place where Thine honour dwelleth,'[24] which place also Faith, Hope, and Charity do spiritually adorn. The cross of triumph is placed in the middle of the church, because the Church

---

[17] Cant. iii, 10. Vulgate.
[18] The fifteen Psalms, cxx-cxxxiv of our version, are called Songs of Degrees.
[19] S. Matthew v.   [20] Ibid.
[21] Here is an allusion to Psalm xlv (*Eructavit cor meum*), 14.
[22] Cant. i, 5.
[23] Psalm xvi (*Conserva me Domine*), 7.
[24] Psalm xxvi (*Judica me Domine*), 8.

loveth her Redeemer in the middle of her heart, and 'the midst thereof is paved with love for the daughters of Jerusalem.'[25] The which as a sign of victory, let all who see say one and all, ' Hail, salvation of the whole world: hail, life-giving Tree!' Wherefore, lest we should ever forget the love of God for us, ' Who gave his only-begotten Son ' to redeem us His servants, the Church armeth herself in her bosom and forehead with this sign, signifying that the mystery of the cross must always be believed by us in our heart, and confessed openly with our mouth. The figure of which went before her in Egypt. But when we cross ourselves from the forehead downwards, and then from the left to the right, we do set forth this mystery, that God ' bowed the heavens and came down,' to teach us to prefer things eternal unto things temporal. But by this sign the army of the devil is overthrown; the Church triumpheth, ' terrible as an army with banners.'[26] ' How dreadful is this place: this is none other but the house of God.'[27] And the Hymn saith, ' The banners of the King come forth: the Cross unfolds its mystery.'[28] Round this do the heavenly legions rally. Of this it is written, ' I saw the holy city, New Jerusalem, coming down from God out of heaven.'[29]

For the Church is militant here; in her home she doth reign: a part is in pilgrimage, a part in glory. That which is in pilgrimage coming up from her exile through the desert, doth sigh for her home, from the 'waters of Babylon for the heavenly Jerusalem;' while the other part, continually seeing peace, doth hold perpetual festival. Thus the heavenly city of Jerusalem is called the 'vision of peace.'[30] How glorious is her kingdom, 'glorious things

---

[25] Cant. iii, 10.   [26] Cant. vi, 10.   [27] Genesis xxviii, 17.
[28] The hymn, *Vexilla Regis*, occurs in the office for Passion Sunday.
[29] Apoc. xxi, 2.   [30] See note 4 on the *Rationale*, I. i, p. 13.

are spoken of thee, thou city of God.'[31] Her guardians be the citizens of heaven, the legions of angels with the glorious company of the apostles, the prophets, and the patriarchs, the armies of martyrs robed in purple, the flowers of virgins, the verdant choir of confessors, compassed about with the universal assembly of all the saints, chaste and glorified! And this wondrous court of heaven is yet more wondrously adorned by that one incomparable jewel, the Virgin Mother, 'whose like there ne'er hath been, whose like there ne'er shall be.' But how great is the admiration of all in beholding the King Himself, and how harmonious be the songs in praise of Him; this is known to those alone, who have deserved to stand amongst the happy throng, and to behold the mystery of the Trinity and the glory of Christ: Who is encircled by the angelic choirs; upon Whom the angels desire continually to gaze. To behold this the Immortal King face to face, the Church below is preparing herself: and while she keepeth here her feasts of time, she is remembering the festivals of her home and of eternity; in which the bridegroom is hymned by angelical instruments. And all the saints continually celebrating the day of great festivity 'which the Lord hath made,' cease not in their nuptial songs to laud the eternal bridegroom, the beautiful in form above the sons of men; Him who hath chosen the Church for Himself of His free mercy. Of whom, as He had seen her from eternity, He saith, 'I will get Me to the mountain of myrrh, and to the hill of frankincense and will speak unto my spouse.'[32] For whom 'He came forth as a bridegroom out of His chamber, and rejoiced as a giant to run his course';[33] when He went forth from His Father, and returned unto His Father—went forth indeed even unto Hades, returned unto the

---

[31] Psalm lxxxvii (*Fundamenta ejus*), 2.
[32] Cant. iv, 6.   [33] Psalm xix (*Cæli enarrant*), 5.

Throne of God—to make all His elect, from the beginning even unto the end of the world, one kingdom in the vision of the Supreme Trinity: in which is glorified 'one God world without end.'

CHAPTER II

OF THE DEDICATION OF A CHURCH

With what carefulness and love Christ doth adorn the bride for Himself and prepare her for her heavenly dedication, is in part signified by the consecration of the material church. The bishop compasseth the church to be dedicated three times, sprinkling it with holy water, the clergy and people following him.

239 A. In the meanwhile without and within there be burning twelve lamps. So often as he cometh to the door (which for a mystical reason is shut), the bishop smiteth the lintel with his pastoral staff, saying 'Lift up your heads, O ye gates, and be ye lift up, ye everlasting doors, and the King of Glory shall come in.'[1] The deacon answereth, 'Who is the King of Glory?' To whom the bishop, 'The Lord of Hosts: He is the King of Glory.' At the third time, the door being thrown open, he entereth with the clergy and people, saying, 'Peace be to this house.' Then he performeth the other ceremonies which pertain to dedication. But whatever things be here done visibly, the same doth God work by His invisible power in the soul, which is the true Temple of God: wherein Faith layeth the foundation, Hope raiseth the buildings, and Charity finisheth it. Also the Church Catholic herself, being made one out

[1] Psalm xxiv (*Domini est terra*).

of many stones, is the temple of God; because many temples make one temple, of which there is one Lord and one Faith. Wherefore the house must be dedicated; the soul sanctified. Water is penitence: salt, wisdom; the threefold aspersion, the threefold immersion in baptism; the twelve lights, the twelve apostles, preaching the mystery of the Cross; the bishop, Christ; his staff, Christ's power; the three strokes on the door, Christ's dominion over all things in heaven, earth, and hell: 'that all the threefold frame of things may bow the knee to Him, their Lord.' Again, the question of the deacon within is the ignorance of the people; the opening of the door, the ejection of sin. The bishop entering, prayeth for peace on the house, and Christ entering the world maketh peace between God and men. Then prostrate he prayeth unto the Lord for its sanctification: and so Christ, humbled in His Passion, prayed for His disciples and them that should believe, saying, 'Father, sanctify them in Thy truth.'[2] Arising he does not give the salutation but only prayeth: because they who be not yet sanctified must not be blessed but only prayed for. The writing the alphabet upon the pavement is the simple teaching of faith in the heart of man. The line drawn from the left corner of the east unto the right corner of the west, and the other line from the right of the east unto the left of the west, do express the Cross, and also the gathering in of both peoples: according as Jacob blessed the children of Joseph with his hands crossed.[3] For although Christ passing from the east did leave the Jews, because they would not believe, on His left hand, and did come unto the Gentiles; to whom, though they had been in the west, He granteth to be on the right hand: yet will he again, passing from the Gentiles who be placed in the

---

[2] S. John xvii.   [3] Genesis xxviii

right of the east, visit the Jews in the left hand corner: who, it is evident, be worse than He first found the Gentiles. The staff with which the alphabet is described typifieth the ministry of teachers, by which the conversion of the Gentiles is effected and that of Jews perfected. In that afterwards the bishop standing before the altar saith, 'O God, make speed to save us'; he doth signify those who having received the faith are preparing themselves to fight. And because they be still in conflict, and as it were amongst sighs, the Alleluia is not yet added. After this the water is blessed with salt and ashes; wine mixed with water being also added. The water is the people; the salt, doctrine; the ashes, the remembrance of the Passion of Christ. The wine mixed with water is Christ, God and Man; the wine His Godhead, the water His Manhood. Thus the people is sanctified by the doctrines of faith and remembrance of the Passion, being united with its Head both God and Man. Whence the altar and the church be sprinkled within; to show that within, as without, the spiritual Church must be sanctified. The aspersory, made of hyssop, denoteth humility; with which grace the Catholic Church being sprinkled is purified. The bishop compasseth the church in lustration and as if bestowing his care upon all. In the meanwhile is chanted the Psalm, 'Let God arise and his enemies be scattered,' with its proper response and antiphon, which is followed by another, 'Whoso dwelleth under the defence of the most high.' Then the bishop chanteth, 'My House shall be called an House of Prayer,' and also, 'I will tell out thy name among my brethren.' And because no work can prosper without God, he prayeth in conclusion that they may be heard who shall enter therein to pray for blessings. After this he approacheth unto the altar, saying, 'I will go up unto the altar of the Lord,' with the whole Psalm: and what remains of the water he poureth away at the base of the altar, committing unto God that which surpasseth human abilities in so great a sacrament. After this the altar is wiped with a linen cloth. The altar is Christ, the cloth is his flesh, brought by the beating of His Passion unto the whiteness and glory of immortality. Next the bishop offereth upon the altar frankincense, which is burnt in the shape of a cross in the middle thereof; and at its four corners he maketh crosses with sanctified oil. Then upon each of the four walls of the church there be made three crosses with the same oil: and the consecration being thus finished, the altar is covered with a white veil. Incense, prayers, and oil do denote the grace of the Holy Ghost. Whose fulness—'like the precious ointment upon the head that ran down unto the beard: even unto Aaron's beard,'[4]—came down upon the apostles and their disciples: who preached the mystery of the Cross through the four quarters of the world, the Lord working with them. The white covering doth typify the joy of immortality: concerning which the Son exulteth, saying unto the Father, 'Thou hast put off my sackcloth, and girded me with gladness.'[5]

[4] Psalm cxxxiii (*Ecce quam bonum*), 2.
[5] Psalm xxx (*Exaltabo te Domine*), 12.

APPENDIX A

CHANCELS

'THE temple of old was divided into two parts by a veil hung in the middle thereof. The first part was called the Holy Place, but the inner part the Holy of Holies. Whatever part then of the office of the Mass cometh before the secret[1] is performed as it were in the outer place: but the secret itself within the Holy of Holies. There were in the Holy of Holies the altar of incense, the ark of the testimony, the mercy-seat above the ark, and over this two cherubims of glory with their faces looking towards each other. Herein the high priest entered alone once in the year, having the names of the patriarchs written upon the breastplate of judgment and the shoulderplates, and bearing a censer of burning coals and blood, and incense, which with prayer he placed in the thurible until the cloud of incense covered him.'[2]

[1] After the *Sanctus*, which, as we shall find, was performed with the full choir and the accompaniment of organs, came the *secret*, which embraced the whole *Canon of the Mass*, performed by the celebrant alone, and the celebration of the Holy Eucharist. 'It is called the secret because these things be hidden from us, since the nature of man can in no wise fully comprehend so great a mystery: for the denoting of which it is rightly performed secretly. To signify the same also, the priest when entering upon the secret is veiled as it were with the side curtains.' See other mystical reasons adduced in the remainder of this passage, Book IV, Chapter 35, and in Chapter 39 an account of the side curtains. Upon the use of these see also the *Dublin Review*, vol. x, p. 339.

[2] See Leviticus xvi; Exodus xxviii, xxxix, and xl.

Afterwards he sprinkled the mercy-seat and the altar with blood, and then he went out to the people, and washed his vestments in the evening. These were types of old, but they have ceased since the things signified thereby have come. But thus the former temple doth denote the present church; the Holy of Holies, heaven; the high priest, Christ; the blood, His Passion; the coals, His love; the thurible, His flesh; the burning incense, prayers of sweet savour; the altar, the hosts of heaven; the ark, Christ in His humanity; the mercy-seat, God the Father; the two cherubims, the twain Testaments, the which do look towards each other because the two do agree; the vestments which be washed, mankind. Wherefore consider what things were done of old, and what things Christ hath done, and then see how the minister of the Church doth represent the same in the office of the Mass. By the ark also is signified the humility of Christ, from which through his mercy all good hath come unto us' (Durandus, Book IV, Preface 13, 14).

In the next section the same subject is further illustrated, though without reference to the immediate subject of this appendix, the necessity of the division of every church into a chancel and nave.

The reader may consult a most interesting series of chapters in Hugo de Sancto Victore (Tituli ii-viii, Ex. Misc. II, Lib. IV) upon this subject: the passages are far too long for insertion here.

The *absolute necessity* of this twofold division is a point which it is more than painful at this time to have to prove. It is only within the last two centuries that our own or any branch of the Church Catholic has dared to depart from an usage which, if any, has universality, antiquity, and consent on its side, and of whose authority was never any doubt in the Church. For some of the arguments which have been adduced in the present controversy we must refer to the publications of the Cambridge Camden Society, and particularly the *Ecclesiologist*. There is nothing more wanted than a careful treatise on the subject which shall in a compendious form put this and several points depending upon it, such as orientation itself, and praying towards the east, in a clear light.

APPENDIX B

ORIENTATION

'Furthermore albeit God is everywhere, yet ought the priest at the altar and in the offices to pray towards the east: according to the constitutions of Vigilius, Pope. Whence in churches which have the doors at the west, he that celebrateth turneth in the salutations to the people: but in churches which have the entrance at the east,[1] as at Rome, there is no need in the salutations for turning round, because the priest always turneth to the people. The temple also of Solomon, and the tabernacle of Moses had their entrance from the east. Pray we therefore towards the east, being mindful, firstly, that He, Who is the splendour of eternal light, hath illuminated 'them[2] that sit in darkness and the shadow of death, rising with healing in his wings':[3] of whom it is said, 'Behold the man, whose name is the East.'[4] For the which cause he saith in the book of Wisdom,[5] 'We

---

[1] S. John Lateran is an instance. We may observe that the reasons for the orientation of churches must have been very strong to have caused an universal disregard of an example thus set at the centre of Western Christendom.
[2] S. Luke i, 79. [3] Malachi iv, 2. [4] Zechariah vi, 12. [5] Wisdom xvi, 28

ought to pray eastward, where the light ariseth.' Not because the Divine Majesty is locally in the east: which is potentially and essentially in all places; as it is written, 'Do not I fill[6] heaven and earth'; and in like manner speaketh the Prophet,[7] 'If I ascend into heaven, Thou art there: if I go down to hell, Thou art there also': but because to those 'who fear His name shall[8] the sun of righteousness arise,' 'which lighteth every man that cometh into the world.'[9]

Secondly, that our souls be thereby taught to turn themselves to the things that are more desirable.

Thirdly, because they who praise God ought not to turn their backs on Him.

Fourthly, according to Joannes Damascenus (who giveth also the three following reasons),[10] to show that we seek our country.

Fifthly, that we may look upon Christ crucified, who is the True East.

Sixthly, that we may prove that we expect Him to come to be our Judge. For Damascenus saith in that place, 'God planted a garden eastward';[11] whence man's sin made him an exile, and instead of Paradise made him to dwell in the west: therefore, looking to our ancient home, we pray towards the east.

Seventhly, because our Lord, at His Crucifixion, looked towards the east: and also when he ascended into heaven, He ascended towards the east: and thus the apostles adored Him: and thus 'He shall come again in like manner as they saw Him go into heaven.'[12]

Eighthly, Daniel likewise in the Jewish captivity prayed towards the temple.

Yet Augustine saith that 'no Scripture hath taught us

---

[6] Jeremiah xxiii, 24. [7] Psalm cxxxix (*Domine probasti*), 7. [8] Malachi iv, 2.
[9] S. John i, 9. [10] *Quatuor orationes.* We should probably read, *rationes.*
[11] Genesis ii, 8. [12] Acts i, 11.

to pray towards the east.' [He, however, says also, 'Though I find not a thing on record in Scripture, yet I receive it as proceeding from the apostles if the Universal Church embrace it ']¹³ (Durandus V, ii, 57).

S. Isidore has a curious passage about orientation. A place, he says, designed so as to face the east was called *templum*, from *contemplating*. Of which there were four parts; the front facing the east, the back the west, the right hand the south, and the left hand the north: whence also when they builded temples, they took their east at the equinox, so that lines drawn from east to west would make the sections of the sky on the right and left hands equal, in order that he who prayed might look at the direct east (Orig. XV, iv).

APPENDIX C

ON THE DESIGN OF THE ANALOGIUM, AMBO OR ROOD LOFT, AND THE READING OF THE GOSPEL FROM IT

1. We have noted afore, that the priest, in the celebration of Mass, when it is not High Mass, himself readeth the gospel. But when a bishop or priest celebrateth High Mass with the highest solemnity, then, in some churches, as at Rome, the deacon having kissed the

---

[13] This section is in several places corrupt: for example—from Damascenus the quotation in the sixth head belongs properly to the seventh.

Our readers may perhaps be reminded of the anecdote of the good Earl of Derby (who, if the Reformed Church in England should ever have a calendar of her own, will assuredly be one of its martyrs), when on the scaffold. The church of Bolton was in sight: and the Earl requested that he might be allowed to kneel on the western side of the block, so that the last object on which his eyes were fixed might be God's house. His executioners showed their poor malice to the last, by denying him this wish.

right hand of the bishop, taketh the book of the gospel from the altar, and giveth it to the sub-deacon to bear, and asketh and receiveth the bishop's or priest's blessing. But in other churches, he first asketh for the blessing before he taketh the book. The benediction having been bestowed, the deacon proceedeth along the south side [1] of the choir to the rood loft, and before him goeth the sub-deacon with the volume of the gospel, and before him the incense-bearer with incense; and before him the torch-bearer with lighted tapers, and before him in some churches the banner of the cross: and thus they ascend the rood loft. And the deacon readeth the gospel: the which being finished, they return to the priest or bishop together. Which things we will more particularly go through. It is also to be noted, that in some churches, the deacon, when about to go to the rood loft, beginneth the antiphon which followeth benedictus in the nocturns, and while he is going thither, it is taken up, and finished by the chorus, to set forth charity: and it is sung without instruments, to denote that God commandeth us to have love alone. And now is the figure changed: for the deacon, who before represented S. John Baptist, now setteth forth S. John Evangelist: because 'the law and the prophets were until John: [2] and after him the kingdom of heaven is preached.'

2. And the word *evangelium* meaneth good tidings; from εὐ, well, and ἄγγελος, a messenger. For the preaching of Christ and His apostles is indeed a gospel, as proclaiming Life after death, Rest after labour, a Kingdom after slavery.

3. And ye are to wit, that as the head hath pre-eminence over the other members of the body, and as

---

[1] As is well known, double staircases to rood lofts appear to have been almost as common in England as single ones: and there are sometimes, especially in Norfolk churches, two corresponding rood turrets.
[2] S. Luke xvi, 16.

the other members obey it : so the gospel is the principal thing of all that are said in the office of the Mass, and hath the pre-eminence, and whatever things be there read, or sung, they consent to it, as may well be perceived.

4. The deacon therefore first kisseth the hand of the bishop in silence, because the preacher must proclaim the gospel for the sake of eternal glory, as saith the spouse in the Canticles, 'His right hand shall embrace me.'[3] Also because the angel which came to announce the glory of Christ's Resurrection did sit on the right hand, clothed in white.[4] In other churches, however, he doth not kiss, but only bowing asketh for a blessing. But the sub-deacon or deacon doth not kiss the hands, but the feet, of the Roman Pontiff, that he may exhibit the greatest reverence to the greatest bishop, and show that he is His Vicar, Whose feet the woman that was a sinner kissed.[5] For his footstool is to be adored because it is holy. Whose feet also, when He had risen from the dead, the woman held and adored. Generally, none ought to kiss the hand of the Roman Pontiff, unless when he receiveth something from his hands, or giveth something to them : to show that we ought on both accounts to give thanks unto Him, Who giveth to all of His own, and receiveth from none.

5. The deacon incontinently thereafter taketh the book of the gospel from the altar, because the 'Law shall go forth out of Sion, and the Word of the Lord from Jerusalem':[6] not the Mosaic Law which went forth of Sinai, but the Gospel Law, of which the Prophet saith, 'Behold the days come, saith the Lord, that I will make a new covenant with the house of Jacob and with the house of Israel.'[7] The book is also taken from

[3] Canticles ii, 6.   [4] S. Mark xvi, 5.
[5] S. Luke vii, 37.   [6] Micah iv, 2.   [7] Jeremiah xxxi, 31.

the altar, because the apostles received the gospel from the altar, when they went about preaching the Passion of Christ. Or the altar in this place signifieth the Jews, from whom the kingdom of God is taken, and given unto a nation that will do its fruits: and from this, that the gospel is taken from the altar, we learn, that it is the Word of God, which is signified by the altar, according to that saying, 'An altar of earth shall ye make unto me.'[8]

6. But he taketh it, according to some, from the right side of the altar: because the Church of the Jews, whence our Church springeth, was situate in the east: and placeth it on the left, as it is written, 'His left hand is under my head, and his right hand doth embrace me':[9] and that for a threefold cause. Firstly, the gospel teacheth that things celestial, which be signified by the right, be preferred to things terrestrial, which the left hand setteth forth. Secondly, the book is inclined on the left shoulder, to signify that the preaching of Christ shall pass from the Gentiles, as it is written: 'In those days Israel shall be saved.'[10] Thirdly, because in temporal life, which is set forth by that side, needful is it that Christ should be preached: and the book of the gospel is in some churches adorned on the outside with gold and gems. But the book remaineth on the altar, from the time that the priest goeth there, till the gospel be read, because it, in this respect, signifieth Jerusalem: since the gospel was first preached in Jerusalem, and remained there from the advent of the Lord till it was published to the Gentiles. As he saith, 'From Sion shall go forth the laws.'[11] For Jerusalem was the place of the Passion, which is also set forth by the altar.

7. Thereafter he seeketh the benediction: because

[8] Exodus xx, 24. [9] Canticles ii, 6. [10] Romans xi, 26.
[11] Micah iv, 2.

none must preach unless he be sent. According to that saying, ' How shall they preach, except they be sent ? ' [12] And the Lord saith to His disciples, ' Pray ye therefore the Lord of the harvest that He may send forth labourers into His harvest.' [13] But Esaias, when he had heard the voice of the Lord, saying, ' Whom shall I send, and who will go for us ? ' [14] made answer and said, ' Here am I, send me.' And the Lord said, ' Go and tell this people,' etc.

8. Again, Moses prefigured this kind of blessing : who, when he had ascended unto the mountain, received the tables of the law and the blessing, and gave the commandment to the people. And the Lord also Himself blessed the order of deacons, and gave it the Holy Spirit and sent it to preach through the whole world. The bishop therefore, or the priest, visibly blesseth the deacon who is about to read the gospel, which he did not do to the sub-deacon when about to read the epistle, because Christ sent the law and the prophets, which be signified by the epistle, while he remained hidden from the world: but after that he had visited it, and conversed with men He sent forth His apostles and evangelists, and taught them, saying, ' Go and teach, saying, the kingdom of heaven is at hand.' [15] ' And they went through the villages, evangelising, and doing cures everywhere.' And he sendeth him to read the gospel, to note that Christ sent the apostles to preach the kingdom of God.

9. But the deacon, laying up in his heart the things which were said in the benediction, must study to show himself pure in heart, clean in words, chaste in deed, that he may be able to set forth the gospel worthily, because the fountain of living waters, that is, the gospel, doth not flow freely, except from Libanus, that is, from a chaste

---

[12] Romans x, 15. [13] S. Matt. ix, 38. [14] Isaiah vi, 8, 9.
[15] S. Matthew x, 7.

heart, and a pure mouth. For praise is not seemly in the mouth of a sinner; nay rather of the sinner saith God, 'What hast thou to do to set forth My ordinances, and take My covenant into thy mouth.'[16] And therefore he is fortified by the sign of the cross, and then having received license and benediction, as is aforesaid, and having made the sign of the cross, that he may walk in safety, proceedeth to the rood loft in silence, with his eyes fixed on the ground: bearing, according to the custom of some churches, nothing in his hand, as the Lord commanded the apostles whom He sent to preach the kingdom of God. 'Take,' saith He, 'nothing for the journey, and salute no one.'[17] But in other churches the deacon beareth a book, as shall be said hereafter. But when he cometh to the rood loft, he saluteth it, as entering into a house to which he offereth peace, and passeth from the right side of the choir to the left, as he had before transferred the book from the right to the left side. For when the Jews had refused the Word of God, it was preached to the Gentiles, who are understood by the left side.

10. In the Roman Church, and in certain others, the sub-deacon ascendeth the rood loft one way,[18] and the deacon another: because the one proceedeth to an increase of knowledge by teaching, the other by learning: and because the minister by the merit of his works, and the preacher by the merit of his words, proceedeth to an increase of righteousness. Whence the Psalmist: 'Thy righteousness standeth like the mountains of God':[19] but they both return to the bishop by the same way, because by final perseverance they attain their reward,

---

[16] Psalm l (*Deus Deorum*) 16.   [17] S. Matthew x, 10.
[18] *Per dextram partem.* We are to imagine, in the whole of this description, the spectators supposed to face the altar. So in the fifteenth chapter of this book, the epistle is said to be read *in dextera parte*.
[19] Psalm xxxvi (*dixit injustus*), 6.

as the Lord testifieth, saying: 'He that endureth to the end, the same shall be saved.'[20] And that preaching sufficeth not without good deeds. For 'Jesus began both to do and to teach.'[21] Therefore the preacher returneth by the same way by the which the minister had gone up. Moreover, he that is about to read the gospel goeth and ascendeth by one way, and returneth by another, according to that saying, 'They returned into their own country another way':[22] because the apostles did first preach to the Jews and then to the Gentiles: as it is written, 'Since ye have cast from you the Word of God,'[23] and the rest.

11. The sub-deacon precedeth the deacon (because John and his preaching preceded Christ and His preaching), carrying in some churches a cushion; which he may place under the book. By the cushion, on which the book resteth, be set forth the temporal things of life, as it is written: 'If we have sown spiritual things, is it a great matter if we reap your temporal things?'[24] For according to the Apostle, 'They which serve the altar, eat of the altar.'[25] For 'the labourer is worthy of his hire.'[26] And the Lord taught us the law, 'Thou shalt not muzzle the ox when it treadeth out the corn.'[27] Again, a cushion is placed under the book to denote that which the Lord saith, 'My yoke is easy, and My burden light.'[28] Austin saith, 'To this yoke whosoever is subject, hath all things subject to him.'

The cushion therefore denoteth the sweetness and pleasure that ariseth from the commands of God. Whence the Prophet, 'Thou, O God, hast of Thy goodness prepared for the poor.'[29] And again, 'O how sweet are Thy words

---

[20] S. Matthew x, 22.   [21] Acts i, 1
[22] S. Matthew ii, 12.   [23] Acts xiii, 46.   [24] 1 Corinth. ix, 11.
[25] 1 Corinth. ix, 13.   [26] S. Luke x, 7.   [27] Deuteron. xxv, 4.
[28] S. Matthew xi, 30.   [29] Psalm lxviii (*Exurgat Deus*), 10.

unto my taste.'[30] Yet in the Roman Church, the deacon goeth first, as the teacher: sub-deacon followeth as the learner: the one precedeth, that he may preach, the other followeth, that he may minister. But after the reading of the Gospel, the sub-deacon, as being now sufficiently instructed, returneth first, having in his hand the gospel, as bringing back the gospel as the fruit of his ministrations: according to that which the Lord promised: 'He that receiveth a prophet in the name of a prophet shall receive a prophet's reward.'[31] Whom therefore the deacon sendeth aforehand to the bishop, to show that he is bringing back the fruit of his preaching: concerning which the Lord commanded, 'I have called you that ye should go and bring forth fruit, and that your fruit should remain.'[32] Moreover, the deacon, bearing back the cushion and gospel, signifieth that the preacher ought, by his good works, to offer his life to God. Whence the Apostle, 'Whatsoever ye do in word and deed, do all in the name of our Lord Jesus Christ.'[33]

12. The deacon also sendeth aforehand the thurible with incense, because the works of Christ preceded His doctrine. As it is written, 'Jesus began to do, and to teach.' But the thurible with incense signifieth prayer with devotion, which the faithful then chiefly ought to employ when they hear the word of God. Again, he doth it, because the preacher must send forth the sweet odour of good works: according to that saying of the Apostle: 'We are a sweet savour of Christ in every place.'[34] He whose life is despised needs is it that His preaching also is contemned.

. . . . . .

The cross precedeth the gospel in token that the

---

[30] Psalm cxix (*Beati immaculati*), 103. [31] S. Matthew x, 41.
[32] S. John xv, 16.   [33] Colos. iii 17.   [34] 2 Corinth. ii, 15.

preacher must follow the Crucified. Whence the Lord saith to Peter, 'Follow Me.' After this, the deacon ascendeth the *ambo* [the rood loft].

17. Now *ambo* meaneth the pulpit, whence the gospel is read, so called from *ambio* [to surround] because that place is surrounded with steps. In some churches also there be two ascents, one left, namely towards the east, where the deacon ascendeth; one to the right, namely towards the west, where he descendeth.

. . . .

18. He ascendeth that he may read the gospel with a loud and clear voice: as that which is to be heard of all, according to that saying of the Prophet, 'O thou that evangelisest to Sion, get thee up into the high mountain.'[35]

. . . .

Also that we may imitate our Lord, Who went up into a mountain,[36] that He might preach the gospel. The gospel is also read in a lofty and eminent place, because it hath been preached throughout all the world: as it is written: 'Their sound is gone out unto all lands.'[37] But the epistle is read in a lower place, as typifying the law, which was confined to Judea alone, as it is written: 'In Jewry is God known.'[38]

. . . .

19. But in a Mass of requiem the gospel is not read in that exalted place, but at the altar, to signify that preaching profiteth not the departed.

. . . .

20. Also the gospel is read from an eagle, according to that saying, 'He came flying upon the wings of the winds.'[39] And the eagle itself is covered with a covering

---

[35] Isaiah xi, 9. [36] S. Matthew v, 1.
[37] Psalm xix (*Cæli enarrant*), 4. [38] Psalm lxxv (*Notus in Judea*), 1.
[39] Psalm xviii (*Diligam Te*), 10

of cloth or silk, on certain feasts, to signify the softness of the heart: as he saith, 'I will take away the stony heart out of your flesh, and will give you a heart of flesh.'[40]

21. But he that readeth the gospel passeth to the left side: and setteth his face to the north, that the saying may be fulfilled, which is written, 'I will say to the north give up, and to the south keep not back'[41] (Durandus, Book IV, chap. xxiv).

APPENDIX D

ON THE SIGN OF THE CROSS

In the second chapter of his fifth book Durandus enters at great length into this subject. The reason for making the sign is to drive away evil spirits, who, as S. Chrysostome says, 'always flee when they see the sign of the cross, as fearing that staff by which they have been wounded.' The pole on which the brazen serpent was raised, the crossing of Jacob's hands when blessing Joseph's children, the mark *tau* (Ezekiel ix, 4) on the forehead, and the seal on the forehead in the Apocalypse, are some of the representations of the cross here alleged. The cross is to be made with three fingers, that is, the thumb and two fingers, in honour of the Trinity. The Jacobites and Eutychians use only one finger. Next the different methods of crossing are discussed. The sign ought to be made at the end of the gospel, the creeds, the Lord's Prayer, the *Gloria in excelsis*, the *Sanctus*, the *Agnus Dei*, the *Benedictus, Magnificat, Nunc dimittis*, at

---

[40] Ezekiel xi, 19. [41] Isaiah xliii, 6.

the beginning of the hours, the end of the Mass, when the priest gives the benediction, and whenever mention is made of the Cross of the Crucified. See also our author in his sixth book *De die Parasceu*.

APPENDIX E

ON THE FOUR COLOURS USED IN CHURCH HANGINGS, ETC.

1. There be four principal colours, by which, according to the diversity of days, the Church distinguisheth her vestments: to wit, white, red, black, and green. For we read that in the garments of the law there were four colours, fine linen, purple, jacinth, scarlet. The Roman Church also useth violet and saffron, as shall be said below.

2. White vestments be used in the festivals of holy confessors, and virgins which be not martyrs, on account of their integrity and innocence. For it is written, 'Her Nazarites were whiter than snow.'[1] And again: 'They shall walk with Me in white:[2] for they are virgins: and follow the Lamb whithersoever He goeth.' On account of the same thing white is used on the festivals of angels; concerning whom the Lord saith to Lucifer:[3] 'Where

---

[1] Lamentations iv, 7.
[2] The bishop here confuses two passages, Apocal. iii, 4, and xiv, 4. Of the same subject Lævinus Torrentius says beautifully in his hymn on the Holy Innocents:
    Ergo supremi parte cœli, lactea qua lucidum fulget via,
    Qua picta dulci stillat uva nectare, et nectar exhalant rosæ,
    Lœti coronis luditis, et insignium mixti puellarum choris
    Sacrum canentes itis agnum candido quacunque præcedat pede.
[3] A misquotation of the bishop's. The words are addressed to Job. Job xxxviii, 7.

wast thou .... when the morning stars sang together?' Also in all the festivals of the Holy Mother of God. In the feast of All Saints: yet some then use red. In the principal festival of S. John Evangelist.[4] In the conversion of S. Paul. In the cathedra of S. Peter.[5] Also from the vigil of the nativity of our Lord to the octave of the Epiphany: both inclusive; excepting the festivals of the martyrs included in that period.[6] In the nativity of our Lord, and also of His Forerunner, because each was born pure. 'For the Lord rode upon a light cloud,'[7] that is, took unto Himself sinless humanity, 'and entered Egypt,' that is, came into the world: as saith the angel to the virgin, 'The Holy Ghost shall come upon thee, and the power of the Highest shall overshadow thee.'[8] But John, although he were born in sin, was sanctified from the womb: according to that saying, 'Before thou camest forth from the womb I sanctified thee.'[9] And the angel saith to Zecharias, 'He shall be filled with the Holy Ghost from his mother's womb.'[10] Also white is used in the Epiphany, on account of the splendour of that star which led the wise men, as saith the Prophet, 'and the Gentiles shall come to thy light,[11] and kings to the brightness of thy rising.' In the purification also, on account of the purity of the Virgin Mary: which, according to Simeon, gave birth to 'a light to lighten the Gentiles, and the glory of Thy people Israel.'[12] On Maundy Thursday, to set forth the anointing, which is consecrated to the purification of the soul. For the

---

[4] That is, on the 27th of December, the day of his 'deposition': the other feast, kept in memory of his deliverance from the boiling oil, before the Latin gate, and therefore called *S. Joannes ante Portam Latinam*, is the 5th of May.   [5] The 22nd of February.
[6] Which are S. Stephen, the Holy Innocents, S. Thomas of Canterbury.
[7] Isaiah xix, 3.   [8] S. Luke i, 35.   [9] Jeremiah i, 3.
[10] S. Luke i, 15.   [11] Isaiah lx, 3.
[12] A very harsh construction: but surely preferable to that by which the Blessed Virgin herself is spoken of as the promised light.

gospel on that day principally setteth forth purity ; ' He that is washed needeth not save to wash his feet, but is clean every whit ' : and again, ' If I wash thee not, thou hast no part with me.' [13] It is also used with the office of the Mass from Easter Eve until the octave of the Ascension inclusive: except on the rogation days and intervening festivals of martyrs. On Easter Day, on account of the angel who brought the tidings of the Resurrection, who appeared in white garments : concerning whom Matthew testifieth, saying, ' His countenance was as lightning, and his garment white as snow ' : [14] and also because children, when baptised, are clothed in white. So also on the Ascension, because of the bright cloud in which Christ ascended. ' For two men stood by them in white garments, which also said, Ye men of Galilee,' [15] etc.

3. And this is to be noted, that albeit in the consecration of bishops, the vestments be of the colour suitable for the day, at the dedication of a church they be ever white, on what day soever the ceremony be celebrated: since in the consecration of a bishop the Mass of the day is sung, but in the dedication of a church, the Mass of dedication is sung. For the Church is called by the title of a virgin : according to that saying of the Apostle, ' For I have betrothed you to one man, that I may present you as a chaste virgin to Christ.' [16] Concerning which saith the bridegroom in the Canticles : ' Thou art altogether fair, my love, and there is no spot in thee.' [17] But this vestment ought to be white, to signify that her garments must at all times be pure, that is, her life must be spotless. Also in the octaves of those of the aforesaid feasts which have octaves, the white colour is used.

4. Scarlet vestments are used on the festivals of

---

[13] S. John xiii, 10.   [14] S. Matthew xxviii, 3.   [15] Acts i, 11.
[16] 2 Corinthians ii, 11.   [17] Canticles i, 15.

the apostles, evangelists, and martyrs, on account of the blood of their passion, which they poured out for Christ. For 'these be they which came out of great tribulation.'[18] Except on the feast of the innocents, as shall be said below. Also on the feast of the Cross, because Christ on the cross poured out His blood for us. Whence the Prophet, 'Wherefore is thine apparel red, as one that treadeth out the wine vat?'[19] But according to others, we then use white vestments: because it is not the feast of the passion, but of the invention, or exaltations.[20] Also from the vigil of Pentecost to Trinity Sunday inclusively: and this on account of the fervour of the Holy Ghost, which appeared in fiery tongues on the apostles. 'For there appeared unto them divers tongues as of fire.'[21] Whence the Prophet: 'He sent a fire in their bones.' Although in the martyrdom of SS. Peter and Paul both red and white be used: and in the nativity of S. John Baptist, white: but in his decollation, red.

5. But when her festivity is celebrated, who was both a virgin and martyr, the martyrdom taketh precedence of the virginity; because it is a sign of the most perfect love: according as the Truth saith, 'Greater love hath no man than this, that a man lay down his life for his friends.'[22] Wherefore on the commemoration of All Saints, some use scarlet: but others, and among them the Roman Church, white: at which time the Church saith, 'They shall walk in the sight of the Lamb with white garments: and palms in their hands.'[23] Whence the spouse saith in the Canticles: 'My beloved is white and ruddy: white in His confessors and virgins,

---

[18] Apocalypse vii, 14.   [19] Isaiah lxiii, 2.
[20] Both retained by our Church. The former (May 3) instituted in commemoration of the discovery of the True Cross, by S. Helena: the other (Sept. 14), which regulates the ember days in that month, in honour of its recapture from Chosroes by the Emperor Heraclius.
[21] Acts i, 1.   [22] S. John xv, 13.   [23] Apocalypse vii, 9.

ruddy in His apostles and martyrs.' For these are the flowers of roses, and the lilies of the valley. Again they who use scarlet on the feast of All Saints, do it with that intent because that feast was first instituted in honour of All Martyrs.[24] But answer may be made that it was also in honour of the blessed Virgin: and that at the present time, after the decree of S. Gregory VII, the Church keepeth that day holy to the memory of confessors and virgins. Also, the octaves of these days follow the colour of the feasts themselves.

6. Black is used on Good Friday: and on days of abstinence and affliction: and also in rogations. Moreover, in those processions which the Roman Pontiff maketh with bare feet: and in Masses of requiem, and Septuagesima to Easter Eve. For the spouse saith in the Canticles, 'I am black but comely,'[25] etc. But on the feast of the Innocents, some use black on account of sadness, some scarlet. The former allege the text, ' In Rama was a voice heard,'[26] etc. And for the same cause canticles of joy are omitted: and the mitre is brought without the orfrey, on account of the martyrdoms to which the Church hath principally an eye, when she saith, 'I saw beneath the throne the souls,'[27] etc.

(So also on Sunday, Lætare[28] Jerusalem, the Roman Pontiff beareth a mitre, beautified with the orfrey, on

---

[24] This alludes to the history of the feast of All Saints. Pope Boneface obtained a grant of the Pantheon from the Emperor Phocas: and dedicated it in honour of S. Mary and All Martyrs. This was on the 11th of May: and the feast of All Martyrs was kept on that day under the title of *S. Maria ad Martyres.* S. John, having confessed before the Latin gate on the 6th, the feast was subsequently kept on that day. But Gregory IV transferred it to Nov. 1st, because the harvest was then gathered in: and because the feast of All Apostles being kept on May 1st, the other would answer to it half-yearly. *All Martyrs* occurs, in a solitary instance, as an English dedication: *All Apostles,* not to be found in this country, has been adopted in Germany.

[25] Canticles i, 5.   [26] Jeremiah xxxi, 15; S. Matthew ii, 18.
     [27] Apocalypse vi, 9.   [28] Palm Sunday.

account of the joy which the golden [29] rose signifieth, but on account of the time being one of sadness, he weareth black vestments.) But the Roman Church, when the festival falleth on a week-day, useth violet, but on the octave, red.

7. In fine, on common days green vestments be employed: because green is the middle colour between black, white, and red; and specially between the octave of Epiphany and Septuagesima: and between Pentecost and Advent, in the Sunday office, this colour is used.

8. As he saith, ' Cypress with nard, nard and crocus.' [30] To these four colours be the others referred; to wit, the scarlet to the red,[31] the violet to the black, the fine linen to the white, the saffron to the green. But some refer the roses to martyrs, the saffron to confessors, the lilies to virgins.

9. It is not unmeet to use the violet on those days for which black is appointed. Whence the Roman Church useth it from the first Sunday in Advent, to the Mass of the vigil of the nativity, inclusive: and from Septuagesima to Easter Eve exclusive. But on the feasts of Saints on Septuagesima and Advent, violet or black is not to be used. And note that on Easter Eve in the whole office before Mass violet is used, except that the deacon who blesseth the taper, and the sub-deacon who ministereth, wear a white dalmatic and tunic, respectively: because that benediction pertaineth to the Resurrection, as doth also the Mass. But the benediction being finished, the deacon putteth off the dalmatic, and putteth on a violet chesible: the sub-deacon, however, changeth not his vest-

---

[29] This refers to the celebrated golden rose blessed by the Roman Pontiff on that day: and sent in token of approval to some Catholic prince. Some of our readers may remember that which was lately exhibited along with the golden altars of Basle.

[30] Canticles iii, 6. But the quotation is not exact.

[31] This passage seems very corrupt.

ments. Some also use white in the procession on Palm Sunday: and in the blessing of the boughs, and while the hymn *Gloria, laus, et honor*, is sung, on account of the joy of that festivity. But the Roman Church useth violet: as it doth also in the procession on Candlemas Day; because that office treateth of the anxious expectation of Simeon, and savoureth of the Old Testament.

10. It also useth that colour in the September ember days, and on the vigils of saints, when the Mass is of the vigil: and on the rogation days, and in Mass on S. Mark's Day.[32] For when we fast, then we bring under our flesh, that it may be conformed to that of Christ, 'By the lividness of whose stripes we be healed.' [33]

The which to express we use violet, which is a pale, and as it were, a livid colour (Durandus, Book III, 18).

APPENDIX F

OF BELLS BEING NOT RUNG FOR THREE DAYS BEFORE EASTER

'On these three days the bells be silent, because the apostles and preachers and others who be understood by bells were then silenced. For the sound of bells doth signify the sound of preaching: of which it is said, "Their sound hath gone out into all lands." For at that time they no longer went round the towns and villages preaching the gospel, but "after they had sung an hymn they went out with Jesus to the Mount of Olives." To whom when the Lord had said, "Behold he is at hand

---

[32] 'Whether there be any superstitious fasting on S. Mark's Day?' is a question which sometimes occurs in the Visitation Articles of Archbp. Parker and his comtemporaries.

[33] Isaiah liii, 5.

that doth betray Me," they slumbered for sadness, and ceased from praises. Whence also from compline, or vespers, when our Lord was betrayed beginneth the silence of the bells. Others, however, do not sound their bells beyond prime of this fifth day of passion week' (Durandus, Book VI, 72, 73).

APPENDIX G

The authority for the dedication festival is our Lord's observing the feast of the dedication of the Temple. This festival has an octave: as also had the Jewish feast, though the Passover and feast of Tabernacles had not.

'But this festival specially denoteth that eternal dedication, in which that other church, the holy soul, shall be so dedicated and united to God that it shall never be transferred to other uses: which will take place in the octave of the Resurrection.' The Psalms for the office of the festival are the *Domini est terra, Judica me Domine, Deus noster refugium, Magnus Dominus, Quam dilecta, Fundamenta ejus,* and *Domine Deus* (Durandus, Book VII, 48).

APPENDIX H

ON THE DEDICATION OF A CHURCH

The following particulars are extracted and condensed from Martene's invaluable work: and as his account is not easily accessible, and somewhat long, it has been thought well to subjoin them here.

Churches were often, in the primitive ages, dedicated by more than one bishop. Constantine having completed a magnificent church at Jerusalem, invited the prelates, then assembled in council at Tyre, to assist in its consecration (Euseb. *Vit. Const.* iv, 43; Sozomen. i, 46).

Constantius his son, having finished a church erected by his father at Antioch, Eusebius of Nicomedia, the intruding patriarch of Constantinople, summoned a council under pretence of consecrating the church, however much in reality to decide against the Catholic doctrine of Consubstantiality. Ninety-seven bishops were present (Sozomen. iii, 5).

So it was also in the Western Church. This is proved by the Preface to the Fourth Council of Arles, holden in 524: which begins, 'When the priests of the Lord had assembled in the will of God to the dedication of the church of S. Mary at Arles.'

In the time of S. Louis, Pope Pascal I consecrated the church of S. Vincent, with the Sacred College of Bishops and Cardinals. About the year 1015, the crypt of the monastery of S. Michael was consecrated by S. Bernard of Hildersheilm and two other bishops; and three years afterwards, the church being finished, it was consecrated by the same S. Bernard with three other bishops (*Vita S. Bernardi.* cap. xxxix, xl).

All these bishops took an actual part in the service. In the consecration of the church of Mans, in 1120, the high altar was consecrated by Gilbert, Archbishop of Mans: S. Julians by Galfred of Rouen: Hildebert of Mans consecrated S. Mary's; Reginald of Angiers that of the Holy Cross. There is a fine passage to the same point in Sugerius's book on the dedication of the church of S. Denis: 'Right early in the morning,' saith he, 'archbishops and bishops, archdeacons and abbots, and other venerable persons, who had lived of their proper expense, bore themselves right bishopfully; and took their places on the platform raised for the consecration of the water, and placed between the sepulchres of the holy martyrs and S. Saviour's altar. Then might ye have seen, and they who stood by saw, and that with great devotion, such a band of so venerable bishops, arrayed in their white robes, sparkling in their pontifical robes and precious orfreys, grasp their pastoral staves, call on God in holy exorcism, pace around the consecrated enclosure, and perform the nuptials of the Great King with such care, that it seemed as though the ceremony were performed by a chorus of angels, not a band of men. The crowd, in overwhelming magnitude, rolled around to the door; and while the aforesaid episcopal band were sprinkling the walls with hyssop, the king and his nobles drive them back, repress them, guard the portals.'

Yet the principal actor on the occasion was the bishop of the diocese. The thirty-sixth canon of the second Council of Arles decrees, 'If a bishop be minded to build a church in another diocese, let its dedication be reserved for the diocesan.' S. Columbanus, being only a priest, dedicated the church of S. Aurelia (Walfrid. Strabo. *Vita S. Gallo*, cap. vi).

The preceding night was spent either in the church or in neighbouring churches in a solemn vigil. S. Ambrose testifies that this was done on occasions of the dedication of the Ambrosian church (*Epist.* 22, *ad Marcellina*). So S. Gregory of Mans, in his dedication of the church of S. Julian, removed the relics of that saint into the church of S. Martin, and there kept vigil (*De Glor. Mart.* ii, 34).

Relics were considered indispensably necessary: so S. Paulinus (*Epist*. xxxii, *ad Sever.*) This church was dedicated in the name of Christ, the Saint of saints, the Martyr of martyrs, the Lord of lords, and was honoured with the relics of the blessed apostles. See also the beautiful epistle of S. Ambrose, translated in 'The Church of the Fathers.' The phrase was, *Consecrare ecclesiam de reliquiis Beati n.*

Yet some churches were consecrated without relics. The second Nicene Council decreed that in this case they should be supplied. Those portions of the consecrated elements were placed with these: to which perhaps that expression of S. Chrysostom is to be referred—'What is the altar by nature but a stone? But it is made holy, when it hath once received the body of Christ.'

These relics occupied different positions. In the church of S. Benedict, consecrated by Pope Alexander II, there were relics in the chapel-apse of S. John, in the bases of the piers, in the four angles of the bell tower, in the cross on the western gable, in the cross of the tower (*Chron. Cass*, iii, 30).

Ashes were sprinkled on the floor, and the bishop with his pastoral staff wrote on them the alphabet, sometimes in Latin alone, sometimes in Greek also.

The whole ceremony concluded with the endowment of the church: or, as it was termed, presenting its dowry.

By way of setting before our readers as clearly as possible the ancient form of dedication, we have chosen, among ten forms preserved by Martene, that of S. Dunstan.

Here beginneth the order of the dedication of a church. The bishops and other ministers of the church advance singing the antiphon, 'Zaccheus, make haste and come down,' *etc.*

Prevent us, O Lord, in all our, etc.

Then twelve candles are to be lighted, and placed round

the church, with the antiphon, three from the east, three from the west, three from the north, three from the south.

God, which by the preaching of Thine apostles, didst open to Thy Church the Kingdom of Heaven, and didst call them the Lights of the world, grant, we beseech Thee, that being assisted by their prayers, by whose teaching we are guided, and splendour illuminated, we may make these our actions pleasing to Thy Divine Majesty.

Here followeth the Litany: the priests going thrice round the church, and beginning from that door at which they be after to enter, namely, the south door.

O Christ, hear us, etc.

Prevent us, O Lord, with Thy tender mercy, and by the intercession of Thy saints, receive our prayers graciously.

Let our prayers, O Lord, come up before Thee, and expel all wickedness from Thy Church.

God, which rulest heaven and earth, graciously give us the aid of Thy defence.

Then one of the deacons entering the church, and shutting the door standeth before it, the others remaining without: and the bishop striking it with his staff, saith:

Lift up your heads, O ye gates, and be ye lift up, ye everlasting doors, and the King of Glory shall come in.

The deacon within answereth, and saith: Who is the King of Glory?

The Bishop. Lift up, etc.

The Deacon. Who is, etc.

The Bishop. Lift up, etc.

The Deacon. Who is, etc.

Chorus. The Lord of Hosts, He is the King of Glory.

The bishop again striking the door it is opened: and

he entereth: the chorus singing after him, Lift up your heads, etc., *to the end of the Psalm.*

The Bishop. The Lord be with you.

Response. And with thy spirit.

The Bishop. Let us pray:

We beseech Thee, O Lord, of Thy mercy, to enter Thy house, and to make for Thyself an habitation in the hearts of the faithful. Through, etc.

Then the bishop entereth the choir, saying:

Peace be to this house, and to all that are in it; peace to them that come in, and to them that go out.

Bless, O Lord, this house, which the sons of men have built for Thee: hear those which shall come up to this place: hear their prayers in the lofty throne of Thy glory.

The clerks begin the Litany; the bishop, with certain priests and deacons, remaining prostrate at the altar.

Lord have mercy upon us, etc.

As soon as Agnus Dei *is said, the bishop, rising, saith:*

Let us pray.

Be Thou exalted, Lord, in Thine own strength, etc.

Then the bishop shall write the alphabet along the pavement,[1] *first from east to west, then from north to south, the chorus saying the Psalm,* Fundamenta ejus.

---

[1] In the treatise of the Mart. Remigius, *De Dedicatione Ecclesiæ*, we have the following explanation of this singular custom: 'A thing which might appear puerile, unless it had been instituted by men, great in dignity, spiritual in life, apostolical in discipline. In all things of this kind, the Lord by His example hath gone before us: and what He hath done, remaineth unchangeable in his successors. What is understood by the alphabet save the beginnings and rudiments of sacred doctrine? Whence S. Paul, "Ye have need that one teach you again, which be the first principles of the oracles of God." Therefore the bishop writeth the alphabet, to signify that he teacheth the pure doctrine of the gospel. He writeth the alphabet twice, and that in the figure of a cross, to signify that the Passion of Christ is set forth by the gospel in its purity. He writeth it in the angles of the church, because by them be set forth the four corners of the world. He beginneth from the east, because the gospel began from the Jews.'

There is probably some reference to the Saviour's stooping down, and writing in the sand. We may also compare those singular and rare bells, in which the only inscription round the crown consists of the letters of the alphabet.

The Bishop. O God, make speed, etc.
Response. O Lord, make haste, etc.
The Bishop. Glory be, etc.
Response. As it, etc.

Then followeth the exorcism of the salt, and the water, and the ashes.

Then the bishop maketh the sign of the cross at the four corners of the altar, with hyssop, going round it seven times. The chorus sing the Psalm, Miserere mei Deus. *Then the bishop sprinkleth the water three times round the church: the chorus singing* Deus noster refugium. *Then the bishop sprinkleth the water over the altar: the chorus singing* Qui habitat. *Then the bishop sprinkleth the whole church inside with the water thrice: to signify the Church's inward faith in the Trinity: and once outside, to signify the one baptism. The chorus sing* Fundamenta ejus; *and while the priests are ascending the turrets,* Jacob beheld a ladder, *etc., and the Psalm* Deus noster refugium.

Then the bishop entereth the church: and sprinkleth water on the pavement in the form of a cross: the chorus singing Benedicite, omnia opera.

The Bishop. Lift up your hearts.
Response. We lift, etc.
The Bishop. Let us give thanks, etc.
Response. It is meet, etc.

Then the bishop goeth to the altar, and poureth the remainder of the water at its base.

Then he blesseth the altar-stone, the altar clothes, the sacerdotal vestments, the corporal, the paten, the chalice, the thurible.

Here followeth the Mass of Dedication.

The post communion ended, the Bishop saith:

Incline, O Lord, Thine ears unto me, and hear me: Look down, O Christ, from heaven, on thy flock and thy sheep : stretch Thine hand over them : bless their bodies and their souls : that in the communion of the saints they may receive celestial benediction, light angelical, the Holy Ghost, the Paraclete.   Amen.

They who be regenerate of water and the Holy Ghost who be redeemed on earth by Thy precious blood, who have received Thy sign on their foreheads, grant them to be Thine on the day of judgment.   Amen.

And as Thou didst bless patriarchs and prophets and apostles, martyrs and confessors, virgins and priests, so bless this flock, who are assembled to-day in Thy name in this church.   Amen.

And as by Thine angel Thou didst free the three children from the burning fiery furnace, so free this flock from everlasting death and the power of the devil, and from earthly lusts and all manner of weaknesses. Amen.

Spare their faults, remit their sins, and present them pure and undefiled in the day of judgment: as Thou didst receive Enoch and Elias into the kingdom of heaven.   Amen.

God Almighty bless and keep you, and make this house to shine with the glory of His presence, and open the eyes of His pity upon it day and night.   Amen.

And grant of His mercy, that all, who have assembled together at this dedication, by the intercession of Blessed N., and all other saints whose relics rest here, may obtain the remission of their sins.   Amen.

That ye may be made a holy temple in the spirit, where the Holy Trinity may ever deign to dwell ; and after this short life ye may attain to everlasting felicity. Amen.

Which He grant, Who liveth and reigneth, world without end.   Amen.

APPENDIX I

ADDENDA

Page 6.—It shows how little Durandus can rightly be charged with fancifulness, when we find him classing among ceremonial precepts, rites for which the Rabbis and many modern expositors have given a symbolical reason.

Page 23.—'The lattice work of the windows.' Wrongly translated in Lewis, 'the screens before the windows.'

Page 25.—This passage proves that in the time and country of Durandus seats or chairs except in the choir were unknown. Though in England Early English or Early Decorated open seats do occur, as in Clapton-in-Gordan, Somersetshire, they are very rare, and take up much less of the church than is the case in later examples. See 'Hist. of Pews,' 3rd ed., pp. 19, 20, 79.

Page 39.—The reader is aware that the words *in medio* of the early Christian altars gave rise to the warmest disputes between the Puritans and the Catholics of the 17th century. The Puritans insisted that they meant in the *body* of the church: the Catholics generally, and more particularly that most able defender of altars, Dr Laurence, insisted that when the fathers spoke of an alter *in medio*, they only meant one so placed as to be where all might see it. The words undoubtedly may bear this meaning: yet perhaps it is better to understand them, as they must be understood in this passage of Durandus, of an altar placed in the chord of the segment of a circle formed by the apse. See *Ecclesiologist*, vol. ii, p. 13.

Page 46, note 2c.—This is a mistake. The fresco alluded to represents a priest repeating the Pater Noster (which is written in his open book) at the N. W. angle of an altar. Upon the altar are two candlesticks and a ciborium: rising out of the latter is the figure of our Blessed Lord. There can be no doubt of the objectionable nature of such a representation.

Page 54.—The nimbus of the Saviour, it is perhaps needless to observe in explanation, is always inlaid, as it were, with a cross: at least the exceptions are excessively rare.

Page 54.—These 'carved figures' probably signify the corbels.

Page 54, note 54.—There is a valuable article on the nimbus by M. Didron from the *Revue Générale de l'Architecture* in the *Literary Gazette* for Dec. 1842. An example is there given of the square nimbus in the case of Pope Nicholas, as represented in a contemporary MS. The whole is well worth reading.

Page 102.—Dedication crosses. We have seen a valuable example of these in the church of Moorlinch, Somersetshire. There are four circles containing crosses pattées on the north and south sides of the chancel; and two at the east end, in all ten: the other two have disappeared.

Page 146.—The bodies of good men called horses. The same idea is worked out at great length in S. Chrysostom's earlier homilies on the Statues.

Page 170.—But how great is the admiration, etc. Compare S. Hildebert's hymn, *Exrta portam*, towards the conclusion:

> Qauntum tui gratulentur,
> Quam festive conviventur
> Quis affectus eos stringat,
> Et quæ gemma muros pingat,
> Quis chalcedon, quis jacintus,
> *Norunt isti, quis sunt intus!*

The last line has the same beautiful turn with the expression of Hugh of S. Victor.

Page 180.—Most of the following practices are observed to this day in the Metropolitical Church of Seville. There are two ambones, but no rood loft: the sub-deacon chants the epistle by himself, in the southern ambo; the deacon, preceded by a taper, chants the gospel from the northern.

Page 182.—So S. Bernard in his commentary on that verse of the 90th Psalm, 'A thousand shall fall at thy side, and ten thousand at thy right hand.'

INDEX

Abbots, how represented, 52
Agathensian, the Council, 45
Agnus Dei, The, 47
Alexander, Pope, 124
Alphabet, inscription of, 98
Allegory, 6
Altar candlesticks, 58
Altar rails, 26
Altars, stripped on Good Friday, 61
Altars, their consecration, 113
Altars, why encircled seven times at consecration, 119
Altare distinguished from ara, 34
Anagoge, 7
Analogium, *see* Rood Loft
Angels, how represented, 47
Antioch, Council of, 197
Antiphonal chanting, 21
Apostles, the, how represented, 50
Appodiatio, explained, 62
Ark of Testimony 35
—— its contents, 36
Arles, Fourth Council of, 197
Arnaldistæ, 139
Augustine, S., 49, 84, 85, 136, 152
Basilica, 13
Baruth, legend of, 89
Bell rope, 74
Bells, when first used, 71
—— what they signify, 72
—— silent, when, 196
Bernard, S., 131, 139
Beverstone church, 46
Bishop, the consecration of a, 145
Bishopstone, 19
Black, when used, 194

Boneface IV, Pope, 94
Breastplate, how made, 10
Burchardus, S., 64
Burial of heretics in cemeteries, 111
Cambridge Camden Society, 85
Cambridge, S. Sepulchre, 55
Cambridge, S. Giles, 26
Capella, whence derived, 14
Carthage, Council of, 158
Cavilla, 74
Cellar, 30
Cement, its symbolism, 17
Cemetery, 82
Cœnobium, 14
Chalices, their materials, 68
Chancels, lower than nave, 26
Chancels, 175
Chancel, more holy than nave, 20
Chrism, 137
Christmas, how churches are to be adorned at, 65
Chrysologus, S. Peter, 49
Church, its meanings, 12
Churches, when to be moved, 32
Clement, S., of Rome, 46
Cloister, 29
Cobham church, 46
Cothelstone church, 54
Cock, the, 165
Commands, moral, 5
Cone, 23
Confessors, how represented, 52
Consecration of a church, 88
Constantine builds a church at Jerusalem, 197
Cosins, Bishop, 154

Ciampini, 103, 126
Cross, the sign of the, 188
Cross triumphal, 28
Cross churches, 21
Crosses, the five, that mark an altar, 114
Crypts, 22
Curtains, of the tabernacle, 15
Cymbalum, 77
Dedication crosses, 98
Degrees, songs of, 43
Depulsare distinguished from compulsare, 78
Derby, the Earl of, 179
Divine Majesty, the, how represented, 53
Division, of the whole work, 11
Door, 24
Dormitory, 30
Dorsals, 56
Dowsing, William, 26
Dunstan, S., his form of dedication, 199
Durandus, his many occupations, 161
Dying, the, lay in sackcloth and ashes, 149
Egleton church, 55
Epiphany, what events celebrated thereon, 155
Evangelistic symbols, 48
Evaristus, Pope, 158
Exeter cathedral, 21
Extreme unction, 139, 148
Faustinus, S., his legend, 84
Felix III, Pope, 89
Ferculum, 28, 167
Frescoes, 45
Glass, 23
Gospel, the, fixed on the altar, 60
—— why not read from the rood loft in a Mass of requiem, 187
Green, when used, 194
Gregory, S., 54, 73, 75, 91, 152
Greeks, the, how they paint saints, 43
Haddenham, 14
Henry, S., his shrine, 48
Holy, distinguished from *sacred*, 81
Horologium, 27
Horses, the bodies of good men, why so called, 146
Hours, the, explained, 75

Hugh of S. Victor, his 'Mystical Mirror' 163
Human body, its resemblance to a church, 19
Hyssop, its virtues, 95
Idolatry, a protest against, 44
Ingoldsby Legends, their profanity, 84
Isidore, S., 83, 137, 155, 156
Jerusalem, its variety of significations, 8
—— rebuilt, 18
John, S., Evangelist, his confessions, 38
Journeys, the Saviour's seven, 119
Kilpeck church, 19
Kyriake, 13
Lateran, S. John, its altar to the west, 177
Lattice-work, 23
Litter, 34, 167
Llandanwg church, 46
Ludlow church, 21
Lyons, Council of, 41
Machpelah, 83
Mans, dedication of a church there, 198
Marriages, when forbidden, 154
—— second, 159
Martyrs, how represented, 52
Martyrium, 14
Mary, S., Magdalene, 126
Maundy Thursday, 153
Mende, 2
Mirror of Magistrates, 9
Moleon, De, his 'Voyage Liturgique,' 67
Montague, Bishop, 31
Murderers, limits of right of sanctuary, 32
Mystical, its meaning, 5
Nola, 77
Nolula, 77
Nimbus, the, 54
Orientation, 19, 177, seq.
Orfrey, the, 59
Ornaments of churches not to be profaned, 69
Ostrich eggs, why hung in churches, 67
Oxted church, 50
Palmers, 52
Paradise, how represented, 54

Parthian skins, 19
Patriarchs, how represented, 51
Pavement, 24
Phylacterium, difference between it and phylacteria, 57
Pictures, their use, 45
Piers, 24
Piscina, 27
Pity, how five-fold, 130
Podium, 85
Portfolio, the, what it represents, 56
Priests, unlettered, 4
—— allowed to consecrate churches, 16
Prophets, how represented, 51
Preston church, 54
Prothesis, table of, 3
Prynne, 21
Pyx, the, 56
Pulpit, 26
Rationale, reason of the name, 10
Reconciliation of a church, 107
Reconsecration, when to be practised, 105
Remigius Monk, 201
Relics required for the consecration of a church, 198
Richard of Cremona, 139
Ring, the wedding, 156
Ringing, various kinds of, 77
Rod of weathercock, 23
Rood loft, 26
—— turrets, two, common in Norfolk, 180
Round churches, 21
Sacraments defined, 152
—— their nature, 2
Sacramental, distinguished from ceremonial, 5
Sugerius, 197
Sambuca, the, 100
Sanctuary, the, 20
Saviour, our, various representations of, 46
Savinianus, Pope, 75
Scarlet, when used, 189
Scuta, the, 59
Seal, the, of an altar, 105

Second Day, why it had no blessing, 79
Senses of Holy Scripture, 5
Separation of men and women, 30
Signum, 77
Sion, distinguished from Jerusalem, 13
Snuffers, the, 58
Sacristy, 27
Stalls, 25
Squilla, 76
Stephen, Pope, 70
Stones of a church, their symbolism, 17
Sylvester, S., 139
Synagogue never applied to a church, 13
Te Deum, method of chanting, 78
Temple, Aslackby church, 21
Thiers, Father, 26
Tie-beams, 25
Tiles, 27
Toledo, Council of, 41
Tongs, the, 59
Torrentius, Lævinus, 189
Towers, 22
Treasures of the church, why exhibited, 66
Unctions, 134
Variety of rites, 8
Veils, their various kinds, 61
Vigilantius, 57
Vigil, of the dedication of a church, 198
Violet, when used, 193
Virgins, difference between and continent, 20
—— how represented, 52
Vladimir, S., his conversion, 55
Walls, why four, 20
Water, Holy, 115, 171
Weathercock, 22
White cloths cover the altar, why, 40
White, when used, 189
Widford church, 46
Women, their heads to be uncovered, 31
York, S. Lawrence, 55

www.ingramcontent.com/pod-product-compliance
Lightning Source LLC
Chambersburg PA
CBHW030321240426
43673CB00040B/1238